POPULAR REALITY

Journalism, Modernity, Popular Culture

JOHN HARTLEY

ARNOLD

A member of the Hodder Headline Group
LONDON • NEW YORK • SYDNEY • AUCKLAND

First published in Great Britain in 1996 by
Arnold, a member of the Hodder Headline group
338 Euston Road, London NW1 3BH
175 Fifth Avenue, New York, NY10010

Distributed exclusively in the USA by
St Martin's Press Inc.,
175 Fifth Avenue,
New York, NY10010

British Library Cataloguing in Publication Data
A catalogue entry for this book is available from the British Library

Library of Congress Cataloging-in-Publication Data
Hartley, John, 1948–
    Popular reality: journalism, modernity, popular culture/John Hartley.
        p.   cm.
    Includes bibliographical references and index.
    ISBN 0-340-58489-0 (pb). – ISBN 0-340-66294-8 (hb)
    1. Journalism.   2. Popular culture.   I. Title.
PN4731.H337   1996
070.4–dc20   96-11676
                  CIP

ISBN: 0 340 58489 0 (Pb)
ISBN: 0 340 66294 8 (Hb)

Composition by Scribe Design, Gillingham, Kent
Printed and bound in Great Britain by St Edmundsbury Press,
Bury St Edmunds, Suffolk and J W Arrowsmith, Bristol.

To Tina Horton

Contents

Acknowledgements

Thanks are due to some people I've never met (and not all of them are still alive), but who really are the inspiration for this book, because their fine contributions to the 'colloquy of large scale' which comprises the republic of letters provided the intellectual insight and political passion which made the field of study both clearer and more inviting than it seemed at first sight. They are Yuri Lotman (peerless scholar), Thomas Richards, Ernesto Laclau, Chantal Mouffe, Marshall Sahlins, Jon Klancher, Michael Hechter, Jack Censer, Robert Darnton; and, in their different ways (as you'll see in what follows), Tom Paine, Tom Hopkinson, Nelson Mandela, Marcia Langton.

Luckily (for me) I have met some pretty inspiring people actually as well as virtually, some of whom have had a direct and decisive influence on this book. They are Bobby Allen, Richard Ericson, Rita Felski, John Frow, Stuart Hall, Terence Hawkes, Sophie Lee, Toby Miller, Meaghan Morris, Graeme Turner. Among those whose work and conversation have reminded me of why intellectual life matters – and why it has a glowing future – are Paula Amad, Tara Brabazon, Abigail Bray, Alison Bunbury, Mark Gibson, Catharine Lumby, Alan McKee, Steve Mickler, John Richardson, McKenzie Wark. Of these special mention must be made of Steve Mickler: friend, colleague and sometime graduate student – I wish he could know how indebted to him I have been, but perhaps if he reads what follows he'll find out!

Special thanks are also due to Alan McKee, who took on the entire burden of chasing permissions for the pictures and, while awaiting faxes from Paris, London, Sydney, Melbourne, Los Angeles and New York, he read the manuscript, played with my children, and shared unstintingly his time, abilities, and friendship, all of which show in the book.

The 'onelie begetter' of this book is the person who not only let me write it, but also waited long enough for that to happen, providing encouragement throughout the provocatively long gestation period. Thanks then to Lesley Riddle of Arnold; I hope the book repays your trust, even if it isn't quite the one you expected.

Parts of *Popular Reality* have been rehearsed at conferences, and I'm grateful to the organizers and participants of:
The *Mass Communications and Technology: A Cultural/Critical View* symposium at the Communication Arts Research Institute, Fu Jen Catholic University, Taiwan, in May 1994. Thanks to Dr Tain-Dow Lee and his amazing student-assistants for their invitation and hospitality; also to Kuan-Hsing Chen and Albert Tang Wei-Min.
The *Citizenship and Cultural Frontiers* conference at Staffordshire University, England, in September 1994. Thanks to Derek Longhurst, Deborah Chambers and the organizers for restoring my faith in the British Polytechnic sector just after it had ceased to exist.
The *Cultural Studies: Pluralism and Theory* conference at the University of Melbourne in December 1992. I thank David Bennett for the invitation.
The *Crossings* Biennial Oceanic Architecture and Design student conference in Perth, Western Australia, April 1995. Thanks to Hootan Golestani for the invitation.
The *International Communication Association* conference in Sydney, July 1994. Thanks to Mike Griffin of the University of Minnesota, and Lawrence Grossberg of the University of North Carolina at Chapel Hill, for asking me to contribute.
The *Cultural Theory Group*, Green College, University of British Columbia, Canada, in September 1994. I thank Sharon Fuller for her enthusiasm (and her driving skills), and Richard Ericson for his generosity.
The *Intellectuals and Communities* conference of the Cultural Studies Association of Australia, University of Technology, Sydney, December 1994; I thank David Marshall, Frances Bonner and Graeme Turner for inviting me to sit on the virtual verandah of their bright and airy intellectual Queenslander.
The *Centres and Peripheries* conference of the Australian and New Zealand Communication Association at Edith Cowan University in 1995. Thanks to David McKie for the invitation.
The *Culture and Identity: City, Nation, World* conference organized by *Theory, Culture & Society*, in Berlin, August 1995. Thanks to Mike Featherstone for the invitation.
The *Whose Cultural Studies? Politics, Risks, Voices* conference at Charles Sturt University, New South Wales, in December 1995. Thanks to Paul Washington and John Tulloch for the invitation.

Material from this book has appeared as articles in *Arena Journal* (New series, 3, 1994) and *The Australian Journal of Communication* (22(2) 1995). Parts of Chapters 6 and 7 have been published as 'The sexualization of suburbia: the diffusion of knowledge in the postmodern public sphere,' in Roger Silverstone (ed.) (1996) *Visions of Suburbia: Symptoms and Metaphors of Modernity*. London and New York: Routledge, to whom I am grateful for permission to publish the material here.

The draft MS was finished during my last few months at Murdoch University, when I was sustained in my efforts by Niall Lucy and Tom O'Regan, to whom many thanks, and by a period of long-service leave which happily coincided with a writing frenzy. Thanks to all the staff and students of that strange, self-doubting university, especially to its Chancellor during my time, Sir Ronald Wilson, who knows the mutual importance of academic work, the media and social justice, and has been energetic in bringing them together in fruitful dialogue. The final revisions were completed at Edith Cowan University, and I thank the staff in the Media Studies Department, especially Robyn Quin, for their support and encouragement. Thanks are also due to Dr David Elder, who generously translated all those letters to Paris into (very effective) French.

It is conventional but quite proper to save one's most heartfelt gratitude to last, and to mention those whose very existence is both the reason for trying to write a decent book and a substantial contribution to the process. A kiss, then, to Tina Horton, and to Karri Hartley, Rhiannon Hartley, Sophie Hartley. And for similar but different reasons, the same to Oona O'Casey Connell and Paul Connell. Freedom and comfort to you all.

And finally, citizen reader, in whose textualized shadow I stand in this book – if you do, I thank you for reading it.

JH
Fremantle

The publishers and I would like to acknowledge gratefully the following for the use of visual materials for the illustrations:

Introduction
Waiting for the Times – painting by B.R. Haydon. *The Times* Archive, Times Newspapers Ltd.
'Sunday Funnies' – Sally Mann and Aperture Foundation, Inc., New York.
'Skin and Bone' – Kirsten Galliott for *Who Weekly*, Sydney, and Sante D'Orazio, New York.
'Photography's Top 100' – Christine Orobello for *American Photo*, and Sante D'Orazio, New York.
Common Sense – Penguin Books.
'Common Sense' – Julie Phillips for Kellogg's.
'Alien Backs Clinton' – Reuters.

Chapter 5
'Vogue par Nelson Mandela cover' – Véronique Chaubin for Joan Juliet Buck, rédactrice en chef du magazine *Vogue*, Paris.

'Homage to Nelson Mandela' – photo Ellen von Unwerth, Kelly O'Neill for Art + Commerce Anthology, and *Vogue*, Paris.
'Liberté' – photo Colin Paterson Jones, and *Vogue*, Paris.
'Fraternité' – photo Derek Hudson, and *Vogue*, Paris.
'Douleur' – photo Derek Hudson, and *Vogue*, Paris.
'ANC rally' – photo Louise Gubb, and *Vogue*, Paris.
'Double mixte' – photo Dominique Isserman, and *Vogue*, Paris.
'Mandela signs off' – photo Louise Gubb, and *Vogue*, Paris.
'"Judy Lamour" in "Vogue"' – Terry Blamey for Kylie Minogue, Pamela Reid Chauvet for photo by Bert Stern, Patricia Watson for *Vogue*, Australia.
'Nicole Kidman's kiss' – Nicole Kidman, Ann Churchill Brown at Shanahan Management and Katherine Olim at PMK for Nicole Kidman, Megan Lowe at *Visages* for photo by Rocky Schenck, and *Vogue*, Australia.
'Leading men' – Baz Luhrmann and *Vogue*, Australia.
'Athletes kiss' – photo Agence Vandystadt, and *Vogue*, Paris.
'Together we can't lose' – photo Craig Golding, Fairfax Photography, and Council for Aboriginal Reconciliation, Canberra.

Chapter 7
'They've used me' – Sophie Lee, photo Rob Austen, and Lawrie Masterson, Editor, *TV Week*.
'Sophie set to shock us again' – Sophie Lee, photo Barry Sproson, and Bunty Averson for *Woman's Day*.
'Sophie Lee in style' – Sophie Lee, photo Warwick Orme, and David Willis for *Cosmopolitan* Australia.
'Helena Christensen in Versace' – *Mirabella* Magazine.
'Winking Kylie' – Kylie Minogue, Beat, and Mushroom Records.
'Kylie remade' – Kylie Minogue, photo Andrew Macpherson and *The Face*.
'Close friend Kylie' – Sophie Lee, photo Daniela Federici, and Dawn Swain for Richard Walsh at ACP Publishing Pty. Ltd.
'TV Extra' – photo courtesy Channel Seven Perth, and the *Sunday Times*.
'Elle Macpherson' – Paul Murray, Editor, *The West Australian*, and West Australian Newspapers.

Chapter 8
'Have you ever wondered . . . ?' – Reg Bryson at The Campaign Palace, Sydney, and *Marketing World*.
'Top people's pin-up' – Vivien Neves, photo Michael Boys, and Lisa Hyland for Macmillan Publishers.
'Gang of Four' – Professor David Goodman, University of Technology, Sydney.
Pears' Soap, Sunlight Soap, and Lux advertisements – Abi Linz for Lever Bros.
Australian gunners – Andy Cole.
'Iwo Jima' – photo Joe Rosenthal, Associated Press, and the *Los Angeles Times*.

'Postcard from Arlington cemetery' – Terence Hawkes.

'Postage stamps' – Martin Barker.

Danas – Dona Kola-Panov.

'New Internationalist' – James Rowland for *New Internationalist.*

'Thanks Central Lancs' – Central Lancashire Development Corporation.

'Big Noise' – illustration by Patrick Archibald. Adbuster Magazine, Volume 2, #2. The Media Foundation, 1243 West 7th Ave, Vancouver, BC, Canada, V6H 1B7.

'Spring break' – Martin Barker.

'Nifty serve' – Koichi Iwabuchi.

'Rush-hour in Sydney' – *Picture Post*, Hulton Picture Library.

'A Plan for Britain' – *Picture Post*, Hulton Picture Library.

'A day in the life of Picture Post' – *Picture Post.*

'A Plan for Education' – *Picture Post*, Hulton Picture Library.

Every effort has been made to obtain permission to reproduce copyright material. If any proper acknowledgement has not been made, copyright holders are invited to contact Arnold's (Hodder Headline) London office.

INTRODUCTION

What is Popular Reality?

(The Politics of Kissing)

1-5

> *The individual human intellect does not have a monopoly in the work of thinking. Semiotic systems, both separately and together as the integrated unity of the semiosphere, both synchronically and in all the depths of historical memory, carry out intellectual operations, preserve, rework and increase the store of information.*
> YURI LOTMAN[1]

Meanings and Modernity

Popular Reality is an attempt to treat the subject of journalism and modernity from the perspective of cultural studies, and from the point of view of journalism's (popular) readerships and textual system. There are some unusual features to this study. It treats modernity as a reasonably coherent mental space, which is of course arguable in itself, but useful as an analytical strategy because it allows comparisons to be made across the time during which modernity has developed – roughly the last two to three centuries. While journalism is produced in conditions of present-tense organized chaos and consumed in the routine expectation of being thrown away and forgotten, it is neither reinvented anew each day nor necessarily very different from what was being done decades and even lifetimes ago. Since my focus is on journalism from the readership's point of view, it follows that what journalism is 'made of', as it were, is not only or even primarily its industrial productive apparatus – technology, corporations, finance, work practices, occupational ideologies, institutional policies and so on – but also, and perhaps more fundamentally, it is 'made of' something at once more modest and elusive, namely meanings, and more pervasive and general, namely readerships themselves – the public.

At one level meanings are much more stable than technologies; we're still arguing about the same things via satellite that people were worrying about via wooden presses. Journalism is a 'mentifact' not an artifact, and while the most decisive political development of modernity, the French Revolution, was reported via journals printed on wooden presses whose basic design hadn't changed since their invention by Johann Gutenberg (c.1398–1468),[2] it has to be admitted that more than two centuries after 1789, when technology has totally transformed printing, and in any case more people get their daily news from electronic than from print media, the ideas we're arguing about are still those promulgated by the French Revolution. You probably don't know what a platen, forme, tympan or frisket is, never mind a 'coffin' or 'skeleton', nor that these crucial components of the wooden press were held together by 'cheeks', a 'cap', a 'winter' and a 'summer'.[3] Equally, you might not have heard of the illustrious iron presses which began to transform this technology: the Stanhope, Columbia, Albion, the Koenig-cylinder, and finally the Hoe-Crabtree-Vickers rotary presses, which eventually raised the speed of production from around 250 single sheets per hour (i.e. 1000 quarto or 2000 octavo pages) in a 12-hour working day on the hand-press, via 1100 sheets per hour (for *The Times* in 1814) on the first cylinder press, to 70,000 copies per hour of a 144-page complete letterpress newspaper (that's ten million pages), 24 hours a day (for the *Toronto Star* in the early 1970s).[4] But you have of course heard of freedom, equality, fraternity and sisterhood, popular sovereignty, comfort; these were among the ideas being popped out at so many sheets per hour throughout the whole period. So *Popular Reality* is concerned not with technology as such, but with the communication of ideas; it's more interested in democracies than dot matrices, even though it is clear that the two share the same history.

At another level than that of their historical stability, meanings are far from stable. They are very hard to pin down analytically, since they arise in the live interactions and relationships of myriad personal, social and textual encounters. Meanings change constantly, they're subject to quite sophisticated taxonomies of genre and import, and what any one event, text, or encounter 'means' will be plural and dependent on the point of view of both the participant and the observer. Meanings are almost too ubiquitous – everywhere you look, think, speak, know, and in everything you do, there are meanings, because the human brain and human culture live inside an enclosing universe of them – a 'semiosphere' as it is called by the Russian cultural semiotician Yuri Lotman (to whom I'm much indebted in this book).[5] Meanings are however not susceptible to the most routine forms of 'scientific' research, because they're not things or objects which can be reduced and standardized in order for their properties and actions to be understood (almost the reverse is true); they cannot be observed, tested, counted, sampled, experimented with, or even interrogated. Though many have tried, it has usually transpired that 'scientific' treatments of meanings tell us more about the investigating institution or its clientèle in official policy-making circles than about the social production and actual signification of meanings (see Chapters 2 and 9). Meanings are produced by and expressive of relations between an *addresser* (which may be a person, text, or institution) and an *addressee* (person, readership, or public). They are thus dialogic, and the dialogue itself requires not only two parties but also a *medium* of communication to which both can contribute, and with which both can make some sense of the other, despite the difficulties of difference, distance, untranslatability and even conflict which may come between them. The result of any encounter between any addresser and addressee in any medium is a *text*. And journalism is, as I shall argue below, *the* textual system of modernity.

In general, the relations between addresser and addressee in modernity are the object of study – the 'subject-matter' – of *cultural studies*. While traditional studies of journalism have tended to concentrate on the corporate and social power of the addressers, such as media moguls and organizations, it has to be admitted that if journalism is going to have any impact at all, whether political, social, behavioural, cultural or even ethical, it must have addressees, and plenty of them. *Popular Reality* redresses the relative neglect of questions of *readership* in the study of popular journalism (the term 'reader' or 'readership' will be used throughout this book to include audiences, viewers, listeners, etc.; see Chapter 2).

But to make a study of journalism from the point of view of the readership, and in the light of the history of meanings, requires a greater attention to *texts* than is usual in journalism studies. Texts are the objective traces of dialogue, relationship, meaning and communication. They are recoverable for analysis, and can be argued over because there is something material – and external to the analyst – to which others can refer to test an argument or asser-tion. This book therefore concentrates on texts, taking the term 'text' to refer to any combinations of spoken or written words, and/or still or moving pictures, in print and audio-visual media, whether short or long, 'live' or recorded, and using them to 'read' (apprehend, comprehend and analyse critically from a given perspective) the relationships which have been established and made meaningful in modernity between media and their readers.

Journalism is in fact a gigantic archive of textuality, a huge store of human sense-making, unselfconsciously generated by and documenting the social, personal, cultural and political interactions of contemporary life, while at the same time displaying its own particular properties and characteristics, its own patterns, histories, quirks and accidents. It is therefore a resource which has to be studied and understood in its own terms, but which can also be used to pursue questions about matters outside of itself; questions about meanings, for instance. As the quotation from Lotman at the head of this chapter makes clear, 'thinking' is not an individual but a social and historical practice; journalism is one of the socio-histori-cal forms that it takes.

Thus, journalism is a wonderful archive for exploring the social production of meaning in the historical circumstances of modernity. But because 'meaning' is so elusive and all-encompassing at once, it is simultaneously hard to observe and hard to avoid. Analysts of textual systems are both caught up in the sense-making practices they're observing (both you and I, gentle reader, are caught up one way or another in the processes of modernity, democratization, comfort and knowledge production), and also they are creative of meanings themselves – any 'reading' of evidence from a textual archive is creative in the sense that what is produced in this context is . . . *more text*, which can itself be circulated and interpreted, and become influential over subsequent thinking. This cannot be avoided, but it is still possible to attempt scrupulous analysis of textuality. Two quite important approaches to the study of 'meaning' are, first, to study only those meanings which can be recovered for analysis (i.e. words on a page, not supposed thoughts in a presumed head), and, second, to adopt some *other* perspective than that represented by the participants in a given sense-making relationship (the addresser/addressee).

Theory Shopping

An example may help to show some of the analytical possibilities and complexities. It so happens that in the course of researching this book I came across a 'politics of kissing' (for which, see Chapters 4 and 5 below). Kissing is in fact a serious and thought-provoking subject in itself (both as a social practice and as a representation in texts), and it is also a remarkably apposite metaphor for thinking about the relationships between producers, texts and readers. For instance, a kiss is a communicative encounter between two parties and is obviously meaningful, though differently for each partner; it's a form of dialogue. What it means depends not only on the kiss itself, but also on the relationship of the participants – they may be lovers, parent/child, or two rival politicians – and a kiss may signify betrayal as easily as love. Kisses are universal (they belong, like language and fire, to the species), but there are culturally specific codes of display for kissing – in some contemporary and many past societies, public kissing would be understood as scandalous if done between lovers but quite proper if done as a 'political' greeting between two men, as a mark of respect, not affection. In Western societies, heterosexual private relationships between adults of child-bearing age may be publicly displayed via kissing, but in such societies there may remain a strongly prohibitive socio-legal prejudice against the public display of homosexual kissing, or kissing between more than two people, or between people of widely differing ages or ethnicities, or by very old or very young people, or on certain parts of the body. Kisses are thus very like meanings, being soft, fleeting, immensely important, sometimes telling the truth, sometimes not, sometimes holding the universe still for a moment, sometimes betokening very little; always highly coded according to existing socio-cultural, historical and political systems for both performers and observers, and always marking, changing and renewing the boundaries between public and private.

But kisses cannot be recovered for observation without retextualization. If observed by a third party, the meaning of a kiss changes completely. What it now means also depends on who's looking (rival, parent, pervert, social scientist, journalist). To observe a kiss from a perspective other than that of the participants is a form of *reading*, while kissing itself may be seen as a form of *writing*. The meanings that can be 'read' from watching a kiss require the skills of a textual analyst, because (you must remember this) there are kisses in stories, sights and songs, on screen and page, in fact and fiction, drama and journalism. Kisses are textualized, and the 'text' can be recorded on film or paper as well as performed 'live'. In such cases kisses are not only available for textual analysis but are also expressive of more than the relationship between the kissers, be it romantic, revolutionary, treacherous or true. The way textualized kisses are 'written' in the media is expressive of the public, three-way relationship between '*textmakers*' (publishers, photographers, writers, etc.), the *medium* in which they appear (journalism, cinema, cultural studies, pornography, etc.), and a *readership* (the public construed as citizen, audience, voyeur, expert, policymaker, moralist, etc.). What's more they'll also be expressive of (and can serve as evidence for) the historical and cultural context within which they are produced, circulated and read, since no one kisses outside of the semiotic conventions of their time and place.

Equally, no one can do textual analysis outside of the cultural and intellectual traditions and trainings in which their literacy is formed and practised. So someone from a cultural background where public kissing is seen as embarrassing or 'Western', might simply disagree with someone trained to analyse press photographs about the 'meaning' of a given image, and of course both of them would be justified in their reading. Kissing then is not just an interesting component of life and journalism (as will be seen later), but because it works as a metaphor for the producer/text/reader relationship it can illustrate some of journalism's general textual properties. Journalism (like kissing) changes according to whether it is being practised or observed, and according to the training and tradition of the observer. But a semiotic hot spot like kissing is more interesting to observe, analyse and discuss than is 'meaning', 'relationship', and other large but abstract concepts. Hence this book tends to pursue general issues through such examples. It seeks to work 'upwards' from a textualized kiss (or whatever) towards a recognition and understanding of the relevant textmaker/medium/readership/observer relationships, not 'downwards' from a fixed methodology or interpretative framework towards the 'scientific' meaning of a kiss.

Another unusual feature of this book compared with most treatments of the topic is that it does not confine journalism to news, if by that is understood the daily reporting of the political public sphere as traditionally defined. It is just as interested in what has become known as 'style', 'consumer', and 'lifestyle' journalism, especially that which addresses a feminized readership. Clearly 'hard' news is an important component of journalism, perhaps its professional cutting-edge, but it is not a self-explanatory, self-evident object of study. Journalism has always included coverage of the private as well as the public sphere, and it is in fact a fundamental thesis of this book that these 'two' spheres have never been as separate as is sometimes supposed; on the contrary, new political movements have tended to develop in the private sphere, while public politics has progressively been privatized over the past century or so. Hence, in this book, no hierarchical distinctions are made of the kind which tend to privilege certain styles and genres of reporting, certain outlets, media, or personalities, on the basis of their supposed seriousness, centrality or historical significance.

The method of analysis adopted in this book is to refer as much as possible to journalistic and academic texts, both of which are regarded as 'primary' since they contribute equally to the development of ideas, arguments (and understanding). I tend to concentrate on what I take to be emblematic texts or moments, using these to tease out the implications and significations involved, rather than attempting objective methodologies like sampling, surveying or statistics. This is because I'm interested in meanings, which are rarely encountered in the form of generalities. You can reduce a kiss to information for the benefit of scientific enquiry, of course, but it's not a method which yields complete understanding of what a given kiss means in specific circumstances to its participants and onlookers. So the methods employed in this book are documentary, forensic, historical, argumentative, metaphorical and textual. Rather than insisting on a spurious unity or comprehensiveness, or claiming for some methodological 'key' an explanatory power it cannot command, I have adopted something called by Paula Amad 'theory-shopping'. Writing about Benetton advertisements, which among other things challenge traditional Left analysis of commercial media advertising by proposing 'the radical producer and the unknowable consumer', and adding to this the tendency of media to address a global constituency, Amad writes:

It goes without saying then that the tools for understanding such maverick producers, consumers and media voices will have to be refashioned in order to indicate a deviation from traditional analyses which would bind them respectively by the forces of market imperative, behavioural submission and global imperialism. Only a form of theory shopping *may suit this task, that is, not a brand-loyalty devotion to one product nor a drive-your-dollar-further bargain hunt. By contrast,* theory shopping *takes advantage of the skills of browsing, seeing and*

*not seeing the products, according to the specific situated-ness of one's
needs.*[6]

Such a procedure has risks; you need to practise doing it, not everyone does it with the wonderful panache shown by Amad herself, you
don't always find what you're looking for, and different selections
may clash with each other. The net result depends quite obviously
on the browser's astuteness as a reader, and on how deft they are at
putting found objects – theories, texts – to new and interesting uses.
But it is my view that what Amad describes here is not just an
anything-goes postmodernism, designed to imitate a no-holds-barred
postmodern commercial media marketplace; on the contrary it is a
scrupulous and *responsible* (albeit exciting and purposeful) model of
intellectual work which has perhaps always been more like this than
traditional (modernist) 'scientific' and Left rhetorics would admit.
In other words, instead of placing our conceptual hemlines according to the dictates of the couturiers of intellectual fashion (from
France, Frankfurt and Birmingham), it is now necessary to take
personal responsibility for the choices made and the uses to which
they are put, within that challengeable public arena of critical
readership which Valentin Voloshinov has called 'colloquy of large
scale'.[7] So it is in this book: 'theory shopping' is combined with 'text
browsing' to produce what I hope is a *dialogic* (literally 'colloquial')
rather than an orthodox account of journalism in modernity.

One very important reason for adopting this type of methodology is that in my opinion journalism has been as badly served by
political and cultural critics as has advertising. It is part of the
argument of this book that journalism has enjoyed a history, from
the very beginning, of 'radical producers', not to mention 'unknowable consumers', and the mechanical application of the pessimism
of both the Left and the right-on to journalism has produced a kind
of academic orthodoxy which completely misses what popular
journalism has been up to for the past two hundred years. So a strategy of this book has been to trace the neglected history of popular
and *commercial* radicalism, without obsessively going through the
catalogue of its supposed crimes (which are the 'binding' of readerships mentioned by Amad in the quotation above). There's little in
here about ownership and control, partly because I think ownership
neither causes nor explains the way meanings are made and communicated, partly because it's all very familiar ground in the study of
the media. There's not much in here about how the media manip-
ulate the masses, because I don't think they do (I think they may
want to, as would quite a few so-called critics). Furthermore, media
are more voluntarist and avoidable than, say, school, family and
government; all of which I have personally found a good deal more
coercive, anti-democratic and manipulative than popular media. My
own sense of it is that if advertising, propaganda and mass manipulation actually worked, we wouldn't need any of it, because everyone
would in fact be buying, doing and believing what they were told.

The continual investment in mass persuasion is the strongest evidence that it doesn't work.

Instead, it is my view that popular media are effective – sometimes historically decisive – when their producers, texts and readers are ideologically, politically and semiotically in touch with each other. When that happens, as for example in America in 1775–6, France in 1789, and even in Britain for a while in the 1640s, the 1800s and again in the 1940s, then the results can be quite startling, and not at all reactionary. As a consequence, I've spent more time than I meant to browsing through the amazing archive of the French Revolution (see especially Chapters 3, 4 and 5). It keeps coming back to comment on or to enlighten issues which are still important today, for the very simple reason that modern public and political life is still dressed in its costumes and performed on its stage.

Revolutionary Modernity

Perhaps a word or two is necessary at this point to explain why I've concentrated on the French rather than the American Revolution to show how journalism, modernity and popular culture were co-created, unleashing democracy and comfort upon a sometimes astonished public. After all, as American readers will doubtless protest, the American Revolution occurred in 1776, a decade before the French Revolution began in 1789. Doesn't it follow that the American Revolution takes analytical as well as chronological precedence?

In fact the American Revolution was and is of major importance in the history of journalism: so much so that I have given it precedence in another book, *The Politics of Pictures*, where I showed that the United States of America was founded in journalism.[8] It was in the period 1775 to 1776, with the publication of Tom Paine's pamphlet *Common Sense*, that the American colonies swung behind the idea of independence, and it was Tom Paine himself who named the 'United States of America', just as it was his political philosophy and liberatory rhetoric that inspired Jefferson's Declaration of Independence.[9] Paine's contribution to American independence and to its political vision was both decisive and *journalistic*. That is to say, without *Common Sense* it is not clear that there would have been a majority for independence among the colonies, their legislators or their populations. After *Common Sense* a declaration of independence became inevitable, and this difference was made by converting a dispersed, isolated and numerically very small collection of settler communities, numbering little more than one and a half million people, into a united but adversarial *readership*, which Paine was able to transform via his pamphlet into a community that imagined itself as a continental power of global significance. I suggested in *The Politics of Pictures* that the American Revolution showed 'just what could be done by addressing argumentation to a pervasive anonymous multitude of common readers, united across social divisions, in order for them to decide and act on the resulting truth for themselves'.[10]

But although the American Revolution was a wonderful example of what could be done with popular sovereignty and popular readership, it was just that – an example. In 1776 the USA was hardly the world power it later became (except perhaps in Paine's imagination); political change of historic and international significance was not going to be provoked by colonial backwoodsmen living weeks away from anywhere, across the Atlantic Ocean. The great powers of Europe were poised on the brink of political, industrial and ideo-cultural modernization, and they were locked into a longstanding competitive 'dialogue' of mutual attraction and war (alternately copying and occupying each others' palaces). A conspiracy of semi-rural settlers whose economy was based on land-grab and slavery was indeed a sideshow to the grandees of Europe (though it made a very good rehearsal stage for expatriate Europeans like Paine and Lafayette). But to compare the Virginia of 1776 with the Versailles of 1789 in terms of political importance would be foolish; just as it would be now to compare the power of, say, Western Australia (whose population currently numbers a little over one and a half million people) with that of the United States itself. While various interesting events and experiments may well occur in Western Australia, they do not assume global-historical significance until they shake the ground between Los Angeles and New York. So there's a real sense in which the (later) French Revolution takes precedence over the (earlier) American – it was in France that it mattered.

For the same reason, I have not followed a well-established Anglo-Saxon tradition which locates the opening of modernity in the 'early modern' political, economic and cultural developments of seventeenth-century England. In this period Britain went through some of the same political convulsions as were experienced well over a century later in France – specifically a regicide and a transformation of government from monarchical to republican, along with a civil war to subdue political opposition to the Revolution and to unite several feudal kingdoms into a national state. At the same time, the economy began to display unmistakably modern characteristics (the establishment of modern markets in commodities ranging from capital to culture, including banking and Shakespeare's theatre), while ideo-culturally notions of individualism, secularism and even democracy began to stalk the land. Furthermore, one of the chief guises in which such stalking went forward was journalism – the revolutionary period in England was marked by striking increases in popular literacy, in liberatory pamphlets and in proto-newspaper 'mercuries', 'intelligencers' and 'advertizers' – a phenomenon which was later to characterize revolutionary France in and after 1789 (and revolutionary Russia in 1917 too; there seems to be some positive correlation between modernizing political revolution and a national per capita literacy rate of between one- and two-thirds).

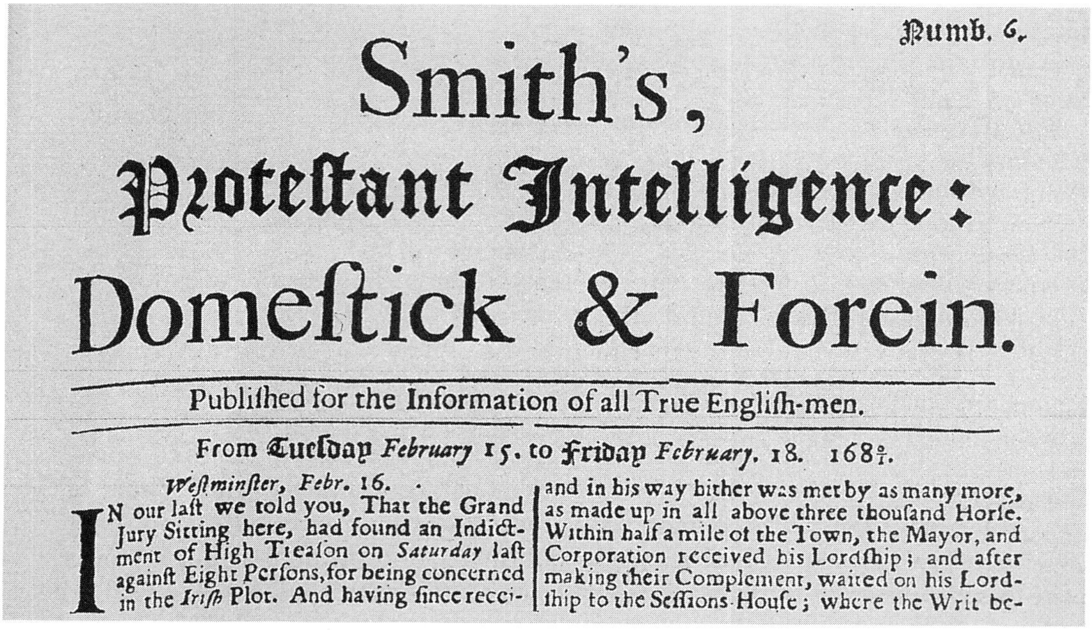

> **Numb. 6.**
>
> # Smith's,
> # Protestant Intelligence:
> # Domestick & Forein.
>
> Publiſhed for the Information of all True Engliſh-men.
>
> From **Tueſday** *February* 15. to **Friday** *February*. 18. 168⁷⁄₈.
>
> *Weſtminſter, Febr.* 16.
> IN our laſt we told you, That the Grand Jury Sitting here, had found an Indictment of High Treaſon on *Saturday* laſt againſt Eight Perſons, for being concerned in the *Iriſh* Plot. And having ſince recci-
>
> and in his way hither was met by as many more, as made up in all above three thouſand Horſe. Within half a mile ot the Town, the Mayor, and Corporation received his Lordſhip; and after making their Complement, waited on his Lordſhip to the Seſſions-Houſe; where the Writ be-

Fig. 1 'Intelligence': journalism, revolution, modernity

But there were differences between the English and the French revolutions, not the least of them being that the English Revolution of the 1640s and 1650s was conducted within a much narrower social stratum than the French, without the pervasive popular involvement that so radicalized Paris; and (perhaps concomitantly), the English experiment failed, and was eventually replaced by the class-supremacist 'Glorious Revolution' of 1688. This settlement produced a strange hybrid polity whose legitimacy was still founded on inherited monarchy, but whose power base was a parliament dominated by landed aristocratic capitalists, who managed to 'represent' the 'commons' or common people without ever having to take the trouble of consulting a popular electorate. And yet the 'Glorious Revolution' is still taken 'officially' as the origin of British parliamentary democracy, as for example by the issue of a celebratory £2 coin in 1989 to mark 300 years of grudging compromise. The coin was issued by the Royal Mint 'to Celebrate the TERCENTENARY of The Bill of Rights and the Claim of Rights', according to a commemorative envelope issued with it by Jif, Jif Spray'n'Foam, and Frish, who gave the coin to supermarket customers at the time. According to Jif, the Bill of Rights 'effectively confirmed the shift in the balance of power from Crown to Parliament', and its current benefits include: 'free and regular elections, freedom of speech in Parliament, proper distribution of governmental power, protection of the rights of subjects and citizens'.

The English Revolution had some very radical, liberatory and democratic tendencies, but it never achieved that simple but decisive moment of *popular sovereignty*, even during Cromwell's Commonwealth, and it was always as much a religious as a secular experiment, especially for the *most* radical writers. Along with the eventual abandonment of republicanism after the 1660 Restoration went a decline in popular literacy and in popular engagement with political questions via the radical press (these did not revive until after the French Revolution). For English popular readerships the energies of the period were turned inwards and 'upwards', as it were – from Milton to Bunyan, from freedom of the press (Milton's *Aeropagitica*) to freedom of the soul (Bunyan's *Pilgrim's Progress*), in a process where literacy became dedicated to textualizing the self (into the imaginary Pilgrim) and Progress was the practice of self-reading (of which the paradigm example is Bunyan's confessional *Grace Abounding to the Chief of Sinners*).[11] Once more, then, it can be said that while the kettle of modernity was evidently brewing in seventeenth-century England, it did not boil over until popular sovereignty spilled into unlikely existence in Paris after 1789.

However, despite the fact that the English Revolution was a failure and that it occurred over three centuries ago, it should not be concluded that it has left no mark, for the consequences of incomplete revolution are quite visible today, and not just in historical legacies like the emigration of so many radicals to the American colonies, or like the peculiarities of British governmental institutions which purport to be operating on behalf of the Crown (not the people), and are therefore apt to be secretive, snobbish and anti-democratic. The vicissitudes of British political history, wherein democratic reform has been so hard, delayed, begrudged and denied, show that the consequences of a failed revolution persist like a running sore in the body politic – a sore which is compulsively scratched by what are commonly regarded as the most 'postmodern' examples of contemporary popular journalism, namely the 'trash', 'tabloid', 'gossip' and 'paparazzi' media. These overheated but underrated journalistic watchdogs worry and tug incessantly at the most fundamental problem that the incomplete revolution has bequeathed to the British political system – its royal family. Since popular sovereignty and monarchy are mutually exclusive forms of government, the persistence within a 'parliamentary democracy' of a form of political legitimacy based on the transmission of monarchical seminal fluid makes the bodies which contain or receive that fluid more than usually anomalous. The popular media, whose 'allegiance' is not really to the Crown but ultimately to their own vast but virtual popular readerships, are performing what can be seen historically as a crucially *pre-democratic* role in their coverage of the British royals, especially the Prince and Princess of Wales (Charlie and Di), who are currently the principal royals of heir-bearing age.

Just as the illicit pre-revolutionary press in France (see Chapter 4) inevitably focused on the gossip, glances, affairs, scandals, sexuality, potency and sexual performances of Queen Marie Antoinette (a proto-Di) and King Louis XVI (a proper Charlie), so the contemporary popular media are actually quite right, in straightforwardly political as well as more broadly anthropological terms, to insist on foregrounding the bodies, sexuality and infidelities of those who constitutionally don't represent but *are* the legitimacy of the state, and through whose bodies must pass the inheritance of monarchy itself. Just as doubts about the political legitimacy of monarchy were expressed in pre-democratic France by lampooning the sexuality of the royals – the king was said to be impotent, the queen rampantly unfaithful – so the contemporary media can be seen to be preoccupied with the consequences of an incompleted move towards popular sovereignty. The sexual comportment of the heirs to the throne is not at all a matter of their private sexual preferences, but is something that cuts to the core of the constitution. But on the other hand, since Britain is *effectively* (isn't it?) a democracy based on representative popular sovereignty, the sexual behaviour of the royals is evidence of their real political impotency, their unfitness to 'rule' countries when they cannot govern their own bodies, and ultimately the absurdity of the very idea of a 'constitutional monarchy' of over fifty million people at home and seventeen sovereign states in the Commonwealth whose continuing 'legitimacy' depends on the sleeping arrangements of one man and one woman. The 'tabloid' and 'gossip' media's obsession with the royal gonads is at the cutting edge, as it were, of political journalism in this context. Far from being *postmodern*, the 'Charlie and Di' saga is strictly *premodern*, and in these pre-democratic circumstances the 'gutter' press is doing what it must: bringing to the attention of popular readerships what court coteries and government cliques already know, namely, the *politics of kissing*.

Conversely, it has to be said that the 'respectable' British media (the so-called newspapers of record and the broadcasters) display a long history of serious bad faith: they have been suppressing information about royal love-lives throughout modernity (from the Prince Regent and successive princes of Wales to Edward VIII, Princess Margaret and Prince Edward); they have colluded actively with official censorship, and even now that D-Notices are a thing of the past, self-censorship sympathetic to the Palace is still routine; and they even refuse to run pictures of royal bodies in unflattering or revealing poses. This shows the dangers of loyalty to a crown rather than towards the real – popular – source of both political sovereignty and media readership. However, the fact that information about royal sexuality has long counted as an official secret, more closely guarded by successive governments than military intelligence, suggests just how unstable this pre-democratic 'constitutional monarchy' really is. From this perspective, the received critical wisdom about popular journalism might need to be revised, for it may very well be that the incessant parade of the bizarre spectacle of Diana's gym wear, Fergie's toes, Andrew's prattishness, Charles's phone conversations, Camilla's tampons, Edward's sexual proclivities, and even Anne's bottom (a picture of which, taken by the Sydney *Daily Mirror*'s Warwick Lawson during a breezy, dress-billowing moment of her tour of Papua New Guinea in 1976 was banned in the UK and Australia, but published on the front cover of – where else? – *Paris Match*), is actually trying to tell us something important.[12]

Morphing the Readership

Since the English Revolution has not yet been completed, and the American one (for all its eventual significance) served at the time as a dress rehearsal for the real thing, I have continued to feel justified in locating the decisive moment of modernity – the transfer of sovereignty from monarch to people – in 1789 Paris rather than 1640s London or 1776 Philadelphia. But this does mean that while my arguments about modernity can be *illustrated* by reference to the events of the French Revolution, they are by no means *confined* to those events. I think what I've tried to show about the co-creation of modernity, popular sovereignty, the politics of comfort, popular journalism and popular readership, holds not just for Paris in 1789 but for westernized/modernizing countries ever since. It is the creation of popular readerships in the name of democratic equivalence that makes the French Revolution both interesting in itself and the model of what I've called the 'mediasphere'.

Without wishing to pre-empt later discussions about the 'mediasphere', I think it might be helpful here to point out one or two of its general consequences by working through some emblematic textualizations. Most importantly, attention to the 'mediasphere' focuses attention on the context within which mainstream journalism actually circulates, rather than on its industrial mode of production. I've suggested that this context has two main features: meanings and readerships. An interesting way to show how this perspective might alter the way that mainstream journalism is approached (i.e. moving analytically from a social science to a cultural studies perspective) is to ask what people look at over the breakfast table.

The most 'mainstream' of any newspaper is perhaps *The Times* (see Chapter 3); dating back to 1785, it is one of the oldest surviving titles in the world, and was once called 'The Thunderer' for the tone of its editorial address to governments (one of which, in the 1850s, was said to have fallen as a direct result). *The Times* has always liked to portray itself as the paper with the most powerful readers (its advertising slogan in the 1950s and 60s was 'Top People Take The Times'), and perhaps that is why both Lord Northcliffe and Rupert Murdoch – who made their fortunes from popular but downmarket newspapers – bought it. What makes the reputation of such journalistic institutions as *The Times* is clearly a combination of its meanings (what it says) with its readership (who reads it), but in the end it's the readership, both real and imagined, that matters most. Over the breakfast tables of England, Very Important Personages, and those who wished to become, associate with, or

Fig. 2 *Waiting for The Times.* Painting by B.R. Haydon, 1835 (*The Times* Archive, London. © Times Newspapers Ltd. 1996)

know what was on the minds of Very Important Personages, would commune with one another, and share their sense of their Very Importance, via a close perusal of *The Times.* So eloquent is this vision of the old radical press adage, 'knowledge is power', that it has even resulted in a painting; an artistic rendition of class *consciousness* as it might actually be experienced, but in B.R. Haydon's 1835 painting *Waiting for The Times* (Fig. 2), it is the ruling rather than the radical class whose consciousness is displayed.

The 'consciousness' on display is not so much 'power' as 'impatience' – the would-be reader of *The Times* (on our right) is present in the picture but absent from the imagined community of VIP readership. The painting captures the longing and desire for participation via textuality in the decisive affairs and stories of the day, just as it captures both the plenitude of information for those in possession of the appropriate technology (on our left), and their open-legged smugness at being thus empowered. It's an image of readership triumphant, of the militant appropriation of meanings and thence of the socio-political sphere that they signify, by a class whose consciousness of itself as a class resides precisely in the knowledge of each reader that the same newspaper and stories are simultaneously being read by his or her peers, often enough the very people whose actions and decisions are being reported, or those whose lives are caught up professionally in the matters being debated, or whose economic and political clout may determine the

Fig. 3 'Sunday funnies 1991'. Photograph by Sally Mann (Sally Mann and Aperture Foundation)

outcome of events which are deemed newsworthy for that very reason.

This is the archetypal image of mainstream journalism, but it is intrinsically anti-democratic. It cannot be extended to mass – popular – journalism without straining beyond breaking point the implied addresser/addressee relationship, for the whole point of the *Waiting for The Times* model of readership is that news is a resource for government *over* rather than *by* the people. But it was in fact the radical, democratizing press which originally coined the phrase 'knowledge is power', as a slogan that *The Poor Man's Guardian* used in the early 1800s to oppose government repression of the 'pauper press'. This tradition of journalism is far from 'mainstream', but it is for me at least the wellspring of democratic journalism and 'mass' readership in modernity, as I've argued both elsewhere and throughout this book.[13]

However, in recent years, during the period often dubbed 'postmodern' by media and academic commentators alike, the image of journalism and of its popular readership has changed; it is neither an image of the 'powers that be' nor of their organized or disorganized radical opponents. Currently – and often to the horror of those brought up in the modernist tradition of 'mainstream' adversarial journalism – the image of both readerships and the meanings circulating via popular journalism suggests a different kind of breakfast reading altogether. Here, and now, the emphasis is not on public life but private meaning, and the readership has morphed from:

male to female
old to young
militant to meditative
public to private
governmental to consumerist
law-making to identity-forming

There aren't many sympathetic portraits that capture the *internal* consciousness of this readership, but I think a sense of it is caught in one of Sally Mann's astonishing and challenging photographs of her own children from the book *Immediate Family* (Fig. 3): the photograph called 'Sunday Funnies'.[14] This picture shows what Mann herself has elsewhere described as 'a common humanity and a durable continuum'; an 'intricacy of particulars' within which lie 'all those universal intangibles: love and light, time and grace'.[15] But it's also, within all this, undoubtedly a picture of *readership* – familial, informal participation in quite a different 'mediasphere' from that of the *Times* reader. It's the Sunday paper's cartoons that hold the eye, on a bed rather than a breakfast table, for children whose unselfconsciousness about their own comportment bespeaks a similar nonchalance about being part of the biggest imagined community ever imagined, the readership of popular media.

Interestingly, the reputation of this readership is at stake in the fate of Sally Mann's own photographs; the *Immediate Family* exhibition was denounced by certain American conservatives when it was first shown, precisely because Mann does make public the most intimate moments of 'love and light, time and grace', in the form of her children's bodies. In my view, sustained by the analysis upon which this book is based, a large part of the reason why Mann's pictures are both so compelling and so controversial is that they show exactly what the privatized, feminized, postmodern *public* actually looks like: irreducibly complex, certainly, but also widely imagined as childlike.

To a tradition of thinking which likes to dress its images of public life in heroic, militant and preferably masculine costumes before sending them out to do gladiatorial battle in the world of information technology, the sight of three largely undressed children idly making their own sense out of mass media in the most private of circumstances is not seen as what Sally Mann calls 'truths, but truths "told slant," just as Emily Dickinson commanded',[16] but as an offence to decency. It's a governmentalist tradition which cannot handle the idea of what it preconceives as a vulnerable, impressionable, untutored, inexperienced population being in fact able to think, act, feel and grow for itself. And so it has produced an image of the public as an infantilized and unenlightened female, for ever in need of correction and protection, hidden out of sight and away from the light – away from the glare of publicity. When someone ('without fear and without shame', as Mann puts it) actually produces public images of this youthful femininity, showing it to be anything but infantilized (and far from sentimentalized), the results can seem shocking, precisely because they transgress the established boundary between public and private.

Sally Mann works in the genre of 'art' photography, rather than journalism or even documentary realism. She takes pictures of a family living an essentially rural existence in backwoods Virginia, in direct line of succession from Stonewall Jackson and Robert E. Lee, back to the founding fathers of the American nation whose 'common sense' has indeed come to this. But still she captures something of the most contemporary mediasphere – although her artistic vision is her own, I think what she depicts is much more general, and can be seen as a staple of popular media. The media-sphere is suffused with images and issues which connect popular readerships and popular meanings together, and there too the focus has moved from masculine command to feminized juvenation and domestic privacy; the mainstream of contemporary journalism is fashion, gossip, lifestyle, consumerism and celebrity, and 'news' is private, visual, narrativized and personalized.

The Mediasphere – Kate's and Kellogg's Common Sense

The icon of the contemporary mediasphere is therefore not the superpower but the supermodel. Kate Moss, hailed as 'the face of the nineties', at the time when Sally Mann's art photography was stirring controversy, is one supermodel who's had more than her fair share of the very same kind of criticism as has been levelled at Mann. Oddly enough, it seemed that those in the know valued Moss for her 'ordinariness', her 'natural' look; qualities which *connected* her to the target readership, as opposed to the first wave of supermod-els (exemplified, perhaps, by Claudia Schiffer).

This is how Australian *Who Weekly* reported her professional appeal:

> *I don't think the fashion world could have got any more excessive in the '80s', says Ashley Heath, a fashion editor at Britain's* The Face *magazine, whose March 1990 photos of Moss were her first in a major publication. 'The models couldn't have got any taller, boobier. Models like Kate Moss represent a more natural look . . . they are young, ordinary girls.*[17]

Kate Moss was seen by her peers as not only the 'quintessential "new look," skinny, young, and knowing', but also 'a great model. That is

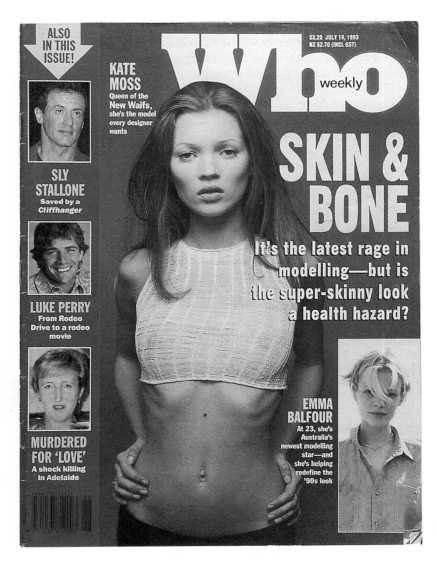

ALSO IN THIS ISSUE!

SLY STALLONE Saved by a *Cliffhanger*

LUKE PERRY From Rodeo Drive to a rodeo movie

MURDERED FOR 'LOVE' A shock killing in Adelaide

KATE MOSS Queen of the New Waifs, she's the model every designer wants

$2.20 JULY 19, 1993
NZ $2.70 (INCL GST)

Who weekly

SKIN & BONE

It's the latest rage in modelling—but is the super-skinny look a health hazard?

EMMA BALFOUR At 23, she's Australia's newest modelling star—and she's helping redefine the '90s look

Fig. 4 Kate Moss in *Who Weekly*: anorexia or art? Photograph Sante D'Orazio

to say, Kate is highly adaptable, looks good in lots of make-up, and in no make-up at all, is easy to work with and puts everything into her job'[18]. But whatever the facts of the case, or the socio-demographics of her appeal, it was not her compliance with the routines of modelling or her 'ordinariness' that propelled her into international notoriety, but her size. Calvin Klein (with whom she signed her first international contract) was quoted as saying: 'She *is* tiny and she *is* young and innocent, and at the same time she can be very sophisticated and very woman-like. There are not a lot of models who can do all of these things'.[19] Moss became famous because she *looked* as though she was transgressing the boundary between childlike 'innocence' and adult 'knowing', a position which produced a very interesting 'reading' of her in the popular media. If looked at as a

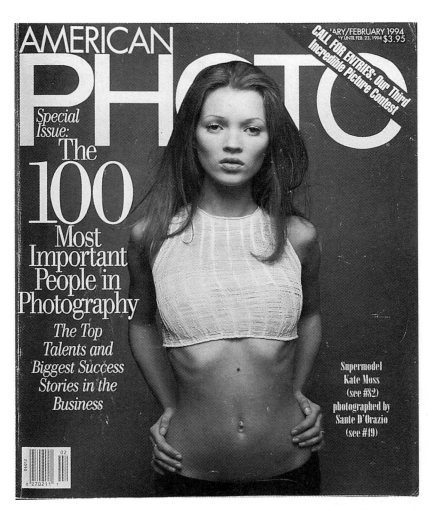

Fig. 5 Kate Moss in *American Photo*: art or airbrush? Photograph by Sante D'Orazio

child, then she was too 'knowing' and was accused of encouraging paedophilia; if looked at as a *woman*, then she was too skinny, and was accused of encouraging anorexia. Naturally, because she straddled the boundaries, she was accused of both; attracting the complaints of

> *some readers of the June [1993] issue of British* Vogue, *whose knickers were in a knot over an eight-page lingerie layout featuring a vacant-eyed, make-up-less Moss, which, they huffed, had overtones of paedophilia and pornography. The* Daily Mail *concurred, saying 'The attempt to make a glamorous ideal of a look that, in reality, is achieved by fasting or starvation seems perverse...' Not surprisingly, Alexandra Shulman,* Vogue*'s editor, has disagreed. 'Personally, I think they're beautiful. The kiddie-porn accusation is ridiculous'.*[20]

In short, while the art circuit was debating Sally Mann, the popular media were thinking about the 'superwaifs', and, quick as a flash, that became art.

The very photograph that *Who Weekly* used on its cover to illustrate 'SKIN & BONE: It's the latest rage in modelling – but is the super-skinny look a health hazard?' (Fig. 4) turned up again within six months on the cover of *American Photo*, whose New Year special issue was devoted to 'The 100 Most Important People in Photography' (Fig. 5). This time Moss signified not anorexia but art. Her cover photograph was used to illustrate the entire 'Top 100', even though 'The Supermodels' only made #82. The supermodels' entry is the only one on the whole list to be given to a collective category of people rather than to a named individual, but nevertheless it claims great power for their 'class':

> *The* New York Times *recently asserted that more kids today know the names of models than ex-presidents . . .. But don't assume that such clout is necessarily a negative for photography. In an era when we can read all about Kate Moss and Cindy Crawford in almost any copy of* People, *supermodels have given photography a superglamorous image.*[21]

Elsewhere in the Top 100 we find – fully fifty places higher than Sally Mann at #77 – Calvin Klein at #26, of whom it is said:

> *From Brooke Shields . . . in her Calvin Klein jeans to Kate Moss . . . in nothing at all for Obsession perfume, Klein's advertising imagery has an artistic life of its own. . . . ample testimony to his belief that art can rub off on commerce.*[22]

It's this combination of art, advertising and the commercial capitalization of eroticized looks, that signals not only success but also the energy of the mediasphere, where the previously incommensurate domains of the public (art) and the private (ad) coalesce and kiss, often enough *in the form of* images of supermodels like Kate Moss, whose 'look' for a time textualizes in one body both the demands of fashion and a simulacrum of the public itself (see also Chapter 7 for further discussion of this phenomenon, whose personalized form I call the 'frocks pop').

As *American Photo*'s editor grudgingly concedes, the current 'clout' of the supermodels is not 'necessarily a negative for photography', for the makers of the negs themselves become stars of the public sphere. For instance, position #49 in the Top 100 is held by photographer Sante D'Orazio, whose picture of Kate Moss graces the covers of both *American Photo* and *Who Weekly*. His entry says:

> *In answer to the question . . . what is erotic? – Sante D'Orazio has an answer: Nearly every image he makes. . . . D'Orazio's become one of the country's [USA] most in-demand celebrity portraitists, a photographer with a reputation for making nearly everyone he shoots, including the most beautiful people in the world, look even better.*[23]

Despite this accolade, and despite the fact that *American Photo* placed D'Orazio more than thirty positions higher than the supermodels themselves, the photograph on the magazine's front cover is not *exactly* the one that he took, nor is it the same as the one that *Who Weekly* published. *American Photo* has not only flopped the picture (reversing its left/right symmetry), but the airbrush has been at work too. There's no trace of Kate Moss's nipples, nor of a mole on her breast (she's anatomically correct in the *Who* version). It is of course speculative to wonder whether the airbrush is wielded routinely on US magazine cover pictures destined for the general newsstand, or whether Kate Moss's image has been singled out by *American Photo* because of the furore about her juvenated and skinny sexuality, in which case we are in the presence of simple have-your-cake-and-eat-it bad faith by the magazine, which erases signs of Moss's gender while celebrating D'Orazio's eroticization of her body. But whatever the reason for the airbrushing, *American Photo*'s cover serves as an example and a reminder that even in the West, in the land of the First Amendment, truth (even 'told slant') doesn't always make it on to the front page: this is exactly the same kind of censorship, though less clumsily done, as is used by totalitarian regimes to rewrite history – for instance the airbrushing of the 'Gang of Four' from the official photograph of the funeral of Chairman Mao in 1976 (see Chapter 8).

Meanwhile, Kate Moss herself was plagued by 'labelling' problems in the press (both popular and up-market), routinely having her body confused for her image, to the extent that she spent the early 1990s having constantly to deny she was anorexic herself. In her own book, *Kate*, published in 1995, she reproduces a couple of newspaper articles – one from an unidentified British tabloid which (disbelievingly) headlined an informal airport photo of her with: 'So this is one of the most beautiful women in the world'. The caption-story ran: 'Kate, 19, became a superstar overnight after appearing in *Vogue* earlier this year. Pictures of the waif-like model clad in sexy underwear were branded obscene by some readers.' The other headline in Moss's book is from *The Independent*, a top-of-the-range 'quality' paper, whose photo of the 'superwaif off duty' is sub-headlined: 'She's still only 19, a gauche teenager, and is endearingly polite. It's enough to restore your faith in supermodels.'[24] The restoration is only partial, however, as the picture is taken not from *The Independent*'s news coverage but from its 'Living' section – what used to be called the 'women's page'. Moss writes in the foreword to her book that 'A lot of horrible, unfair, untrue things have been said about me. I've been labelled viciously by the majority of the media', and signs off with a PS: 'I am just on my way out to dinner, to eat a massive steak and loads of very fattening potatoes, with loads of butter.'[25]

We have moved from what people look at over their breakfast table to what Kate Moss – the very image of newsworthy, eroticized readership – eats for dinner. It seems we've come a long way since the founding moments of both modernity and journalism, when America's revolutionary households read Tom Paine's *Common Sense* to each other over the waffles and hash browns. In fact we've come

Fig. 6 'Common Sense' – from modernity to postmodernity

to postmodernity, where people don't read newspapers at all at the breakfast table, but lounge around on Sundays with the 'funnies', and follow the trials, tribulations and tear-sheets of the supermodels in the glossies, the tabloids, and the supermarket weeklies. At breakfast, the only reading material left is the cereal packet, which might well be a box of Kellogg's Common Sense – a concoction of oatbran flakes released in the UK market to appeal to people with worries about heart disease and fitness:

> *Keeping your heart in shape doesn't have to mean a tiresome and taxing regime. Try a swimming costume and a little common sense. Swimming a few lengths, three times a week at the local pool could turn out to be quite fun. And* Kellogg's COMMON SENSE *every day.*

While Kellogg's doesn't seem too convinced about the swimming, 'common sense' is now its registered trademark.

Perhaps this explains why cereal boxes have themselves become icons of 'readership' – but only as part of a widespread tendency to belittle the textual study of popular culture, by implying that 'reading' such trivial objects of study is self-evidently (in the very name of 'common sense') absurd. Toby Miller quotes the celebrated line in Don de Lillo's 'postmodern' novel *White Noise*, where a character complains about a certain American university's specialization: 'I understand the music, I understand the movies, I even see how comic books can tell us things. But there are full professors in this place who read nothing but cereal boxes.'[26] The joke may be understandable, but at the same time it is clear that cereal boxes can indeed 'tell us things', and that 'reading' them alerts us to the semiosphere whose interconnections allow – encourage – dialogue between revolution and heart disease, modernity and swimming, political philosophy and breakfast.

Postmodern Journalism and the Knowledge Class

Meanwhile, what of the events that used to give stout men apoplexies? As everybody knows, the real world of politics and power, the stuff of proper journalism, is not untouched by the developments outlined above. Even presidents of the United States (who may be less familiar to popular readerships than Kate Moss) have to run the gauntlet of media interest in their diet, their fitness regime, their sexuality and private lives. At election time it is as much the personal, private and bodily behaviour and image of candidates that decides the issue as policies – perhaps more so. Under such conditions, candidates need all the friends they can get.

For those nostalgic modernists and news junkies who still read the morning broadsheet over their bowl of Common Sense, the 'quality' press still provides a service, but it is fully integrated into the mediasphere. Here's how. During the 1992 Bush/Clinton presidential election campaign a story from *The Times* was syndicated around the world (of Murdoch outlets), appearing for instance in *The Australian* under the headline 'ECONOMY DEALS BLOW TO BUSH'.[27] The story was a round-up of evidence showing how badly President Bush was doing in the election run-up, concentrating on new figures which indicated a poor rate of growth in the US gross domestic product. But this economic story (substance) was prefaced by something deemed really significant (style): 'The greatest indicator of public disillusionment with the President is the first spate of anti-Bush jokes doing the rounds of Washington ... .' Accompanying the story is a photograph captioned 'Mr Clinton laughs at a headline in Arkansas yesterday' (Fig. 7). And well he might, for this image completely overwhelms the three-column, twenty-six-paragraph story: it shows him holding up one of the supermarket weeklies and sharing the joke of its outrageous headline: 'ALIEN BACKS CLINTON!' With friends like those, Bill Clinton could hardly lose; he rides to the White House not only on the back of Bush's 1.4 per cent GDP, and not in a flying saucer, but at least partly on the positive image of a candidate who, despite intense media speculation about his own private and sexual affairs, could still come up laughing at (with) the excesses of the popular media. This photograph (which I'm tempted to call a portrait *of* 'democratic equivalence') combines neatly the

Mr Clinton laughs at a headline in Arkansas yesterday — Reuters pictur

Fig. 7 'Alien Backs Clinton!' (Photograph © Reuters)

two worlds of the 'trash' and 'quality' mainstream media, coalescing fact and fantasy, politics and personality, and encapsulating the contemporary mediasphere, where the most powerful public office on the planet may be reached with the help of backers who don't exist on it; that's the curious world of modern popular reality.

It is part of the argument of *Popular Reality* that things have not suddenly degenerated to this point, nor that these strange liaisons, dialogues and kissings in the mediasphere are indicative of any supposed decline from a once pure and rational public sphere, but that such connections have constituted the mainstream of journalism from the very start. Later in the book (Chapters 6 and 7) I try to show what the 'postmodern' public sphere (the mediasphere) looks like – it is textualized, privatized, suburbanized, feminized and sexualized. But it is still part of the mediasphere created in the opening moments of the French Revolution; it's a product of history, certainly, a history which goes back further than the familiar 'nowist' rhetoric of postmodernity might suggest. But at the same time the period of two hundred years or so covered in this book is not all that long in terms of cultural or discursive developments. According to semiotic time and cultural space, we're still in the same universe that was created in modernity's 'big bang' on that warm Parisian Tuesday of 14 July 1789. In this sense, the French Revolution has the status of central, mythic 'law-formation' for the West, while the American Revolution remains at the level of newsworthy 'anomaly' or 'surprise' (see Chapter 4 for a further explanation of these terms, which are Lotman's).

In tracing the modernizing energies of the French Revolution, I've also quite self-consciously concentrated on the progressive and democratizing side of public, political and journalistic events, and on the radical rather than the reactionary press. I think the radical press deserves the credit for some of the most important positive developments of modernity: for the idea of taking popular sovereignty literally, for instance; and for inventing a politicized public of citizen readers; as well as for working out in public the implications of 1789, not only for the activists in that struggle but for activists in other causes, on behalf of women and colonized peoples for instance, who were able to use it as a model to argue for their own 'democratic equivalence', and for previously non-politicized areas of private and personal life, from clothes to the calendar (see Chapter 4).

At the same time, I recognize the long-term contribution of the modernizing commercial and right-wing press, which has been less in the realm of ideas (their political catch-cry is 'Don't!'), than in the pursuit of that other goal of modernity, comfort. The commercial media were also, obviously, at the forefront of the industrial, organizational and institutional development of journalism, as part of a larger tendency towards the commodification of culture and language into entertainment and information. For their own reasons, they had a major influence on the transformation of volatile, intermittent, active but disloyal revolutionary readerships into a reading public who would consume their news as regularly as (and with) their breakfast cereals – a transformation of readers from citizenship to circulation, as it were. The commercial media eventually created a variegated but pervasive landscape of habituated media-readers stretching across the social and geographical spectrum, for whom journalism became not only liberating but pleasurable and even useful (see Chapter 3), from one end of the imperialized globe to the other. The semioticization of public, private and personal life, the transnational communications of postmodern media, would not be possible without such capital investment.

But of course the uses to which such resources can be put do not always coincide with the intentions of their 'owners', who are not only the personalized gladiatorial barons of popular image, but also institutional investors like insurance companies and pension funds. Indeed, if there is a 'class struggle' in the empire of information, it is not so much between owners and readers, producers and consumers, as an internecine struggle between different elements of what John Frow has identified as the 'knowledge class'[28] – among whose factions would be journalists (media textmakers) on the one side and critical intellectuals on the other, fighting out with each other who gets to speak on behalf of an increasingly unknowable audience, in whose name so much contemporary media 'representation' seeks to gain power for its own point of view. The interesting thing about the 'knowledge class' is that its members rarely own and control, in the economic sense, the media and discourses they produce, deploy, and fight over. This is why I have spent some time in this book (especially in Chapters 2 and 9) criticizing not the popular media but my own 'trade' – critical intellectual academic work – for developing a technology of control, i.e. 'mass communication studies', every bit as anti-democratic as anything the media moguls have invented.

The political Left and Right don't emerge from this study without swapping a few of their clothes, and neither does 'popular reality'. In fact part of my purpose in this book is to go beyond the tradition of binarized, adversarial criticism of the kind to which John Frow himself falls victim when he recognizes that journalists are part of his 'knowledge class', only to dismiss them wholesale (along with priests and teachers) on the grounds that their class function is simply to 'inculcate ruling class ideology'.[29] This is a standard leftist denunciation of journalism – especially popular ('commercial') journalism – and Frow uses it in a self-evident, throw-away manner, in the course of a book which is actually arguing the reverse: namely that culture cannot be reduced to class, and that intellectual cultural critique cannot be sustained around the binarization of the 'high culture' (ruling class)/'low culture' (popular class) distinction, even where there's an effort made (as in cultural studies) to reverse the evaluative polarity by valorizing the low/popular pole of the binary. Frow's point is well made; it is important to go beyond such cold war metaphorics, and the reason why is clear when Frow himself momentarily reverts to them. For a theoretical approach which simply denounces journalists as 'inculcators of ruling class ideology' gives itself no reason to investigate journalism further – there's no more to be said.

Binary Kissing

But of course journalism has a varied history, and while there are plenty of capitalist running-dog lick-spittles (as we used to call them) in the trade, there are other traditions entirely: some that aspire to 'inculcate' revolution, or at least alternative ideologies, such as feminist, multicultural, ethnic, indigenous, environmental, youth or subcultural points of view (see Chapter 9); there are others that don't have ideological aspirations at all. It is important to go beyond a characterization of journalism which lumps all this together and prejudges whatever is said, done or shown as 'ruling class ideology'. It is equally important, however, not to take the industry's self-evaluations at face value either, for professional journalists are not exempt from the cultural values they live among. All too frequently within journalistic and 'opinion-leader' circles there is an uncritical acceptance of high/low-type distinctions, such as:

(positive evaluation) v. (negative evaluation)

newspapers of record v. tabloids

information v. entertainment

'hard' news v. 'soft' news

'quality' v. popular press

substance v. style

leftist v. rightist

politics v. gossip

words v. pictures

press v. television

culture v. consumerism

public sphere v. private lifestyle

public service media v. commercial media

Unfortunately for the apparently pure binarism of the above set of distinctions, not only do many journalists *espouse* the values on the left while *working* for those on the right, but also the intellectually respectable media (associated with the terms on the left) are just as suffused with the values on the right as is the most virulent trash-tabloid, which is itself just as likely to display – at the textual if not at the boardroom level – the values on the left, and for vast readerships.

Furthermore, the above distinctions may well have a long history as 'common sense' in the media industry and among policy-makers, academics and listeners to breakfast radio, but that doesn't make them any the less prejudicial as a mental map of modern media. Not only do such binaries reinforce a systematic bias against popular, screen and commercial media, but they also tend to reinforce other prejudices, principally the one which considers many of the terms on the right as 'women's issues', with the (silent but inescapable) implication that serious politics and the public sphere is men's stuff (see Chapter 2). As a result, while it is important to be aware of the *existence* of these binary tendencies both in journalistic discourses and in critical accounts of the media, and to notice how they may underlie the very real institutional structures within which media organizations operate, it is equally important to remember that such binaries belong to the discursive universe that analysis is trying to explain, and not to the framework of explanation. In short, it is necessary to test out what work such categories are doing 'empirically', as it were, by looking at the institutional and discursive form they may take, without assuming that such forms are either natural or inevitable, and without accepting what Frow calls their 'regime of value' – the 'regime' of understanding in which it seems so obvious that quality papers are 'better' or even 'more serious' than the tabloid media.[30]

For example, the above binary prejudices may, historically, structure a nation's whole cultural policy and thence its journalistic institutions, as for instance in the post-imperial world (from Britain via Malaysia and Singapore to Australia, to my own knowledge, and doubtless elsewhere too, and not only in the old white dominions) where 'public service broadcasting' on the BBC model has been sustained for generations precisely in order to *preserve* the above prejudicial distinctions, by placing cultural value and public investment on the left, and leaving the entire domain represented by the right-hand set of terms to 'market forces' (plus government regulation). Even when, as during the past decade or so, governments move towards deregulation and 'market forces', this does not represent an abandonment of the distinctions, but merely a policy swing towards the values on the right. One effect of this history has been to train media participants and observers alike that 'quality' is somehow naturally opposed to 'width': that is, the output of prestige media organizations is reckoned to be of high quality but of minority appeal; conversely, commercial journalism is conceded to be popular, but worth doodly-squat. And an effect of this ideology is that public service people value their work but not their readers, while commercial people value their ratings but not their writings.

Such presuppositions leave in place the very prejudices that need to be analysed and superseded (see Chapter 1). Journalism is not explained by what its proponents like to claim for it, nor by what its detractors claim against it. In order to take proper account of it, it is necessary to adopt a perspective on journalism which neither takes sides between the above binary oppositions nor simply reproduces them. In this book (see especially Chapter 1), I characterize journalism as 'the textual system of modernity', a formula which allows it to be considered as a whole (i.e. across and beyond the various binary divides) and at the same time allows its changes to be viewed historically (i.e. across modernity). Such a perspective yields new insights into journalism, as I've already suggested. But the formula also allows something to be said about *modernity*, for an analysis of journalism as a textual system is *also* an analysis of modernity, I would argue. Journalism forms a mediasphere which connects readerships not only (perhaps not even primarily) with the public domain, but also with the culture at large – indeed journalism is one of the chief mechanisms by which different (and sometimes mutually incomprehensible) cultural domains are kept in dialogue with one another. In this context it may be that the most fundamental changes are occurring at the margin or in the most despised media. Thus it is unwise to retain too rigid a view as to what counts as mainstream journalism today.

Popular reality emerges as the textualization of social relations, the advancement of the logic of democratic equivalence, and the pursuit of comfort, in modernizing societies. It's a democratized mediasphere which not only textualizes debate and decision-making, but also the public in whose name all this is done (the readership), and the participants in the developing dialogue, from politicians to entertainers and supermodels. Popular reality is also a politicized private sphere, a feminized, privatized, suburbanized, consumerist domain of popular sovereignty, linked by a popular and pervasive journalism which both creates and serves this strangely disembodied postmodern public. Popular reality, then, is what happens when producers, texts and readers, in the integrated unity of the semiosphere, are in 'virtual' touch with each other, kissing.

Notes

1. Yuri (Iurii Mikhailovich) Lotman (1990) *The Universe of the Mind: A Semiotic Theory of Culture.* Trans. Ann Shukman. Bloomington and Indianapolis: Indiana University Press, 273.
2. Hugh Gough (1988) *The Newspaper Press in the French Revolution.* London: Routledge, 183–7.
3. James Moran (1973) *Printing Presses: History and Development from the Fifteenth Century to Modern Times.* Berkeley and LA: University of California Press, 32–4.
4. Moran, 108, 218–19 (and *passim*).
5. Lotman, Chapters 8–13.
6. Paula Amad (1994) *Radical Inauthenticity and Cultural Anxiety: The Benetton Advertising Phenomenon.* MA thesis, Department of English, University of Melbourne, 13.
7. Valentin Voloshinov (1973) *Marxism and the Philosophy of Language.* New York: Seminar Press, 95.
8. John Hartley (1992) *The Politics of Pictures: The Creation of the Public in the Age of Popular Media.* London and New York: Routledge, 166–9.
9. Thomas Paine (1976, first published 1776) *Common Sense.* Edited with an introduction by Isaac Krammick. Harmondsworth: Penguin.
10. Hartley, 166.
11. John Milton (1974) *John Milton: Selected Prose.* Harmondsworth: Penguin, contains *Aeropagitica.* John Bunyan (1928, first published 1666) *Grace Abounding to the Chief of Sinners; or, A Brief Relation of the Exceeding Mercy of God in Christ, to His Poor Servant, John Bunyan.* London: Dent, New York: Dutton, Everyman's Library.
12. The source for the picture of Princess Anne in PNG is the Perth *Sunday Times,* 24 September 1995, which issued a four-page liftout to celebrate publication of a book featuring a century of Australian press photography, called *The Pictures Tell the Story* (1995). Sydney: Angus & Robertson.
13. Hartley, Chapter 7.
14. Sally Mann (1992) *Immediate Family.* New York: Aperture. The book is unpaginated. 'Sunday funnies' is reproduced within Sally Mann's foreword, as if to illustrate her discussion of her photographic relationship with her children.

15. Sally Mann (1988) *At Twelve: Portraits of Young Women*. New York: Aperture, 13.
16. Mann, *Immediate Family*, foreword.
17. Allison Lynn (1993) Slim pickings. *Who Weekly*, July 19, cover story, 46–53.
18. Kate Moss (1995) *Kate*. London: Pavilion Books. Flyjacket, and foreword by Liz Tilberis, Editor-in-Chief of *Harper's Bazaar*.
19. Calvin Klein (fashion designer and parfumier), quoted in *Who Weekly*, 46.
20. *Who Weekly*, 47.
21. David Schonauer (ed.) (1994) Photography's Top 100 [#82 The Supermodels]. *American Photo*. January/February, 95.
22. *American Photo*, 73.
23. *American Photo*, 80.
24. Moss, n.p.
25. Moss, foreword.
26. Toby Miller (1990) 'There are full professors in this place who read nothing but cereal boxes.' Australian screen in academic print. *Media Information Australia*, 55, 5–13.
27. Economy deals blow to Bush. *Weekend Australian*, 1–2 August 1992. Bylined 'Bryan Boswell in Washington and The Times'.
28. John Frow (1995) *Cultural Studies and Cultural Value*. Oxford: Oxford University Press. See especially 120ff.
29. Frow, 121.
30. Frow, Chapter 4.

CHAPTER

1 *Journalism and Modernity*

(Journalism, Media, Popular Culture)

For their part, citizens are relatively sceptical.   RICHARD ERICSON *et al.*[1]

Journalism, Media, Popular Culture

This chapter is in three parts: journalism, media, popular culture; it comprises a reworking of each of these familiar terms into the terms of this book. My starting position on *journalism* is that it can be studied as a whole, despite its size and variety; it may be understood as the sense-making practice of modernity. I see *media* not as so many technologies or industries, but as the ground upon which modernity has been textualized, as the forms taken by a textual system like journalism. And I'll argue that the crucial feature of *popular culture* is the creation of readerships (a term which includes audiences, and listening and looking as well as reading graphic text), which can be understood narrowly as the readerships of specific media and forms, and more widely as 'readerships by any other name', as it were – collectivities imagined as unities which are only united by common readership of media and journalism (for example, the people, wo/men, the nation, the empire, the species). Meanwhile, I am pursuing a line of historical thought which seeks to trace the bringing together of the 'public sphere' and the 'semiosphere' into the 'mediasphere'.

All this may suggest a very neat and coherent object of study, a unified whole that can be known and which explains its composite parts. But it has to be said that the only ground from which 'modernity' can be seen 'as a whole' is the ground of *postmodernity*, which is not a ground at all and which would have no truck with anything 'as a whole'. Postmodernity is however one of the developments in knowledge-culture which has led to such non-canonical forms as journalism being taken seriously in the first place, and which is just as interested in popular culture, mass media, and the ephemera of throwaway consumerism as in the tenets of high-art high modernism. What follows, then, is postmodern in topic and in sympathy, but nevertheless it does try to look at the textual system of journalism as a whole, even if that 'whole' must in the end be recognized as a convenient analytic fiction designed to impose some order on a chaotic field; an imposition which is clearly in the eye of the beholder, as I survey a socio-semiotic scene which is even messier than the mythical teenager's bedroom, and my pathetic attempts to tidy it up are, equally obviously, designed not to produce a tidier reality, but for your benefit (dear reader), in the vain hope that if I do this you'll be able to find things more easily. However, as in teenagers' bedrooms, so in journalism – the 'natural condition' is more *strewn* than structured, and of course a proper tidy-up can only be done by the well-meaning outsider when the life-force which leaves traces of itself in such startling disarray is temporarily absent.

Journalism

Female journalists in training are often amused by the macho rhetoric which permeates newsrooms. Good news is 'hard' news rather than 'soft' news, reporters talk about 'getting a good story up' and feature writing is often maligned as a slightly effeminate 'fluffy' practice. There is no question that traditional news values split both format and content along traditional masculine and feminine lines. Facts, objectivity and the public sphere belong to the men. Women line up with feature writing, subjectivity or domestic issues. It's a rhetoric, however, which is entirely contradicted by contemporary news practice.
CATHARINE LUMBY[2]

Journalism as an Object of Study

As the sense-making practice of modernity, journalism is the most important textual system in the world. Of all the means by which language is capitalized and communicated, only drama competes with it for the same global extension, social pervasion, formal variety, and scope of subject-matter. But unlike drama, journalism purports to be true; its importance lies not only in its giantism as a physical product, but also in its real and imagined power to affect other systems, actions or events. Its reputed powers are almost miraculous – it is said to affect individuals and bring down governments, to expose evils and wreck lives, to be the defence of democracy and the cause of decline, to extend knowledge and spread ignorance, all at once, all over the world.

Journalism is so big, however, that it can be persuasively argued that there's no such thing as journalism in the singular; nothing that unites all the things that may be associated with the term 'journalism' except the term itself. It seems to exceed any category that might be used to encompass it – it is found in so many different forms, media, times, places, contexts, genres and industries, with so many different styles of writing and representation, so many ways of presenting itself as true, addressing so many different types of reader, that any suggestion that something called 'journalism' even exists would be foolhardy, a totalizing projection of the false unity of a word.

It is important to bear this in mind, since it is clear that at the level of its daily output and cumulative textual archive journalism is far too big to observe, let alone render into a coherent object of study. Journalism is a differentiated part of language, but just as a language cannot be understood by counting its vocabulary, so journalism cannot be understood by looking at the aggregate of its stories; neither can it be understood in terms of any supposed underlying 'grammar' – a set of abstract rules (of differentiating, selecting and combining elements) and competencies (of recognizing and using the rules). Unlike a language, journalism is not shared equally among the members of a community, however defined. It is subject to social divisions of labour (some people produce it, others consume it), and unlike language in general, journalism is a social and historical product – some societies have managed without it altogether, and where it occurs it is subject to change across much shorter timeframes than a language could deal with. In short there is no essence to journalism, no universal.

Having said that, it is possible to argue that journalism does display some characteristics as a textual system which can be described without essentializing it. Foremost among these is its *modernity*. Journalism is *the* sense-making practice of modernity (the condition) and popularizer of modernism (the ideology); it is a product and promoter of modern life, and is unknown in traditional societies. Journalism is more intensive the more 'modern' its context, thriving most in urbanized, developed, industrial and post-industrial contexts; its densest and most exotic flowerings being found where literacy, affluence and social differentiation are highest, where competitive, individuated lifestyles are most developed.

So much a feature of modernity is journalism that it is easy to describe each in terms of the other – both journalism and modernity are products of European (and Euro-sourced) societies over the last three or four centuries; both are associated with the development of exploration, scientific thought, industrialization, political emancipation and imperial expansion. Both promote notions of freedom, progress and universal enlightenment, and are associated with the breaking down of traditional knowledges and hierarchies, and their replacement with abstract bonds of virtual communities which are linked by their media. Journalism and modernity are marked by the co-development of capitalization and consumerism, market expansion and the infinite, fractal differentiation of both product and purchaser, niche and need. Journalism is caught up in all the institutions, struggles and practices of modernity; contemporary politics is unthinkable without it, as is contemporary consumer society, to such an extent that in the end it is difficult to decide whether journalism is a product of modernity, or modernity a product of journalism.

Such an extreme claim, that modernity is a product of journalism, may be going too far, but it does at least focus on the fact that modernity was and is a *campaign* – a political and marketing campaign, undertaken as a definite pursuit by definite agencies with specific goals. Modernity is not a mere accidental condition of being recent or up to date; it's the process and result of modernization, which has taken quite definite forms in Western and more recently global development. The campaign trail of modernity is journalism. It's worth pointing out that even in societies with the most highly developed modernity, there are plenty of pre-modern and some postmodern activities in place – activities which are resistant to modernization. Among them would figure (some aspects of) early childcare (pre-modern or oral), the contractual relations between academic writers and commercial publishers and the relations between university intellectuals and their students (feudal), environmental politics and the use of the internet (postmodern). As it happens, journalism shows every sign of outliving modernity – it has overshot the runway of its destination, and can now be seen careering off into the distant vistas of postmodernity. Postmodernity is among other things a tendency within journalism, especially the outer extremes of popular journalism (trash or tabloid) and academic journalism (avant-garde or hyperliterate) respectively.

Journalism may be taken as the textual system of modernity. It shares the salient features of modernity and of modernism. The most important of these are:

> the people (society)
> science (knowledge)
> progress (politics)
> comfort (capitalist-culture)

From these elements would follow such phenomena as industrialization, urbanization, the market economy, the 'cash nexus' (employment and therefore unemployment), secularization, socialism, developmentalism (dominion over nature), consumerism. Journalism is caught up in all these developments.

Studying Journalism

To study journalism is to deal not only with a body of texts in a variety of media, but also to investigate the very foundations of modern life. As a *textual system*, journalism requires analysis as to its textuality (i.e. the phenomenal form it takes for the reader, viewer and listener) and as to its system (i.e. its mode of production and distribution, and the institutions and practices which sustain it). It is as a textual system that journalism has whatever effects are claimed for it, whether those are regarded as positive (enlightenment) or negative (ideology), progressive (the fourth estate of democracy) or reactionary (social control, passification, consumerization). A textual system needs an interdisciplinary investigation, organized loosely around its textual features (ranging from the minutiae of semiotic organization and generic forms to large-scale discursive regimes and ideologies) on the one hand, and on the other around its social existence (structure, institutionalization, economy, history).

The most important *textual* feature of journalism is the fact that it counts as true. The most important component of its *system* is the creation of readers as publics, and the connection of these readerships to other systems, such as those of politics, economics and social control.

However, journalism has not generally been studied in these terms at all. It entered the realm of formal learning late, reluctantly, and without much of a welcome from the existing inhabitants. Despite the fact that it is one of the biggest textual systems in the world, it is not studied in most departments of textuality (philosophy, literature, the arts, cinema); and despite its centrality to questions of social power, conflict and change it is not central to departments of sociology, politics, government and history; it's divided piecemeal among them or relegated to newer, interdisciplinary fields like communication and media studies which prestige universities don't even teach. Compared with subjects like English and Social Science, it has never achieved stability or prominence as an academic discipline with its own institutional apparatus of courses, professors, methods of enquiry, specialist language, findings and debates, its own books, journals and conferences. These do exist, of course, but they enjoy neither the centrality of established academic subjects nor the widespread support and recognition of organizations like the ICA, MLA, or BSA (see also page 53).

Journalism is taught not as a branch of learning nor even as a distinct research field, but as a professional qualification which foregrounds the technical skill of producing journalistic output in words and (sometimes) pictures. Rarely do journalism courses ask their students to consider the conditions for journalism's existence: where it comes from, what it is for, and how it works, in the context of modernity. Students are simply asked to *do* it without understanding it.

This kind of 'training' is dedicated to producing middle-ranking professionals. Journalism is not like architecture, law and medicine, where the profession itself controls its own conditions of work, from entry and apprenticeship, to the government and regulation of professional knowledges and practices, not to mention maintaining or increasing the value of the service provided. Indeed, journalism has not developed as a profession at all, but as a trade, and a long succession of its own senior practitioners are militantly in favour of that fact, resenting the drift of recruitment and training towards graduates, and insisting that the best qualifications are personal attributes (a nose for news, a winsome face), the best training is on the job. Hence a university training in it does not even guarantee a cadetship, let alone advancement to the top of the career ladder. Journalism is socially constituted as a business, so recruitment is a managerial *droit de seigneur*, and the 'top' is generally not occupied by journalists at all, but by capitalists, both private and state.

Small wonder that those who seek to professionalize journalism as a mode of production have a difficult time of it. Journalists themselves, like teachers, wobble in status between proletarian practices and organization (hiring and firing conditions, unionization) and professionalization (codes of ethics, disciplinary procedures). In this context, it is hard to standardize entry into the practice of journalism, hard to establish what counts as specialist knowledge, hard to set a premium on journalistic labour. It is these difficulties which tend to dominate journalism courses in universities; they too wobble between craft skills and professional ethics, spelling and government, layout and law, turning out graduates with professional aspirations into a market place which in some respects has not even achieved proletarian status, since employers can and do hire people with no training at all and put them straight into the most prominent positions. In a market where years of experience can be outbid by a squirt of hairspray, it is not learning but looks, not the cerebral but celebrity, that mark the winners, and celebrity smiling is not something that can easily be taught in universities or regulated by professional associations; journalism is one of the 'smiling professions' whose aspirants may be well advised to spend more on orthodontics than on books.[3]

Given its insecure professional and academic status, journalism in universities has tended to favour the (mythic) values of quality print journalism – the first few pages of the local or national broadsheet of record – while simultaneously giving students at least a nodding acquaintance with new technologies and desktop publishing; holding on to an individualistic respect for fearless investigative exposé while preparing their graduates for a bureaucratic career in the corporate publicity department. Taught by former practitioners whose own apprenticeship was unlikely to have included a university degree in journalism, and whose allegiances are unshakably fixed on one of journalism's fastest disappearing forms, students are encouraged to rely on their own least professional (i.e. personal) attributes and to lionize people whose knowledge base is local, commonsensical, interpersonal and dedicated to shifting a known and obvious product in a tight market. Even as they gain their diplomas and degrees, cadet journalists are encouraged to get by on native wit, drive and/or personal relations with the boss. As a result, while it's easy to point to individual success stories, it's equally apparent that here we have a 'profession' which cannot police its own boundaries, personnel, standards or price, which has no essential (defensible) body of knowledge and practice. It aspires to the professional status of *architects* while actually turning out *real-estate agents* – petty-bourgeois, self-employed, white-collar workers with no commitment to professionalization in a market which is still governed by individualistic competition and whose knowledges, while requiring talent, are neither mysterious nor scarce.

Journalism as a Field of Knowledge

Following the example of art colleges, and like most courses in the general field of practical text-making from fashion design and music to film and electronic media production, journalism courses concentrate obsessively on the one sector of the industry which is chronically oversupplied with labour – production. Courses tend to get perfunctory when it comes to the business side of journalism (students choose an MBA not a DipJourn to learn How To Be a Media Mogul), and editing is taught as a production skill ('subbing') not as a cultural control function. If students ever learn that it is distribution, not production, that is the key locus of power and profit in journalism as in any of the culture industries, it is usually because some ratbag radical from a theory course has been asked to give a guest lecture, not because the journalism programme has any investment in promoting understanding of the industry as a whole (never mind the cultural form as a whole).[4] Similarly, budding journalists are taught media law without any attention to their own (often feudal) contractual status – 'law' means 'protecting the employer from prosecution'. They are taught too that journalism is a private, commercial industry, a trade in commodities for profit in a free market; but less often explained is the peculiar nature of the cultural commodity, which cannot be standardized, made scarce or used up. Journalism deals in knowledge, symbol, image, information, story – these things are not like potato crisps, which can be manufactured to add value to the raw material, and which are used up when eaten. Journalism is a capitalization of language, adding value to culture, and as such it is displaying an increasing historic tendency to move beyond the form of exchange required in industrial markets, where consumers give cash for commodities which are used up when they are consumed, towards a postmodern form of exchange, where audiences give time for non-material commodities which they don't pay for and which are not used up when they are consumed. Equally strange is the 'free' market which has only ever existed inside a framework of state regulation and government interference, for there never was a 'free press' – only a continuous cha-cha between editors and governors, back and forth from deference to defiance. And of course journalists are not taught to understand their product from the point of view of 'the consumer', their readers, the public; on the contrary, they are encouraged by their own informal peer-system to keep their distance from the punters, whose 'use' of journalism is seen as a matter of marketing (which isn't taught anyway) rather than culture (which is actively despised).

The alienation of journalists from what they write is hardly surprising, since of all workers in the knowledge industry they are among the least secure in their intellectual property rights, and most proletarianized in their mode of production. The texts they make belong not to them but to their employer, even when they have a byline. News stories do not write themselves, of course; it takes individual creativity. But those individuals use the capital resources of the newsroom (which they don't own), and their output is a function of those resources (this is why – and how – it's possible to have left-wing journalists writing for right-wing papers). Journalists are also encouraged to see their work as throughput (continuous reproduction of pre-engineered commodity) rather than as an *oeuvre* (cumulative authorial statement). They are subject to quite extreme divisions of labour, so that what appears is by no single hand, and corresponds to no shaping artistic vision other than that of the corporation which claims copyright. Furthermore, journalists work the field of knowledge in a slash-and-burn, highly capitalized, appropriative manner, not as tillers and recyclers of a semiotic permaculture – in other words, as a colleague of mine has put it,[5] the difference between journalists and academics is simply this: academics must always cite their sources, journalists never do.

It is normal for graduates of art, literary and cinema studies to *like* the textual forms taken by their object of study while harbouring no professional ambitions to paint, write novels or make films. The study of these cultural forms is part of a general education in the humanities, an education that combines the encouragement of astute textual reading with attention to questions of power, knowledge, culture and social structure. Surprisingly, journalism has never been taken up in universities in this way – you cannot study journalism simply because you like its cultural forms (a 'news junkie' is a very different animal from a cineaste, aesthete or bibliophile). Nor can you get far if you are simply interested in journalism's historic importance, even though there's plenty to study. As a textual system, as a mode of knowledge production, and as the sense-making practice of modernity, journalism clearly displays its own distinctive features, its own histories, and establishes specific relations with other institutions and practices. It also provides hard evidence of very large-scale cultural tendencies within modernity (and its unlooked-for consequence, postmodernity), for example: changes in the relations between addresser and addressee in the development of human communication; evidence of the extension of the capitalization of language; the development and transformation of notions of truth, community, the public sphere, nation, personality and conflict in modernizing societies; changes (and continuities) in the history of looking; the extension of journalism to global populations, almost the whole species, pervading billions with the impulse of modernization and the democratic principle, hinting at a reintegrating of our dispersed, fragmented and combative species at cultural if not political levels.

All this is interesting and worthy of investigation, but apart from a round-up of the usual suspects from 'both sides' of the story – here a left-wing pessimist, for whom pervasive journalism spells the end of political modernization, there a right-wing pessimist, for whom pervasion of any kind means loss of culture to consumerism – apart from these ritualized genuflexions to Left and Right, no attempt is made to teach such matters to the very body of people for whom journalism is so pervasive. Despite the fact that citizenship and communal identity are not possible these days without journalism, and despite the continuing efforts to democratize higher education, the penny does not seem to have dropped that students, like everyone else, live in Lotman's semiosphere, which demands a response from tertiary education that goes beyond reducing news to a set of technical operations. For those who were brought up on it, if not by it, journalism is interesting as a field of knowledge, not merely as a corporate duty statement.

Journalism in Theory

But in the arena of academic research and scholarly publication, journalism is elusive, as if it isn't there at all, despite the attention and controversy surrounding the world it renders into corporate narrative. It is not commonly studied as a textual system in its own right, rather it is colonized and plundered by other disciplines, like politics, government, history, etc. In other words, its stories function as a documentary archive, a mere store of knowledge not about journalism (the reporting of the events of the day) but about something else (the events themselves). If you read books on journalism they're usually about politics, while books on politics casually ride roughshod through journalism as if it isn't there in order to provide their own narratives with incident and colour, anecdote and evidence. Journalism is a *terra nullius* of epistemology, deemed by anyone who wanders by to be an uninhabited territory of knowledge, fit to be colonized by anyone who's interested. Linguists raid newspapers to illustrate theories of language. Social scientists exploit news stories as evidence of something real (beyond the stories) which will prove their case. Historians trawl the microfiches to document their chosen biographical figure, social issue or political scandal. Even philosophers watch the news on TV, and wonder. Uncle Tom Cobbley is in there as well, compiling a study of some cultural eccentricity from clippings and press releases, to publish his own bestseller on what is then taken to be culture, not journalism.

All human life is there, but journalism is invisible. Not only as a ('transparent') medium, but journalism *as a whole*, as a field of human endeavour, escapes attention. This is why it is useful to take the risk of thinking about journalism in the singular, as a whole. Naturally, there is already in existence a tradition of media theory which has tried to locate the various components, elements or moments of journalism, and show how they are *articulated* together in some form of complex unity. Generally, such articulations are imagined on a linear, production-line model, using three main elements which correspond to production (journalists), distribution (texts) and consumption (readers). But media theory, following a modernist, realist, Marxist predilection for analysing origins and determinations over destinations and outcomes, has what amounts to an obsession for analysing certain locations in a given textual system and neglecting others. It has become so general that the same basic structure is repeated over and over again in different contexts and using different disciplinary or descriptive terms. The structure of tripartite divisions is extremely common in theoretical and analytical work involving textual systems. For instance:

journalism	*media*	*popular culture*
production	distribution	consumption
addresser	message	addressee
sender	channel	receiver
author	text	reader
producer	cultural commodity	market
performance	genre	audience
discourse	text	subject
state	ideology	citizen
(us)	(to)	(them)

Such simple triplicating is not as innocent as it might look, for there is a crossfertilization between these terms, and a very strong current of causation flowing (from left to right, mimicking alphabetic reading) which suggests that the terms on the left determine the outcomes on the right through the medium in the middle. The terms on the left that come from social theory describe large-scale institutions, while those on the right tend to be thought of as individuated and dispersed. The mixture of such a structure with a simple linear model of communication (mouth-to-airwaves-to-ear) has produced almost irresistible associations between activity on the left and passivity on the right. Analysts of social change and power relations have therefore tended to concentrate on the terms on the left, while formalists and textualists find plenty to occupy them in the middle. But the terms on the right emerge from this intellectual tradition as relatively neglected, since they have been understood as phenomena whose explanation lies not in themselves but elsewhere (i.e. on the left); some of them have even attracted contempt and derision (consumption especially) which perhaps rubs off on the others in the same structural position (popular culture and audiences especially).

Small wonder that analysts have tended not to pitch their tents on the right of this field, and that those who do (for instance theorists of popular culture and postmodernism) have been looked at with bemusement amounting to hostility. It all seems so real and obvious. For instance, if the sentence 'I collect newspaper mastheads' is placed on the right of this structure, it would apply to a consumer/reader, and may describe a person's domestic, amateur hobby, akin to collecting stamps or pictures of movie-stars. Slim pickings for a theory of textual systems there. If, however, you place the sentence 'I collect newspaper mastheads' on the left, it applies to the realm of production, and may describe what Rupert Murdoch does for a living. Enough said? Unfortunately for the cause of neat simplicity, this tendency is itself a classic symptom of modernism, prioritizing process, production, origin, causation and power over consumption, destination, diffusion and meaning. As such it is part of the problem which an adequate account of journalism as the textual system of modernity needs to explain. In other words, while journalism can be (and often is) explained as *a mode of commodity-textual production, channelled through various media, to passive consumers in popular culture*, it must nevertheless be remembered that this formula is itself a product of modernist thinking, and it has its explanatory limits.

The reason for that lies in the *supplementary* status not only of the terms on the right in the above structure, but of journalism as a whole textual system in modernist theories of knowledge. No matter what is actually written, said or shown in any particular journalistic text, it remains the case that distinctions are maintained between journalism and other forms of writing, speaking and visualizing, such as these distinctions:

knowledge	*journalism*
history	news
production	distribution
pure	applied
philosophy	*journalism*
truth	facts
literature	*journalism*
creative	derivative
art	technique
science	*journalism*
original observation	eyewitness experience
method	sources

Journalism is the poor relation of discourse in theoretical writing; it seems to be a classic Derridean supplement,[6] a mode of knowledge production which is not only seen to be derivative of other discursive or textual regimes (of history, philosophy and literature for instance), but also actively to corrupt, vulgarize and endanger those forms of knowledge thought to be purer and prior. Journalism 'counts' as distributive marketing rather than productive art, an application of knowledge technologies not created by it, and so it has attracted no Foucault to analyse its power relations, no Derrida to unthink its presumption of the innocence of its writing, no Williams to historicize its mode of cultural production.

It is important to notice, rather than simply to accept, the supplementary status both of journalism 'as a whole' and of the right-hand columns in the above structures. This status needs to be understood as a feature of the mode of explanation, as much as of the nature of journalism. One of the limits of journalism's supplementarity in hierarchies of knowledge, and of the consumer/reader's supplementarity in hierarchies of journalism, is that very little work has been done to theorize reading and reader-ships in the development and deployment of modernity in general and journalism in particular. Of course, plenty of market research, audience analysis and opinion polling is done, but this is a symptom of the above regimes of knowledge, not an explanation of readership.

Media

Far from disappearing into the mists of the Himalayas, the imperatives of the Victorian imperial mythology of knowledge continue to animate the production of knowledge as a utopian epistemology, a disposition to compre-hensive knowledge, and a will to power. THOMAS RICHARDS[7]

Imperial Information

The media are older, wider and more diverse than journalism. There are media in all ages of human history, and all stages of social organization. In pre-modern or non-industrialized societies, the media are generally associated with religion, royal or priestly propa-ganda, and folk art. These functions remain, of course, in secular-ized societies.[8] Within the media, whether understood in formal ('film') or in institutional ('cinema') terms, journalism co-exists with other things, notably drama-fiction, talk and advertising. Conversely, journalism is not confined to any one medium. Like those forms of expression which spill across the whole semiosphere (music, adver-tising, photography, writing, speech) journalism is ubiquitous in most of the recognizable media forms of the age, from its ancestral home in the daily, weekly, monthly and periodical press, to the electronic news media of television, radio and cinema (newsreel and documentary).

The news is a discursive field, permanently caught between the rock of communication and the hard place of truth, having to distinguish itself from its neighbours by using the very devices it seeks to keep at a distance. Like journalism as a whole, TV news is part of what Mark Poster (following Baudrillard) has called the 'remaking of language'.[9] It has become a communicative end in itself, dissolving the boundaries not only with other signifying systems but even the classic distinctions between text and audience, discourse and society, object and subject, turning the 'knowing subject' into a dispersed, decentred, informational matrix. Looked at visually, instead of being part of the archive of imperial knowledge, television news is just another ad for postmodernity. Perhaps this is a development not to be regretted, for the shift of emphasis from the real to communication brings with it a shift from a technology of control to a technology of interactive semiotic participation, where citizens of media use TV news as their forum, even while it is also their marketplace. But then, that was exactly the status of the Roman Forum too: a mixture of soap and beer, discourse and democracy, power and information, of public sphere and semiosphere.

Popular journalism is an invention of the nineteenth century, and some very nineteenth-century attitudes about it are still circulating as respectable opinion. However, on closer inspection of the historical field three things seem arguable: (i) the sphere of imperial political, economic and military power, which is traditionally taken to be the reality that journalism is supposed to reflect more or less accurately, was by the end of the nineteenth century already a mixture of fantasy, information, fiction and symbol, as much a discursive field as the more obviously textual media which set out to 'cover' it; (ii) that journalism's often poor reputation in the matter of truth tells us more about the realm of knowledge and its internal hierarchies (i.e. another discursive field) than it does about what journalism actually does; (iii) that journalism has been postmodern for over a hundred years. Journalism's presentational aspects, its visuality and its discursive visualizations, can be understood not as the unfortunate contaminants of an otherwise pure and factual realism, but the very purpose of journalism, from the very start.

Thomas Richards, in *The Imperial Archive*,[10] argues that the British Empire was the first to be characterized by the attempt to control knowledge rather than territory. Unable to control their far-flung possessions by military force and seeking coherence in a giant empire whose territories had nothing in common, the British, says Richards, began to think differently: 'The narratives of the late nineteenth century are full of fantasies about an empire united not by force but by information.' While a single nation can be physically controlled by various institutions of Foucauldian power, such as prisons (the law), schools and armies, these are ineffective or temporary when used outside the nation state. Another way of putting this might be to revive the Althusserian distinction between RSAs and ISAs – repressive and ideological state apparatuses – to say that while the full array of coercive RSAs (army, government, police, etc.) were deployed in the Empire, they were not sufficient, and consensual ISAs (civil and discursive institutions, culture) were also developed. And so the Empire was *imagined* as a nation: 'seeing it that way, through the distorting lens of the nation, lent the Empire the sense of symbolic unity that it so often lacked in practice'. A *fictive* nationhood was developed to extend Britishness to the far corners of the earth, using national symbols and discursive institutions of Englishness (like the *OED*, the image of Victoria herself, and others such as Shakespeare, the Anglican church, the British Museum, and later the BBC, etc.) to unite Poona with Purley in the imperial imagination.

Just as national symbolism was exported, so was information imported, according to Richards:

> *From all over the globe the British collected information about the countries they were adding to their map. They surveyed and they mapped. They took censuses, produced statistics. They made vast lists.... In fact they often could do little other than collect and collate information, for any exact civil control, of the kind possible in England, was out of the question. The Empire was too far away, and the bureaucrats of Empire had to be content with shuffling papers.*[11]

These papers became the basis for two new developments: first, the information explosion, including a new statist dimension to 'classified' information and 'intelligence'; and second, a fantasy of control through knowledge which was first manifested in the literature of the period, giving rise to new narrative possibilities through the secret agent and the detective – characters like Sherlock Holmes with access to information, knowledge and sciences beyond the reach of their readers. Richards points out that despite, and then because of, their huge informational archives, the British had no more success in unifying the domain of knowledge into a coherent, comprehensive whole than they had had in unifying and controlling territory. But once again, fiction, fantasy and fabrication came to the rescue of reality. Writers such as Rudyard Kipling, H.G. Wells, Bram Stoker and Erskine Childers achieved in fiction what the imperial bureaucracy and the institutions of knowledge were failing, despite ant-like industry, to achieve in fact: each of these four writers produced work which 'equates knowledge with national security . . . and each goes so far as to see knowledge itself not as the supplement of power but as its replacement in the colonial world'. This is what Richards calls the 'myth of a unified archive, an imperial archive holding together the vast and various parts of the Empire'.[12] In true Derridean style, the power of force is supplanted in the twentieth century by the force of its supplement, knowledge: 'Today we routinely assume that no power can possibly exist without its underlay of documents, memoranda, licenses, and files'.

Richards concludes that the imperial archive was passed over to American intelligence during the Second World War, and 'the Americans learned their lesson well. . . . Today's American Empire thinks not about occupying land but about watching it, and calls its colonies satellites.'[13]

Textualized Reality

Other writers, notably Jon Klancher, have argued that the control of information was a specifically middle-class response to the industrial and imperial development of nineteenth-century England. Klancher suggests that, lacking a direct power base in the economy like the fundamental classes (workers and capitalists), the middle-class reading public sought to take control of the world by textualizing it.[14] He associates this development with the burgeoning periodical press, which the equally burgeoning middle class used both to inform and sustain itself. They also used it to promote new values – hygiene, Christianity, nature study, domesticity, self-help – to the working class, using literacy and mass media for the first time in a process which may properly be thought of as the 'internal colonization' of one class by another.[15] In a summary of his argument Klancher writes:

> *Reading the periodicals, this audience [the so-called 'middle-class public'] learned to operate the interpretative strategies through which it could 'read' a social world, a symbolic universe, a textual field, in order to discover its own purpose within them. In the pages of its public journals, such an audience read the social order as a symbolically instructive text. Thus the 'middle-class' public could often edge away from any declared class identity of its own, standing apart from the social order to the extent that it could textualize it.[16]*

This analysis of the reading public suggests to me at least the origins of the contemporary, postmodern public sphere, where imperialism has given way (if it was not already the same thing) to cross-demographic communication via popular and international media, which are the locus of political participation for populations which should more accurately be thought of as readerships than as citizens of nations.

I take two themes from the cultural history work of Richards, Klancher and others. First, that the unity of Empire ruled by direct, forceful control of global territory always was a fantasy in the modern period; we do not live in a world where simulacra (information) have replaced a previous referential reality (territory) because such a reality never existed on its own. This is not the kind of revisionist statement which is intended to deny the physical force of imperial expansion and exploitation, but rather to say that such force is itself evidence of the power of the fantasies in whose name it was unleashed. The British Empire was an empire of the imagination, of fantasy, information, classification, knowledge, texts and symbols, and it was 'united' *only* in the readerships created and sustained for and by its own textuality – it was itself a simulacrum, created out of the very impossibility of its existence any other way. In short, and to correct Marx and Engels who were poetic but mistaken on this point, all that is solid always was air.

Second, it is clear that the role of national, political fantasy has been taken over from the imperial bureaucrats by the journalistic media; this is the public sphere, the imagined community, the information archive, of the contemporary period. Like the Empire before it, the media sphere has occasioned pervasive political and social anxiety about its power, its tendency to cross national borders, not to mention its apparent disconnection with reality. Today's global empire is not only post-territorial and postmodern, it's post-national, since it cannot be seen *simply* as 'the American' Empire, even if it does specialize in watching, and does colonize by means of satellites (in high earth orbit). Further, this media-public sphere is not merely a realism, it's a fully paid-up member of the semiosphere, where visualization of the community takes precedence over truth, and where the news is only one of various discursive resources available for creation of the public. This media sphere is where its critics see the coca-colonization of the world,[17] the creation of a post-national style community where readerships are created not for nations but for corporations, via logos, advertising campaigns, catchphrases, an earth united by the colours of Benetton, the 'empire of the sign' which Barthes imagined, taking American software on East Asian hardware to numberless infinities of souls at the round earth's imagined corners.

In the context of the cultural and semiotic history I've sketched here truth is not what it used to be. However, the most common and commanding senses of the word today are derived from the imperial archive itself, from the belief that truth could be positive, comprehensive, classified and known. Nineteenth-century truth is that of empirical science, of the eyewitness explorer who reveals the true nature of an independently existing reality by observation, description, classification and publication – in short, by compiling an archive. Richards makes the connection: 'The new disciplines of geography, biology, and thermodynamics all took as their imperium the world as a whole, and worked out paradigms of knowledge which seemed to solve the problem of imperial control at a distance.' Mapping, dating and experimentation were used literally to *discipline* space, time and movement. He says:

> The administrative core of the Empire was built around knowledge-producing institutions like the British Museum, the Royal Geographical Society, the India Survey, and the universities (many of the figures of imperial myth, from T.E. Lawrence to Indiana Jones, started out in some institution of higher learning). The ideology of mid-Victorian positivism had also led most people into believing that the best and most certain kind of knowledge was the fact. . . . The various civil bureaucracies sharing the administration of Empire were desperate for these manageable pieces of knowledge. They were light and movable. They pared the Empire down to file-cabinet size.[18]

The world as a whole is reduced to Bitzer-style facts, but these are the foundation of truth (truth = 'conformity with fact; agreement with reality' – *OED*). The abandonment of territory as the basis of empire, and the abandonment of the dream of unified, comprehensive knowledge, in favour of numberless unconnected but classifiable facts, unified only in an equally dispersed and pluralized readership, seems to be a cue for popular journalism. Like the British Empire and Victorian knowledge, journalism takes as its imperium the world as a whole.

47-

Popular Culture ▬▬▬▬▬▬▬

In short, he so bewildered himself in this kind of study, that he passed the nights in reading, from sunset to sunrise, and the days, from sunrise to sunset; and thus, through little sleep and much reading, his brain was dried up in such a manner, that he came at last to lose his wits. CERVANTES[19]

The Reader in History

Popular culture is another name for the practice of media readership in modernity (I follow Gramsci on this).[20] Jon Klancher, describing new directions in research into nineteenth-century journals and their 'reading publics', suggests that a crucial shift has occurred, where old-fashioned notions of the literary *reader* have given way to the notion of the *audience*. The questions now are 'how readers were produced for texts in history, how readers often resisted their representations, and what these dialogic tensions mean for literary, social and intellectual history'.[21] These issues are at the heart of contemporary cultural studies, and follow from what Klancher identifies as something that 'strikingly distinguishes the new investigations of "cultural production"', namely Marx's contention in the *Grundrisse* that 'not only the object of consumption but also the manner of consumption is produced by [cultural] production ... consumption is created by production not only objectively but also subjectively. ... Production thus produces not only an object for the subject but also a subject for the object.' This is the definitive statement of the theoretical position which has governed the recent study of sense-making practices in modernity. It suggests that publics and consumers are not simply people waiting passively out there for something to consume, but on the contrary that they are brought into being *as* consumers and publics by the process of cultural production itself. By this formula, then, journalism cannot simply be thought of as an industry which produces a throwaway commodity (printed paper), but as a form of cultural production which produces its own consuming subjects – the public, the consumer.

The 'key move from "reader" to "audience" had far reaching consequences', according to Klancher:

> *What we call an 'audience' cannot simply be a generalized 'reader in the text' (as reception theory has had it), or a cultural inference made from the class anatomy of society (as one reading of Marx would imply), or an aggregate of empirical individuals to be identified and described (as the modernizers hoped). Rather it is a historically fluid, constructive category.*[22]

Arguing that the category of 'audience' is therefore part concept, part 'ideological field', part social formation and part representation, Klancher says: 'the "audience in history" cannot be understood exclusively as either a purely textual, socio-structural, statistical, or conceptual entity. Rather the "audience" must be grasped from these diverse angles of view taken together'.[23] This is precisely what happens in the study of popular culture, which has developed over a thirty-year period from the early 1960s as an interdisciplinary inquiry into precisely these matters. The general stance of such work is that 'popular culture' can be understood as the ideological field within the social formation where subjectivities are produced, on the site of persons, in ideological conformity with the productive requirements of capitalism.

But along the way the historical (rather than formalist) concept of the *reader* has been all but forgotten, and nowadays if you mention the word 'reader' or 'readership' in cultural studies it is generally assumed that you are backsliding into 'high culture', with all the baggage of prejudice and disdain for the popular that this so often entails. Meanwhile, much literary theory has dispensed with any consideration of readership at all, settling for immensely sophisticated *readings* of the ideological field of literary and theoretical writing. Hence, while 'popular culture' is suffused with text, and literally made of audience, there's not a reader to be seen. This is a pity since, as Renate Holub has pointed out in relation to Antonio Gramsci's work in the 1930s on popular culture (which she associates with Brecht, Benjamin and hope, rather than with Frankfurt and pessimism), there's a possibility for 'rationally planned cultural intervention' based on a study of readership:

> *The plan follows a tripartite order: first, Gramsci looks at the molecular processes of hegemonic cultural practices, in particular the reading practices, of many social strata, which allows him to research the differences of cultural production; he then asks what these reading practices reveal in terms of inner drives and inner needs, what the cultural production responds to or satisfies; and finally he draws up a balance sheet as to what needs to be done for a counter-hegemonic culture.*[24]

This plan is in fact quite recognizable in the work of the Birmingham Centre for Contemporary Cultural Studies in the 1970s, and I'll discuss that in more detail in Chapter 9. But for the moment, it might be more salutary to note how and with what effect contemporary Left theory has become rather sniffy about readers.

Reading as Hyper-consumption

A radical theorist of literary textuality and global politics in the context of imperialism, colonialism and metropolitanism is Aijaz Ahmad, in his book *In Theory: Classes, Nations, Literatures*. A reading of some of Ahmad's argument will I hope serve to clarify and contextualize some more general questions concerning popular culture, readership, and the politics of theoretical work in the current period. Aijaz Ahmad notes without enthusiasm that:

> one is impressed by how much the increasing dominance of the poststructuralist position has had the effect, in the more recent years, of greatly extending the centrality of reading as the appropriate form of politics, and how theoretical moorings tend themselves to become more random, in proliferation of readings, as much of inter-textual cross-referentiality as in their conceptual constellations.[25]

Ahmad makes clear what he thinks of this a couple of pages on: 'Very affluent people may come to believe that they have broken free of imperialism through acts of reading, writing, lecturing and so forth.'[26]

Ahmad is having a go at poststructuralism and postmodernism in Western literary theory. He is unimpressed by what he calls 'epistemologies which are based on the exorbitation of language' (he means the work of Foucauldians) as opposed to work which addresses the 'realities of autonomy and agency' within the more 'durable realities of class belonging, institutional location and periodization of production' (he means Marxism).[27] Within this context, it is very notable that language, literature, theory, and the practices of 'reading, writing, lecturing and so forth', are consistently understood as mere epiphenomena, with reading especially a mere individualistic sign of 'affluence' hardly distinguishable from conspicuous consumption. Literary theory as a whole – which Ahmad both practises and denounces – is not exempt from this epiphenomenal, supplementary status. Ahmad signals his intention of breaking with 'the existing theoretical formation' and with 'discrete developments within literary theory'. He proposes as his own method the need for:

> negotiating the dialectic between the relatively autonomous status of literary theory as such, as a distinct form of cultural practice, and its determination, in a last instance which is not infinitely postponable, by the world of political and economic materialities which surrounds and saturates it.[28]

For Ahmad, then, it is politics (imperialism) and economics (capitalism) which 'surround' and 'saturate' both theory and the practice of theorizing; never the other way round, despite the 'relative autonomy' of theory. The whole body and practice of theory is suspect and has to be broken with; it is surrounded and saturated – this is a relative autonomy which can hardly be thought of as autonomous, only derivative.

Making fun of theorists who 'centralize *reading* as the appropriate form of politics' and who 'believe they have broken free of imperialism through acts of reading' seems innocent enough – good point-scoring by one who champions the cause of socialism in colonized nations – but it is in fact a damaging departure from its own theoretical protocol, which insists on 'relative autonomy' of the theoretical realm and *dialectic* (dialogue) between such a realm and others. In other words, the possibility must be faced that *reading*, theorizing, and so on *do* determine the materialities of politics and the economy, and that far from being saturated by these apparently pre-semiotic materialities, it is the practice of reading which has some definite determinate effect on them.

Given the obvious in-your-face reality of politics and the economy, this claim may seem wild and peculiar, but it is quite easy to defend historically, and not just because influential modernist *writers* like Marx and Mao were also compulsive *readers* (their books are *readings* of others' theories and of social circumstances), whose own formal *readership* (Marxists) clearly have had some effect on the materialities and practices of modernity. Beyond even this, the claim that reading is a material and determinate practice for large-scale populations of readers only seems odd in the context of uninspected assumptions at work in Ahmad's argument. For instance his real is never semiotic, and (it follows) while theory, language and literature can all be read, the materialities of politics and economics are somehow exempt from this necessity, being 'objective'; his theory also fetishizes production and origin, and has literally nothing to say, beyond the quoted scornful dismissal, about reading itself. This is a pity, since Ahmad's analysis is in fact founded on a presumption of the power of reading, despite his apparent neglect of the issue. The popular media hardly rate a mention in the whole book – one throwaway line about the 'expansion of Hindi literature – and of the language itself, through the electronic media and whatnot – since Independence'.[29] He has zero to say about readerships of literature or media, and nothing about reading as a part of the political or cultural process. Even though he admits the role of 'the electronic media and whatnot' in creating a *vernacular* public in conditions of independence and nation-building, Ahmad doesn't pursue the matter, for he is exclusively preoccupied with 'a very few positions which have been, I believe, seminal and defining'. In other words, his whole project is a new incarnation of the supplementarism outlined earlier in relation to the status of both readerships in general and journalism in particular. For Ahmad, it is only necessary to analyse the 'defining position', not the 'many other writers [who] may come to inhabit the field marked by such a position'. He wants to:

> *interrogate not the variations of subsequent habitation but the modalities of primary definition – hence the emphasis not on cataloguing the numerous names and writings of those who have participated in these debates, but on narrowing the focus to those particular ideas which have generated so many others.*[30]

His structure, then, is binary:

very few seminal and defining positions	many other writers inhabiting the field marked
modalities of primary definition	variations of subsequent habitation
ideas which generate so many others	cataloguing numerous names and writings of those who participate in debates

The ideas in question turn out to be those of Edward Said, Michel Foucault, Fredric Jameson, with a bit of Salman Rushdie and Karl Marx thrown in (it seems women don't have 'seminal' ideas). His Foucault is to theory as imperialism is to India, but more to the present point is that Ahmad is not only explicitly supplementarist but also organizes his preferences around an object/subject distinction – the favoured terms on the left are all objective, or at least things (positions, modalities, ideas), while those on the right are all subjective, or at least people (writers, inhabitants, participants). This distinction casts the sphere of literary theory itself into a hierarchy of writ*ing* over read*ers*; and the more influence that is claimed for the 'seminal' blokes of high theory, the less can be imputed to the process of cultural production in all its socio-historical 'variation'. This oddly top-table approach to the production and circulation of ideas about knowledge in the context of empires, colonies, classes and nations is laudable in its search for 'objective determination', but it has a blind spot at the very point of its 'narrowed focus' – it refuses the possibility that the diffusion of knowledge, and reading itself, are determinate practices with material effects. Ahmad clearly needs readership as the vital amniotic fluid which nurtures those 'many other' ideas 'generated' by his 'seminal' positions. Right at the centre of his own theory, Ahmad tacitly installs readership as a determinate practice – i.e. the academic, intellectual *readers* of his 'few and defining' authorities then become the *writers* of the 'subsequent variations'. It follows (though equally tacitly), that the binary opposition between reading (subsequent, subjective) and writing (primary, objective) that he himself insists upon is not an opposition at all, since the power of his 'primary definers' can only be communicated by a social, public process of reading and *rewriting*, diffusion by *readings* (i.e. formal, written and published reading practices – Voloshinov's 'colloquy of large scale').

The point here is a general one – reading is not a solitary, individualist, consumptive, supplementary act of silent subjection to a series of imperial graphic impressions. On the contrary, reading is a social, communal, productive, act of writing, a dialogic process which is fundamental to (and may even *be*) popular culture. In relation to journalism, the implications of this argument are that it is dangerous to assume that reading is an epiphenomenon. It can take a very visible form in the guise of journalistic 'readings' of the intellectual and material scene – journalists 'read' the economy and politics for their readers, for example, as well as broadcasting critical opinions, intellectual debates and research findings to non-specialist reader-ships. And reading takes the less directly visible form of constructed readerships – virtual communities of ideological interest within an overall social and discursive formation which are constructed on the site of various modes of journalistic production. Such virtual communities can be 'peopled' directly at times of instability, even to the extent of causing people to take direct political action, if readers are sufficiently motivated (successfully interpellated) *prior* to the specific incendiary action. In more routine circumstances, it may not be readers as corporeal bodies which determine actions taken in their name, but readers as discursive representations whose power – the sovereignty of the people – is appropriated by those who claim to represent them, among whom journalists always have figured prominently. In short, readings, readers and representations thereof may be as numerous and as various as the inhabitants of a colonized empire, but that does not mean they are explained by consigning them to the supplementary status of imperial servitors with a habit of over-consumption. Things are not that simple in the republic of letters.

Making Readers

OUR REPUBLIC AND ITS PRESS WILL RISE OR FALL TOGETHER. AN ABLE, DISINTERESTED, PUBLIC-SPIRITED PRESS, WITH TRAINED INTELLIGENCE TO KNOW THE RIGHT AND COURAGE TO DO IT CAN PRESERVE THAT PUBLIC VIRTUE WITHOUT WHICH POPULAR GOVERNMENT IS A SHAM AND A MOCKERY. A CYNICAL, MERCENARY, DEMAGOGIC, [CORRUPT] PRESS WILL PRODUCE IN TIME A PEOPLE AS BASE AS ITSELF. THE POWER TO MOULD THE FUTURE OF THE REPUBLIC WILL BE IN THE HANDS OF THE JOURNALISTS OF FUTURE GENERATIONS.[31]

These four sentences are quoted from an article of May 1904 by Joseph Pulitzer, who according to Michael Lewis not only 'had a bad case of shame for the Spanish atrocities invented by his reporters to goose up the circulation of his newspapers', but also founded the Columbia School of Journalism with a $2 million endowment. Lewis suggests that these sentences 'are about as close to the intellectual origins of the American journalism school as you can get'. They are also cast in bronze (in capital letters) at the entrance to Columbia, the best-known such school in the world. Lewis comments on this:

The first sentence . . . may or may not be true, but it sets a fittingly autocratic, unreflective tone. . . . The last two sentences offer the sort of grandiose vision of journalism entertained mainly by retired journal-ists or those assigned to deliver speeches before handing out journalism

awards. Highly flattering to all of us, of course, but it would be more
true to flip the sentence to read: 'a cynical, mercenary, demagogic people
will in time produce a press as base as itself. . . '.[32]

Here is a classic chicken-and-egg question – does journalism 'produce
in time a people', as Pulitzer has it, or is it 'more true' to argue with
Lewis that 'people will in time produce a press . . .'. The answer to
that question is among other things the subject of this book, but
there's no doubt where Lewis, like many professional journalists,
stands on the issue. He is scathing about any attempt to 'dignify a
trade by tacking onto it the idea of professionalism and laying over it
a body of dubious theory'. For him 'the best journalists are almost the
antithesis of professionals. The horror of disrepute, the preternatural
respect for authority and the fear of controversy that so benefit the
professional are absolute handicaps for a journalist'. He points out
that 'the trade' (i.e. news executives who hire journalists) 'has
somehow sustained a robust contempt for the credential', and he gives
his own views on why 'the desperate futility of journalism instruction
becomes clearer the closer one gets to the deed'. It is because of 'the
instinct to complicate', which produces 'the entire pretentious science
of journalism'. The journalist's task is simply 'to observe, to question,
to read and to write about subjects other than journalism'.[33]

Tucked away in this interesting denunciation of training is the
serious problem of what journalism is for, more serious than the
question of whether journalism schools are good for anything more
than a 'frenzy of student networking' (in order to 'meet someone
who worked at *The New York Times*'), or whether journalism as a craft
is anything more than: 'All we do is ask questions and type and
occasionally turn a phrase.'[34] Lewis's formulation of what a journalist does – 'to observe, to question, to read and to write' – construes
the practice of journalism as astute reading and journalists as active
readers. Like Ahmad in the passages quoted earlier, who construes
the practices of literature and theory as writing (which includes critical reading) by theorists, without ever considering readers, Lewis
confines journalism to what *journalists* do. Both Ahmad and Lewis
work with models of their textual systems which require astute, critical reading by their practitioners, but take no account of the *readership* called into being by these systems. Indeed, it is pretty clear that
Lewis at least does not believe such a readership – the public – is
called into being at all, given his views of the public: 'a cynical,
mercenary, demagogic people will in time produce a press as base
as itself . . .'. Such a proposition has polemic value (though what a
'demagogic people' might be is hard to imagine), but it simply begs
that chicken-and-egg question of which came first, the press or the
public, the textual system or its readers.

While it may seem blindingly obvious at first glance that there
must be a public in existence before a press can be invented to serve
that public, history actually suggests the reverse: reading publics, and
indeed the very idea of the public in the first place, are products of

theory, journalism and literature, and were literally brought into being – out on to the streets, acting as the public – by the press. Pulitzer may have sounded grandiose and self-serving in his claim that 'a press will in time produce a public . . .', but regrettably this does not automatically mean he wasn't right.

The public of modernity is coterminous with the readerships of media, and the contemporary media developed as a means to call certain kinds of public into being. At stake in this process were – and are – some glittering prizes. From the outset (of modernity) it has been those who are able to call on the largest readerships who are apt to carry off the most political and commercial booty, and while the public has rarely acted collectively outside of moments of revolutionary fervour and annual sales, it is true nevertheless that those who have a plausible claim to direct knowledge of the public can take power in their name, act socially and politically on their behalf. And so modernity is characterized by the global acceptance of one of the Enlightenment's first principles – popular sovereignty – a sovereignty which is stimulated, governed and exploited chiefly and most actively by those who invented 'the people'.

Notes

1. Richard V. Ericson, Patricia M. Baranek and Janet B.L. Chan (1987) *Visualizing Deviance: A Study of News Organization*. Milton Keynes: Open University Press, 358.
2. Catharine Lumby (1994) Feminism and the media: the biggest fantasy of all. *Media Information Australia* 72, 49–54.
3. The idea of the 'smiling professions' is explored in my (1992) *The Politics of Pictures: The Creation of the Public in the Age of Popular Media*. London and New York: Routledge, Chapter 5.
4. In this case the guest in question is Nicholas Garnham (1987) Concepts of Culture: public policy and the culture industries. *Cultural Studies* 1(1), 23–37.
5. Thanks to Niall Lucy for this point.
6. For the original supplement, see Jacques Derrida (1976) *Of Grammatology*. Baltimore and London: Johns Hopkins University Press, Chapter 2, esp. 141–57.
7. Thomas Richards (1993) *The Imperial Archive: Knowledge and the Fantasy of Empire*. London and New York: Verso, 44.
8. Hans Magnus Enzensberger (1976) Constituents of a theory of the media. In *Raids and Reconstructions: Essays on Politics, Crime, and Culture*. London: Pluto Press, Chapter 2.
9. Mark Poster (1990) *The Mode of Information: Poststructuralism and Social Context*. Cambridge: Polity Press, 6, 62–3. See also Mark Poster (1994) Baudrillard and TV Ads. In *The Polity Reader in Cultural Theory*. Cambridge: Polity Press, 126–33.
10. Richards, 1–8 (and *passim*).
11. Richards, 1–3.
12. Richards, 6.
13. Richards, 8.

14. Jon P. Klancher (1987) *The Making of English Reading Audiences, 1790–1832.* Madison: University of Wisconsin Press, 51–68.

15. See Michael Hechter (1975) *Internal Colonialism: The Celtic Fringe in British National Development, 1536–1966.* London: Routledge & Kegan Paul; and also R.K. Webb (1955) *The British Working Class Reader 1790–1848: Literacy and Social Tension.* London: George Allen & Unwin.

16. Jon Klancher (1990) British periodicals and reading publics. In Martin Coyle, Peter Garside, Malcolm Kelsall and John Peck (eds.) *Encyclopedia of Literature and Criticism.* London: Routledge, 876–88, this quotation, 886.

17. I've borrowed this term from McKenzie Wark (1993) Suck on this, planet of noise! (Version 1.2). In David Bennett (ed.) *Cultural Studies: Pluralism and Theory.* Melbourne: Melbourne University Literary and Cultural Studies, vol. 2, 156–70.

18. Richards, 4.

19. Miguel De Cervantes Saavedra (1902, first published 1605) *The Life and Exploits of the Ingenious Gentleman Don Quixote De La Mancha.* Trans. Charles Jarvis. London: Sands, 2.

20. See especially Renate Holub (1992) *Antonio Gramsci: Beyond Marxism and Postmodernism.* London and New York: Routledge, 102–16.

21. Klancher, British periodicals, 881.

22. Klancher, 881–2.

23. Klancher, 882.

24. Holub, 105.

25. Aijaz Ahmad (1992) *In Theory: Classes, Nations, Literatures.* London: Verso, 3–4.

26. Ahmad, 11. He goes on: 'For human collectivities in the backward states of capital, however, all relationships with imperialism pass through their own nation-states, and there is simply no way of breaking out of that imperial dominance without struggling for different kinds of national projects and for a revolutionary restructuring of one's own nation-state. So one struggles not against nations and states as such but for different *articulations* of class, nation and state. And one *interrogates* minority nationalisms, religious and linguistic and regional nationalisms, transnational nationalisms (for example Arab nationalism) neither by privileging some transhistorical right to statehood based upon linguistic difference or territorial identity, nor by denying, in the poststructuralist manner, the historical reality of the sedimentations which do in fact give particular collectivities of people real civilizational identities. Rather, one strives for a *rationally argued understanding* of social content and historic project for each particular nationalism. Some nationalist practices are progressive; others are not'. [My italics] I agree (although not with the jibe about poststructuralism), and would only ask for due weight to be given to what Ahmad actually wants: articulation, interrogation, rationally argued understanding – among popular readerships, not just top-table theorists, even radical non-metropolitan ones.

27. Ahmad, 6.

28. Ahmad, 7.

29. Ahmad, 79.

30. Ahmad, 3.

31. Quoted in Michael Lewis (1993) J-school confidential. *The New Republic,* 19 April, 20–7. The word 'corrupt' is in square brackets in the quotation because, according to Lewis, it is used in the pamphlet version of

Pulitzer's article but does not appear on the bronze plaque. I'm grateful to Professor Dick Robison for collecting this interesting piece of Americana for me.

32. Lewis, 27.
33. Lewis, 22–3.
34. Lewis, 26.

2 *Citizens of Media*

(Technologies of Readership)

All the People like us are We,
And every one else is They.
And They live over the sea,
While We live over the way,
But – would you believe it? – They look upon We
As only a sort of They! RUDYARD KIPLING[1]

Popular v. Intellectual Knowledges

Popular culture and intellectual culture are among the largest –
perhaps the most extensive – cross-demographic and global
'imagined communities' of these or any other times, and insofar as
they keep in touch with each other at all, they are kept in touch by
journalism. But this does not have to be characterized as some sort
of latter-day cross-demographic imperialism. Intellectuals routinely
keep in touch with their own globally dispersed colleagues, with
what John Frow has called the 'knowledge class',[2] by active readership; not only consuming or using discourse but producing and
exchanging it, amassing competence and knowledge through
reading practices, and engaging in critical argument and discussion
on the same basis, via books, journals, conversations, and latterly the
internet. I simply suggest that popular readerships do the same.
Looked at as a 'we' not a 'they' community, 'mass' audiences may
be seen to be discursively 'decolonized' (i.e. more free) to a much
greater extent than is commonly admitted in critical coteries. Every
academic's best friend is the 'astute reader', who shares the codes
of the writer down to the subtlest allusion. It is my argument that
this animal is not an imaginary beast confined to the upper reaches
of the knowledge class; astute readership may be understood as a
practice within all reading communities, including popular culture

(including its 'readings' of intellectual culture). That possibility is what this chapter is about: a technology of readership which is widely available and capable of democratization, not in dreams of techno-topia, but here and now, in popular media.

As participation in the traditional public sphere declines in many of the 'old' democratic societies,[3] our understanding of what constitutes 'the political' also has to be rethought, focusing more on issues that are traditionally seen as private rather than public. Such a rethinking would suggest that the traditional idea of the public domain has faded in significance in the twentieth century, to be superseded by a privatized, feminized, suburban, consumerist and international domain of popular media entertainment; a domain constructed in the three-way space between texts, politics and popular readerships. It is here, in a 'public sphere' that is too often condemned in advance by modernist critics reared on the rhetorics of the nineteenth-century realisms, that the most important and pervasive political issues of the late twentieth century are to be found, i.e. gender, environmental, and peace-seeking politics, none of which were initiated or elaborated from within the traditional (Habermasian) public sphere.[4]

Perhaps at this point I should clarify some terms: in this chapter the terms 'reading' and 'readership' are intended to serve as inclusive (though not totalizing) descriptors: 'readerships' are the audiences, consumers, users, viewers, listeners or readers called into being by any medium, whether verbal, audio-visual or visual, journalistic or fictional; 'reading' is the discursive practice of making sense of any semiotic material whatever, and would include not only decoding but also the cultural and critical work of responding, interpreting, talking about or talking back – the whole array of sense-making practices that are proper to a given medium in its situation. In this chapter, 'mass communication studies' includes all formal inquiry into the popular media, from no matter what disciplinary or philosophical perspective, since I'm taking 'mass communication studies' to be the modernist historical discourse within whose terms the very notion of 'mass communication' has been made possible, elaborated, developed, struggled over, re-invented and abandoned throughout most of this century in English-speaking Western intellectual culture. So I include cultural studies as part of 'mass communication studies', even though the latter is a term not often used in cultural studies. And finally, while I'm clarifying terms, by 'intellectual culture' I refer not only to the sphere of formal research and teaching in recognized institutions of learning, but also the informal and much larger culture of theorizing, criticism and reading to be found in journalism and publishing, in governmental and administrative policy-making, and the myriad decentralized practices of intellectual exchange that take place everywhere from coffee shops to hairdressers. I do not mean to perpetuate the opposition between intellectual and popular culture, since I agree with Umberto Eco that they are mutual, reciprocal and interdependent sites of knowledge production. That is why I use one of intellectual culture's most privileged words – reading – to describe one of popular culture's most despised phenomena – media audiences.

I will argue that one of the main impediments to understanding what's going on in the realm of the popular public media turns out – paradoxically – to be the very technology devoted to investigating it, namely the field of 'mass communication studies' itself. While the media do require constant critical attention, it is equally true that common assumptions in many different branches of intellectual culture, including academic, governmental and journalistic writing, also need to be critically questioned, i.e. assumptions that infantilize or 'paedocratize' popular media readerships (audiences), rarely crediting them with critical distance, scepticism or reason, or with being able actively to integrate, compare or triangulate media discourses with others elaborated in different institutional sites. In short, popular readerships are imagined, if at all, as the straightforward binary opposite of intellectual readerships and their supposed critical practices. It is my contention, in response to this, that intellectual discourse has created an entirely imaginary 'other' to itself out of popular media audiences – an 'invisible fiction' whose presumed characteristics can be explained by reference to the purposes, politics and prejudices of intellectual culture at large, rather than by looking at audiences as such. But while intellectual culture continues to pathologize and belittle the practices of popular readerships, the democratization of the sphere of media citizenship will be established and extended – or not – without their assistance.

Technologies of the Self

Before addressing the main issue of this chapter – i.e. that 'mass communication *studies*' is historically a *technology of control* – it is perhaps useful to identify two different ways that technology has been conceptualized in relation to popular media as such.

At one extreme, the concept of media technology seems so obvious that it seems hardly to need explaining. Thus, in a standard introductory book on the subject, Lynne Schafer Gross deals with media technologies as various novel means for the production and distribution of domestic television, like cable, satellite and videodisks.[5] The narrative of glamorous upward spiral in the Reagan era, through to a crash in the 80s, followed by a shake-out and fragmented regrowth into the 90s, is familiar enough – it's the story of world capitalism.[6] Now it seems we are being prepared for another period of upward spiral, with satellite systems vying to cover the whole of Asia along with the information superhighway (an oddly one-way street, so far); but whatever the actual method of production or distribution, it seems obvious in all these accounts that 'technology' is self-evident, simply a matter of corporate investment in the relevant scientific or engineering innovations, coupled with legislative attempts to regulate the play or level the playing field, and then a risky wait while the marketing strategies either do, or do not, pay off.

However, there's the rub. At the very end of her book, having pointed out that it is only 'large companies with deep pockets' which have the economic base to enable them to survive while a given technology gains in popularity, Gross comes up with this:

> *American society engages in a love–hate relationship with its economic base. Capitalism, free enterprise, corporation, profit, and similar terms are sanctified when compared to similar elements of other economic systems such as communism and socialism. But on the home ground, such words usually have negative connotations. A large corporation making a healthy profit is somehow inherently evil, corrupt, and inflexible, and is obviously gaining at the expense of "the little guy."*[7]

In the end, then, even an apologist for 'new media technology' has to acknowledge that it is not so obvious when looked at from the point of view of the consumer; the upward spiral of new technology is glamorous and/or risky only for corporate producers and distributors – for consumers (i.e. readers) it's a matter of technical indifference (they don't care whether a programme is delivered by cable, satellite or microwave); more to the point for the general public is the suspicion of economic rip-off and political manipulation by megacorporations and their mates in state policy-making. Gross identifies a conflict of interest between 'technology' and the consumer, a structural conflict that runs right through the production and distribution of TV and other media, and right to the heart of the *study* of 'mass communication' as well, as I'll try to show in later sections.

But the kind of cultural criticism which characterizes the branch of 'mass communication studies' that I espouse, namely cultural studies, has not had much to say about technologies of production and distribution as such; since Raymond Williams we've been less interested in black boxes than in cultural forms. However, 'technology' has not been neglected in this process – on the contrary, it has been completely retooled. At the other extreme to Gross, the work of Michel Foucault has been influential in a radical reconceptualization of the whole idea of technology – a rethink which follows from his equally far-reaching retheorizations of power and knowledge. Foucault identifies four kinds of technology, each of which has a bearing on the theme of this chapter:

1 technologies of production
2 technologies of sign systems
3 technologies of power
4 technologies of the self.

Foucault glosses technologies of the self as:

> *techniques which permit individuals to affect, by their own means, a certain number of operations on their own bodies, their own souls, their*

own thoughts, their own conduct, and this in a manner so as to trans-
form themselves, modify themselves, and to attain a certain state of
perfection, happiness, purity, supernatural power.[8]

Foucault's explorations in the history of sexuality are an extended
analysis of technologies of the self.[9] Similarly, Teresa De Lauretis has
conceptualized the social institution of cinema – its textual regimes
and productive apparatus – in terms of 'technologies of gender'. In
other words, not only are 'selves' sexualized and gendered by means
of techniques ranging from the medieval confessional to modern
cinema, but also the entire imaginative and discursive apparatus of
what De Lauretis identifies as 'theory, film, and fiction' constitutes
a technology through which such selves are produced.[10]

I will argue that one of these technologies of the self is the practice
of reading, but first it is necessary to indicate how the Foucauldian
notion of technology has been applied to media. This has been done
in his recent book *The Well-Tempered Self* by Toby Miller, who uses it
to describe the production and governance of the self and then its
(our?) self-administration in line with the requirements of cultural-
capitalist policy.[11] At first sight, it seems that his use of the term could
hardly be further removed from Gross's common-sense notion of
technology as corporate innovation in the delivery of information
and entertainment product. But Miller does in fact describe exactly
the same terrain – the terrain of policy, governmentality and the
mechanisms for creating and sustaining a social order in which
capitalist economics and liberal-democratic politics can flourish.

Interestingly, the two extremes of technology analysis (Gross and
Miller) both end on the same note – of consumer resistance.
Corporate technotopia often fails to materialize because, as Gross
concedes:

> *Consumers will be the ultimate judges as to which of the new televi-*
> *sion technologies survive economically. Consumers do not really care*
> *about the technologies themselves. People are interested in watching*
> *programs, not delivery systems.*[12]

People don't care much for corporations either, as she says, nor for
what Miller calls the 'corporate-capitalist state'. And so, having
devoted most of his book to explicating how personal, national, civic
and consumer self-formation results in incomplete but loyal subjects,
Miller comes at length to consider 'the actions of living persons in
opposition, in resistance' to these technologies of governance. He
addresses this 'potential for contradiction' through a study of incivility. Incivility 'operates against the technologies of power' that form
his four kinds of incomplete subject; it is 'a "sovereignty that one
exercises over oneself"'.[13] Thus the unruly incivility that he describes
(and implicitly recommends) is explicitly offered as a 'move beyond
a situation where people can "recognise themselves and their aspirations in the range of representations on offer within the central
communications sector"'.[14]

In fact, it transpires, even as 'mass communications' and other technologies of the self constitute and discipline the consumer-citizens they address, so those citizens escape and exceed the technologies. Miller goes further than most in conceptualizing 'technology' as the cultural-capitalist art or skill of producing and governing selves, but his book nevertheless holds on to a version of self/society dualism, where the 'sovereign' self is precisely the unruly one which resists its status as a 'well-tempered' product of disciplinary discourses. Given my topic in this chapter, it is significant that what sets incivility or 'parodic politics'[15] apart from straight society for Miller is a critical, creative and performative *reading* practice; a very public deconstructive re-reading of received and powerful social truths which are tested to destruction and then reworked into 'messages of subversion' addressed to the 'prevailing social relations'.[16] In other words, Miller's analysis (against the grain of his main thesis) describes not only the formation of the 'postmodern subject', but also what I'd call a postmodern politics of reading, centred on 'the actions of living persons' in relation and reaction to popular media and powerful truth-discourses; his incivility is my media citizenship.

Communication Research as a Technology of Control

I turn now to the 'technology' of 'mass communications studies'. It is not only 'mass media' as such which can be seen as technologies of governance, but, more immediately, our own professional practices and discourses can be seen in the same light. In other words, 'mass communication *studies*' – in which I include cultural studies – has historically and discursively operated as a technology of social control. 'Mass communication studies' has an analytic gaze which ranges far and wide in time and space, overseeing the relationships between populations and media technologies from the stone age to STAR-TV. Spatially, it looks well beyond the bounds of individual nations, at what McKenzie Wark calls the 'global media vectors'.[17] Temporally, it investigates time in all three tenses – past, present and future. A classic example of the attempt to explain media technologies by surveying the entire field of human history (and vice versa) is Marshall McLuhan's *The Gutenberg Galaxy*; for example:

> As we shall see, manuscript culture is intensely audile-tactile compared to print culture; and that means that detached habits of observation are quite uncongenial to manuscript cultures, whether ancient Egyptian, Greek, or Chinese or medieval.[18]

Hans Magnus Enzensberger acidly dismissed McLuhan as the 'ventriloquist and prophet' for the 'apolitical avant garde':

> A new Rousseau – like all copies, only a pale version of the old – he preaches the gospel of the new primitive man who, naturally on a

higher level, must return to prehistoric tribal existence in the 'global village.'[19]

For Enzensberger, McLuhan's dictum that 'the medium is the message' tells us 'with complete frankness' that 'the bourgeoisie does indeed have all possible means at its disposal to communicate something to us, but that it has nothing to say'.[20] In short, Enzensberger wants to stress the class character of 'mass communications' against McLuhan's generalized humanism, but both point to changes in consciousness and social power attendant on media technology.

A recent example of work on new technology which uses a universalist (not to say McLuhanite) perspective, but shifts temporal distinctions into spatial ones, is by Beverly Jones.[21] She summarizes four 'world views' as pre-modern, modern, postmodern and 'new paradigm' (i.e. computer paradigm), but she says: 'In spite of the terminology used, these world views are not to be regarded as chronologically ordered. Rather they continue and co-exist in the present.'[22] Jones uses this schema to criticize the present and predict the future. She says 'the modern view accepts the use of technology to record and view human suffering with no physical, sensual or emotional involvement' (e.g. the use of computer-controlled video in smart missiles and VR to simulate battles). Meanwhile 'the relativistic fragmented view of the postmodern' has 'revealed the problematic nature of broadcast television', but it seems the future belongs to the new age of 'connectivity' with its 'links to the premodern view of a harmonious connected magical view of the world':

> *Will the new user/audiences join technologies of video, computer graphics and virtual reality to the new world view of connectivity to create widespread breakdown of the model of the world as objective manageable information?*[23]

Such questions are endemic to 'mass communication studies': 'how will the future turn out for our technology, country, culture ... species?'; and 'how can we capture and control that future?' But researchers routinely ask their questions from a quite narrowly focused point of view, a single perspective that is posited outside the object of study, scrutinizing it as an object upon which action can be taken. The imagined reader of 'mass communication *studies*' is equally restricted; we rarely address directly those who constitute the 'masses' or audiences of the media we study, but instead we call up our own readers from among those who would take power in the name of audiences by acting on them, from policy-makers in government, the bureaucracies and industry to activists, agitators and artists who want audiences as constituencies or clients for protection or correction.

Studies of audiences abound, of course, but all too rarely do they take on the perspective of the audience itself. A revealing exception to this tendency is an article by Joke Hermes in the journal *Cultural*

Studies. She sets herself up as a young researcher, equipped with both cultural studies and social-science sensitivities and skills, and eager to get viable and useful data from audience ethnography, only to find that within the pragmatic routines of everyday life, it is possible that media texts are 'virtually meaningless'. I should point out that her thoughtful and troubling article could be seen as a direct challenge to my own project in this chapter, since it suggests that audiences are not (always) 'readers' at all; at the very least her findings are a corrective to any (unintended) implication of this chapter that reading practices are necessarily results-oriented and purposeful, characterized by the gaze of concentration, and respectful of textual strategies (including ideology). Equally, as Hermes suggests, reading can be a matter of apprehension at a glance, creating meaning (or not) in ways that defy (escape and exceed) rationalist explanation or even observation (and media receivers can be switched on without being attended to at all). But perhaps more to the point in the present context, Hermes's own disquiet at generating masses of data that according to the expectations of 'mass communication studies' were nearly meaningless, indicates the extent to which it is not the internal rhythms of popular culture (wherein just floating along is just floating along) but the requirements of data-gathering, value-added, quantifiable *information* that governs studies of audiences.[24]

There are good reasons for this. The formal study of 'mass media' was first elaborated to try to understand the workings of 'mass society', but that understanding was of economic or political value not so much to those who lived in and so constituted such a society, but to those who sought to change, govern, or profit by it. Historically, 'mass communication studies' *as a field of inquiry* has been a technology of power, a discourse of control, whether that discourse was radical or conservative, or the control desired on behalf of markets or Marxists. Hence the familiar terms, which have escaped the academy and achieved the status of common sense to think about the relation between audiences and media, are terms like 'manipulation', 'power', 'influence', 'effect' – stressing what happens to audiences, and all too frequently with the extra spin of disapproval or negativity thrown in.[25]

There are reasons for this too. First, what audiences themselves do is notoriously hard to observe, never mind to convert into significant data, partly because 'mass audiences' do not exist as such – they are not people communally assembled in sight of one another to hear and judge (audit) a performance. They do exist as metaphors, dispersed throughout the domain of the social like so many ghosts in the machine – they're everywhere, but one can never quite catch them *being themselves* (they're like Martians or communists in 1950s paranoia movies). Second, what audiences do is not necessarily all that important to those who can afford to pay for the labour of finding out – they need numbers not actions, effects not meanings. In short, 'audiences' – as a discursive category – are a product and an integral part of the technology of governance through which various institutions seek to take power in their name; they're a fiction produced for their own benefit by the disciplinary 'three Rs' of ratings, regulation and research. In such a field, it is not difficult to understand how technology has come to be seen as the very agent of media 'effects', whether the latter are said to result from deliberate campaigns (commercial or political), or as dysfunctional side-effects of entertainment (violence, bad language, bad ideology, sex, passivity); the audience reduced to its own cartoon image, society as Beavis and Butt-head, a teenage nerd sitting in front of MTV with 'one hand on the remote control and the other down his shorts'.[26]

An attempt to circumvent some of these problems can be seen in the 1980s' return to anthropology and ethnography in audience studies. Audience ethnographers have sought to include the suburban consumer among those cultures whose way of life may be described empirically. However, audience ethnographers cannot avoid the analytic gaze, as is recognized by Ellen Seiter and her colleagues in their account of the 'ethnography of reading'.[27] They make the point that:

> *Today, there is an increasing tendency within ethnography to reject 'colonial representations,' i.e. 'discourses that portray the cultural reality of other peoples without placing their own reality into jeopardy.' . . . Audience studies are carried out by academics . . . who 'go out into the field' to learn about . . . groups of viewers with social and (sub)cultural backgrounds usually different from their own. This means that the differences and similarities between participants and scholars in terms of class, gender, race, culture or subculture, educational background, age, etc. have to be reflected.*[28]

Some researchers, for instance Henry Jenkins, have decided simply to refuse the protocols of academic distance (controlling gaze), despite the apparent 'danger of overidentification with the research subject':

> *While conceding that such a risk (media study's particular version of 'going native') is present in writing an ethnography from within the fan community, I must note as well that this danger is not substantially lessened by adopting a more traditionally 'objective' stance. In the past, scholars with little direct knowledge or emotional investment within the fan community have transformed fandom into a projection of their personal fears, anxieties, and fantasies about the dangers of mass culture.*[29]

Jenkins warns against both judging and instructing popular readerships, criticizing studies (he mentions Jan Radway's *Reading the Romance*) which 'cast writers as vanguard intellectuals who might lead the fans toward a more overtly political relationship to popular culture', because these empower not the readership but the academic, enabling 'scholars to talk about a group presumed incapable of responding to their representation'.[30]

I think that the criticisms of vanguard intellectuals and of the controlling gaze of modernist research are well made. But I do not agree that the alternative is a 'hands-on' approach to audiences, a touchy-feely technologized 'connectivity' (even if only on the internet) which seeks to understand audiences by magically becoming them.[31] For one thing, such an understanding defers too much to informal, experiential knowledge and belittles too much the practice of formal knowledge production with its attempts to be scrupulous, testable and open. Rather than 'putting their own reality into jeopardy' (which may be just another kind of acid trip), researchers need to admit not their identity but their art (for which the Greek word is *techne*); they are skilled in the use of a particular technology and need to take responsibility for it within and beyond the academy. It ought to be possible to do justice to and to learn from popular readerships without de-skilling intellectual culture.

Audiences are Readerships, not People

To do this, however, to study 'mass communication' from the point of view of the audience, requires us, paradoxically, to abandon the unwarranted supposition that audiences are people. Instead, we need the much more modest concept of audiences as readerships. Reading is not an intrinsic property of one's subjectivity, whether that is seen as sovereign or as constructed by technologies of governance. Reading is a practice – a part of a cultural repertoire of actions that people may undertake from time to time. Like speech it is distributed throughout human culture in ways that are relatively autonomous from economic, political and cultural identity (i.e. barring accidents, everyone can talk). All cultures produce texts for reading as well as speech; all cultures are semiotically affluent,[32] suffused with reading practices ranging from the decoding of bodies and landscapes to the enjoyment of ceremonies, songs, stories and spectacle (what might be called stone age television).

But like spoken language, reading is also subject to historical development. For instance:

- capital investment (training or education in literacy),
- colonization (turning people into readerships of particular textual regimes),
- division of labour (e.g. some reading is for consumption, other kinds for further discursive production),
- appropriation (intellectual culture has a massive investment in reading technologies and guards them jealously),
- divide and rule (disempowering hierarchies of reading and readerships, e.g. popular romance readers vs. philosophers),
- economic gain (commercial media).

Like speech, reading is a universal technology of communication, but it is not an already-existing attribute of persons, nor are readerships 'natural' self-present communities with an existence beyond their production by the media they read. Reading is a discursive practice by means of which an individual will sometimes be called into being as an audience, sometimes not. It follows that audiences are discursive productions, but nonetheless real. Once this notion of audiences as readerships is established, along with the idea of reading as a technology capable of historical development, then it is possible to pose quite different questions in relation to the media than would be possible if we persist in thinking of audiences as people.[33] For instance, what would constitute 'best practice' in the realm of media readings?

A persistent idea about what might, in line with contemporary managerialist protocols, be called 'industry best practice'[34] in the domain of reading, is what public intellectuals – 'we' – are reputed to do; the 'tradition of critical discussion',[35] a tradition Karl Popper traces back to ancient Greece. The ideal of critical discussion or critical rationality, of reasoned speech and argumentation (i.e. 'forensics' – pursuit of the truth by argument in the public forum), is also central to the Enlightenment idea of the public sphere; a domain of rational discussion between free and informed citizens in an open, public forum in which decisions can be made, and the powers-that-be can be criticized and held to account. Thus, both in the scientific philosophy of Popper, and in the political philosophy of (especially) Jürgen Habermas, an image has developed of 'an association of free and equal individuals who regulate their communal life themselves through democratic will-formation'.[36] According to Popper, reason followed reading – it was only when discourses were 'exosomatic' or developed outside the body in some communicable medium (like writing), that rational discussion could proceed and build upon itself.[37] The same applies to Habermas's public sphere – its participants were already and only *educated readers,* and the public sphere itself was a 'discursive community' bound together by Popperian 'critical reason'.[38]

Feminist Public Sphere as Technology of Readership

Can the notion of a public sphere comprising an open society of rational readers be imagined in relation to contemporary popular media and their gigantic, international readerships? Both Popper and Habermas (along with most other critical social theorists from the Frankfurt School onwards) would emphatically say no. But their militant modernism is perhaps too absolute and exclusive, too binary in its construction of a 'we' community opposed to 'the masses'. It offers no insight into ways that the public sphere, the domain of critical argument, and the 'mass' media, might develop and change historically, not least in relation to each other, nor how readerships may be formed, changed and democratized over time.

Turning to the one branch of learning that has traditionally taken some interest in reading and readerships, namely literary theory and criticism, may be of some assistance here, although historically the prevailing wisdom of critical common sense has held either that training in critical reading is itself a technology of governmentality,[39] or else that it should be used by radical conservatives whose catch-cry is still the Leavisite: 'The citizen . . . must be trained to discriminate and resist'! – and what s/he is supposed to resist is, of course, the temptations of 'mass communication'.[40]

However, the powerful notion of a public sphere within an 'open society' has been used by literary theorist Rita Felski to identify what she has called the 'feminist public sphere'.[41] She notes the changes that have had to be wrought in the Habermasian notion of the public sphere along the way. That is, the emancipatory ideal of the public sphere, where equal access is guaranteed to all citizens, is compromised in point of historical fact by gender and class blindness, since the sphere is actually a segment, restricted to 'an educated male bourgeoisie and enlightened nobility'. Even the limited achievement of the bourgeois public sphere was (according to its proponents) progressively lost, as:

> *the commodification of the mass media and the influence of state bureaucracies on individual life experience (the colonization of the life world) makes it increasingly impossible to identify any independent arena for the critical and informed formation of public opinion.*[42]

Felski's formulation here makes it clear that the Habermasian public sphere is imagined as outside of and in opposition to the 'life world' of social experience,[43] and also that the formation of public opinion was a specialist job which had to be undertaken by someone other than the public, in opposition to the popular media.

But at this point (the 1960s), according to Felski, the growth of 'counter-public spheres' can be discerned, spheres which appeal not to universality but 'toward an affirmation of specificity in relation to gender, race, ethnicity, age, sexual preference, and so on'. Such counter-public spheres:

> *seek to define themselves against the homogenizing and universalizing logic of the global megaculture of modern mass communication as a debased pseudopublic sphere, and to voice needs and articulate oppositional values which the "culture industry" fails to address.*[44]

Felski identifies feminism as a 'counter-public sphere' in this oppositional sense (although it's important to note that the 'counter-cultures', including various feminist ventures, were fully integrated with as well as oppositional to 'mass communications' in the 1960s and 70s). But at the same time this *counter*-public sphere has two *universalizing* tendencies. First, it seeks to erase differences between women (age, class, ethnicity, etc.), so that as Felski puts it, 'the "we" of feminist discourse is intended to represent all women as collective cosubjects'. Second, because it does seek to address/interpellate all women, not just specialist activists in the oppositional counter-public sphere, feminism is itself a form of mass communication, calling into being a readership from within those same mass media whose inadequacies as a 'pseudopublic sphere' have just been criticized:

> *Insofar as [feminism] is a* public *sphere, its arguments are also directed outward, toward a dissemination of feminist ideas and values throughout society as a whole . . . . The feminist public sphere also constitutes a discursive arena which disseminates its arguments outward through such public channels of communication as books, journals, the mass media, and the education system. The gradual expansion of feminist values from their roots in the women's movement throughout society as a whole is a necessary corollary of feminism's claim to embody a catalyst of social and cultural change.*[45]

Felski conceptualizes a dual role for the feminist public sphere: '*internally*, it generates a gender-specific identity; . . . *externally*, it seeks to convince society as a whole of the validity of feminist claims'.[46] This formulation strains to breaking point the critical-outsider approach to the mass media – 'mass communication' surely cannot remain the 'debased pseudopublic sphere' of 'global megaculture' that feminists first opposed if it is at the same time the vehicle for feminism to communicate across gender, class and demographic boundaries, both to address other women, and to engage in critical discussion with 'male-defined cultural and discursive frameworks'. At some point (or on some occasions), the popular media must be understood as *constituting* the feminist public sphere, and media audiences must be recognized not only as the recipients of 'public opinion' formed in an 'independent' critical domain located somewhere over their heads, but as the readership which *constitutes* the public of the feminist public domain. Given this combination of critical and communicational forces, I would argue that Felski's notion of a feminist public domain which is at once oppositional to and part of the media, is the most useful conceptualization of 'media citizenship' to date.

The possibility of such a mediated public domain is hinted at in a most unlikely context: in the writings of Karl Popper. In line with Felski's dual-function feminist public sphere, he posits a dual function for language as a whole. He divides human language into two 'lower' and two 'higher' functions (evaluative terms which I quote without wishing to transform Popper's rationalist preferences into natural facts), and he makes bold claims for the latter:

> *The most important of human creations, with the most important feedback effects upon ourselves and especially upon our brains, are the higher functions of human language; more especially, the* descriptive function *and the argumentative function.*[47]

Popper argues that the two 'lower' functions of language, namely '*self-expression*' and '*communication*' (or '*signalling*') are always present, even when the two 'higher' functions are also present, which explains why 'the most important of the higher functions have been overlooked by almost all philosophers'. I suggest that the self-expression and communicative functions of language correspond here to Felski's 'internal' identity-forming and experience-sharing function of the feminist public sphere. Meanwhile, within and 'higher' than them are the descriptive and argumentative functions, corresponding to her 'external' function which 'seeks to convince' (argument) society of feminism's 'validity' (truth). In other words, the same forum can have two functions; the obvious one of expression and communication, which 'mass communication' has in abundance, together with the descriptive and critical discussion function, which the media also display (in fact whole genres are devoted to it), but which philosophers may fail to notice.

For Popper, 'with the descriptive function of human language, the regulative idea of *truth* emerges, that is, of a description which fits the facts', while critical argument is what makes the human species human and not animal:

> *Human languages share with animal languages the two lower functions of language . . . It is to this development of the higher functions of language that we owe our humanity, our reason. For our powers of reasoning are nothing but powers of critical argument.*[48]

These claims about what makes 'us' human are highly provocative. Popper gives the technology to which we 'owe our humanity' a spatio-temporal origin, coincident with 'the development of a descriptive language (and further, of a written language)'. 'That great spiritual revolution, the invention of critical discussion, and in consequence of thought that was free from magical obsessions' had taken place 'by the sixth century B.C.'[49] This formulation not only leaves outside of humanity people living before 599 BC or beyond the sway of Hellenism, but it also seems to deny human status to those who are non-literate or inept at scientific method!

Since this is unlikely to be his intention, Popper's conception of humanity requires a technology to generalize reason and so produce those 'feedback effects on our brains'. This technology is language, which he argues is subject to historical development[50] when society commits its knowledge to exosomatic forms (writing, books, media) and to the error-eliminating practices of public critical discussion and argumentation in search of descriptive truth. Here Popper is at one with the Foucauldians that selves are formed historically, not given: 'In order to be a self, much has to be learnt; . . . not only perception and language have to be learnt – actively – but even the task of being a person.'[51] This learning task (a form of reading) is presumably not confined to intellectuals. Popper thus hints at a theory and a technology of reading in which self-expression and communication are the ubiquitous but not the only functions, and are shared by all utterance whether rational or not. Applying this to Felski's history of the feminist public sphere, it could be argued that the 'higher' functions of language – truth-seeking description and critical argumentation – are not only the 'external' function of the feminist public sphere, they are also the general cultural function of 'mass communication' itself.

Citizens of Media

Just as the bourgeois public sphere was far from universal, so, as Henry Tudor reminds us, the classical public forum was far from general, being an accidental by-product of noble men's self-aggrandizement. In the classical tradition:

> *A virtue which was not exercised, or was exercised only in the obscurity of private life, was no virtue at all. . . . To become real, virtue . . . had to achieve public recognition, for only in so far as a man's virtue was acknowledged by others did it attain an existence outside of his own private self-appreciation. Of course, the public before whose eyes the citizen performed his deeds and which awarded glory was narrowly circumscribed. It was the ruling class itself, and not the mob, whose judgement was the standard of excellence.*[52]

Small wonder then, that for the Roman nobility, according to Tudor:

> *To be denied citizenship was to be excluded from the public sphere and thus to be condemned to obscurity and a kind of living death. It was the despised condition of slaves, women and strangers.*[53]

It is my feeling that we have inherited a little too much of the evaluative distinction inherent in this male/nobility model of the public sphere. Slaves, women, strangers, minors – or workers, women, migrants and children in today's parlance – still form the readerships of popular media, and are still despised insofar as they remain 'condemned to obscurity' as the denizens of mass-media culture (see Chapters 6 and 7). The reason I am harking back to these classical myth-origins of contemporary political practices is not to praise but to bury them; to show how the concepts of intellectual culture and the public sphere (critical reason and argumentation) still retain evaluative prejudices dating back to gender and class supremacisms which ought to have no place in contemporary media theory but which have hung on since ancient times (with an extra medieval twist that separates a Latinate learned class from a vernacular populace).[54]

I've tried to show that even the most radical and progressive discourses, such as feminism and cultural studies, persist in denigrating the mass media, even when they see ways of using 'mass communication' for their own purposes. What they have not done sufficiently is to conceptualize the way in which the readership of 'mass communications' constructs itself into an imagined community whose public sphere is symbolic, but much more real than the Roman Forum ever was for the general public. 'Mass communications' and their readerships can be reconceptualized as citizens of an emergent, globalizing, postmodern public sphere, which is situated, via the pervasive popular media, in the privatized, feminized, so-called 'contemptible, obscure living death' in fact of the private domain. This is in fact the place where you'll find the reasoned speech of the Habermasian public sphere, Popper's critical discussion, Felski's feminism, not to mention Miller's sovereign parodic politics and Frow's knowledge class (plus some game shows). It's the home, suburbia and television.

Broadcast television is far from being an outmoded technology – it is the exemplary form of what can be called a 'technology of society'. It's a distribution system, a mechanism for communicating across class, gender, ethnic, national, and other boundaries, by means of which readerships can act for the time being as citizens of a symbolic community which is simultaneously as small as their home, town or faction, and as big as humanity, and in which the 'three Ds' of drama, didactics and democracy are continuously in play to engage readers not only in self-expression and communication, but also in truth-seeking description and critical argument, in both fictional and factual forms. In the end, what's on TV is no more 'representative' of the general community than the classical public sphere was, but because access to it is general and daily, and because its regime of reading is non-coercive, the public sphere of television is an extensive and supple 'technology of society' for its readerships, who have no other exosomatic mechanism for constituting themselves as society.

In such a context, the masculine, elite and exclusive world of the traditional public domain – 'representative' politics and administration, along with its critics – is certainly not neglected, but alongside it, virtually unnoticed, other knowledges, other politics, are established and generalized, creating a new political agenda. Where, for example, new ethnic, gender, environmental, youth, and peace-seeking politics are produced and sustained in the interstices of drama serials, nature documentaries and current affairs, or in the relationships between certain stars, styles or musics and their fans, it is not of the first importance to decide who owns and controls this technology of society,[55] nor is it wise to ignore the politics simply because it is communicated in banal and showy formats. 'Mass communication studies' might do well to learn from Lynne Schafer Gross's 'consumers', who as we've seen 'do not really care about the technologies themselves' because they are 'interested in watching programs, not delivery systems'. This is a lesson 'we' in 'mass communication studies' could learn from media readerships, since watching programs – more astutely than they're given credit for – is the very technology by means of which readerships turn themselves into citizens of media.

Notes

1. Rudyard Kipling (1977) *Selected Verse.* Ed. James Cochrane. Harmondsworth: Penguin, 289–90.

2. John Frow (1993) Knowledge and class. *Cultural Studies* 7(2), 240–81. Frow extends the concept in the (1995) book where this article is reprinted, *Cultural Studies and Cultural Value*, Oxford University Press.

3. As measured by a decline in numbers of people voting in nations where this is voluntary (especially the USA), and even where it is compulsory, as in Australia, opinion polls indicate increasing disaffection with politics; for instance an April 1994 poll among young people gave between 78 per cent and 93 per cent responses for various negative statements about politicians, and showed that a quarter of 18-year-olds failed to register to vote in the 1993 Federal election (ABC-TV *Attitude* 4 April 1994). A 1987 Newspoll (on the eve of the Bicentenary) showed that 46 per cent of respondents did not know Australia had a constitution, while among 18- to 24-year-olds this figure rose to 70 per cent (*Weekend Australian* 2 May 1987). The 1994 *Attitude* poll showed young people placed greater trust in musicians – i.e. in the political credibility of the new privatized public domain of so-called entertainment media.

4. See Ross Poole (1989) Public spheres. In Helen Wilson (ed.) *Australian Communications and the Public Sphere: Essays in Memory of Bill Bonney.* Melbourne: Macmillan, 6–26.

5. Lynne Schafer Gross (1990) *The New Television Technologies.* 3rd edn. Dubuque, IA: Wm. C. Brown, 3.

6. Gross writes: In 1983, the new television technologies seemed to be on a continuously upward spiral. Most were healthy, exciting – even glamorous. By . . . 1986, I felt like I was writing obituaries. Most of the technologies were facing economic reality – and not dealing with it very well. By now [1990], there has been a shakeout. Two of the media – cable TV and VCRs – are doing quite nicely. Others are dead (STV, videotext), dying (teletext, videodiscs, DBS) or low key (MMDS, SMATV, LPTV).' Gross, xiii. The technologies referred to by initials in this quotation are: VCR = video-cassette recorders; STV = subscription television (a form of pay TV where scrambled signals are broadcast and subscribers pay for a decoding box); DBS = direct broadcast by satellite (i.e. direct from satellite to individual home satellite dishes); MMDS = multichannel multipoint distribution service (multichannel TV broadcast at extremely high frequencies [over 2000 MHz] and requiring a 'down converter' in subscribers' homes); SMATV = satellite master antenna television (i.e. a communal satellite dish feeding an apartment building or other restricted community); LPTV = low power televsion (i.e. localized broadcasting). Clearly this account refers only to the USA in 1990.

7. Gross, 215–16.

8. Michel Foucault (1988) *Technologies of the Self: A Seminar with Michel Foucault.* Ed. Luther H. Martin, Huck Gunman, Patrick H. Hutton. London: Tavistock, 18.

9. See, for instance, Michel Foucault (1979) *The History of Sexuality: Volume One – An Introduction.* Trans. Robert Hurley. Harmondsworth: Penguin, 58–64 (on confession as a technology of the self); Michel Foucault (1987) *The Use of Pleasure: The History of Sexuality Volume Two.* Trans. Robert Hurley. Harmondsworth: Penguin; and Michel Foucault (1988) *The Care of the Self: The History of Sexuality Volume Three.* Trans. Robert Hurley. New York: Vintage Books.

10. Teresa De Lauretis (1989) *Technologies of Gender: Essays on Theory, Film and Fiction.* London: Macmillan.

11. Toby Miller (1993) *The Well-Tempered Self: Citizenship, Culture, and the Postmodern Subject.* Baltimore and London: Johns Hopkins University Press.

12. Gross, 215.

13. Miller, 173; the phrase is quoted from Michel Foucault (1988) *The Care of the Self: The History of Sexuality Volume Three.* Trans. Robert Hurley. New York: Vintage Books, 85.

14. Miller, 172. The internal quotation is from Peter Golding and Graham Murdock (1989) Pulling the plugs on democracy. *New Statesman and Society* 2, (56), 11.

15. An account of the Sisters of Perpetual Indulgence, an order of gay male nuns active in the politics of sexuality in Australia, especially in relation to a papal visit in 1986. Miller, Chapter 5, esp. 202–17.

16. Miller, 203.

17. See, for instance, McKenzie Wark (1990) Vectors of memory . . . seeds of fire: the Western media and the Beijing demonstrations. *New Formations*, 10, 1–12; and McKenzie Wark (1991) From Fordism to Sonyism: perverse readings of the New World Order. *New Formations* 15 (Winter), 43–54.

18. Marshall McLuhan (1962) *The Gutenberg Galaxy: The Making of Typographic Man.* London: Routledge & Kegan Paul, 28. The section of the book's 'mosaic' from which this quotation is taken is entitled: 'Civilization gives the barbarian or tribal man an eye for an ear and is now at odds with the electronic world.' McLuhan's denial of 'detached habits of observation' to the Greeks is in direct contradiction to the assessment of Greek rationalism by Karl Popper (see below).

19. Hans Magnus Enzensberger (1976, first published 1970) Constituents of a theory of the media. In *Raids and Reconstructions: Essays in Politics, Crime and Culture.* London: Pluto Press, 42–3. This is not the place to conduct a debate between these two worthy sparring partners of the late 1960s, but it is salutary to note that the opposing media futures each of them imagined a generation ago still remain the industry standard, as it were, the educated common sense, for positive (McLuhan) and negative (Enzensberger) visions of the culture and politics of media technologies.

20. Enzensberger, 44. One response to this would be to shift attention from the communicator to the readership.

21. Beverly Jones (1993) Cultural maintenance and change. *Media Information Australia*, 69 (special issue on *Art and Cyberculture* edited by Ross Harley), 23–37. See also the article by David Tafler and Peter d'Agostino, The techno/cultural interface, in the same issue, 47–54.

22. Jones, 23.

23. Jones, 35–6.

24. Joke Hermes (1993) Media, meaning and everyday life. *Cultural Studies*, 7(3), 493–506.

25. See James W. Carey (1977) Mass communication research and cultural studies: an American view. In James Curran, Michael Gurevitch and Janet Woollacott (eds.) *Mass Communication and Society.* London: Edward Arnold, 409–25.

26. *The Face*, October 1993.

27. Ellen Seiter *et al.* (1989) Don't treat us like we're so stupid and naive: Toward an ethnography of soap opera viewers. In Ellen Seiter, Hans Borchers, Gabriele Kreutzner and Eva-Maria Warth (eds.) *Remote*

Control: Television, Audiences and Cultural Power. London and New York: Routledge, 223–47.

28. Seiter *et al.*, 227. The internal quotation is from James Clifford (1983) On ethnographic authority. *Representations* 1(2), 133.

29. Henry Jenkins (1992) *Textual Poachers: Television Fans and Participatory Culture.* New York and London: Routledge, 6.

30. Jenkins, 6.

31. Jones.

32. On semiotic affluence, misrecognized by modernist anthropology, see Marshall Sahlins's 'The original affluent society' (first published in insurrectionist Paris in 1968): 'Current low opinions of the hunting-gathering economy need not be laid to neolithic ethnocentrism, however. Bourgeois ethnocentrism will do as well. . . . If modern man, with all his technological advantages, still hasn't got the wherewithal [to beat scarcity], what chance has this naked savage with his puny bow and arrow? Having equipped the hunter with bourgeois impulses and paleolithic tools, we judge his situation hopeless in advance.' Marshall Sahlins (1972) *Stone Age Economics.* London: Tavistock, 3–4. See also his table-turning anthropological reading of the contemporary American clothing system in Marshall Sahlins (1976) *Culture and Practical Reason.* Chicago: Chicago University Press.

33. See Eric Michaels (1985) Ask a foolish question: on the methodologies of cross cultural media research. *Australian Journal of Cultural Studies* 3(2), 45–59.

34. See John Clarke and Janet Newman (1993) The right to manage: a second managerial revolution? *Cultural Studies*, 7(3), 427–41.

35. Karl Popper (1983) *A Pocket Popper.* Ed. David Miller. London: Fontana, 26.

36. Jürgen Habermas (1989) The new intimacy between culture and politics: theses on enlightenment in Germany. In *The New Conservatism: Cultural Criticism and the Historians' Debate.* Ed. and trans. S.W. Nicholsen. Cambridge, Mass.: MIT Press, 203.

37. Popper, 72, 58–9, 60.

38. Rita Felski (1989) *Beyond Feminist Aesthetics: Feminist Literature and Social Change.* Cambridge, Mass.: Harvard University Press, 164–5.

39. Ian Hunter (1988) *Culture and Government: The Emergence of Literary Education.* London: Macmillan. See also Holly Goulden and John Hartley (1982) 'Nor should such topics as homosexuality, masturbation, frigidity, premature ejaculation or the menopause be regarded as unmentionable': English, official discourses, and school examinations. *LTP: Journal of Literature Teaching Politics,* 1, 4–20.

40. F.R. Leavis and Denys Thompson (1933) *Culture and Environment: The Training of Critical Awareness.* London: Chatto & Windus, 3–4. The full passage reads: 'The school-training of literary taste does indeed look a forlorn enterprise. Yet if one is to believe in education at all, one must believe that something worth doing can be done. And if one is to believe in anything, one must believe in education. We cannot, as we might in a healthy state of culture, leave the citizen to be formed unconsciously by his environment; if anything like a worthy idea of satisfactory living is to be saved, he must be trained to discriminate and resist.' On reading publics see also Q.D. Leavis (1932) *Fiction and the Reading Public.* London: Chatto & Windus; Richard Altick (1957) *The English Common Reader: A Social History of the Mass Reading Public*

1800–1900. Chicago: Chicago University Press; Jon Klancher (1987) *The Making of English Reading Audiences 1790–1832*. Madison, Wis.: University of Wisconsin Press; Harvey Graff (ed.) (1981) *Literacy and Social Development in the West*. Cambridge: Cambridge University Press.

41. Felski, 164–82.
42. Felski, 165–6.
43. Note also that the Habermasian 'life world' is implicitly granted some kind of natural existence prior to its 'colonization' by media and state bureaucracies. This formulation wrongly supposes that populations exist independently of their production in line with economic forces (it would be better to remember, bluntly, that no capitalism = no working class), and it wrongly supposes a kind of *a priori* semiotic purity which *can* be 'colonized' by media.
44. Felski, 166.
45. Felski, 167.
46. Felski, 168.
47. Popper, 71.
48. Popper, 72.
49. Karl Popper (1950) *The Open Society and its Enemies*. Princeton: Princeton University Press, 172.
50. It would doubtless have come as a surprise to Popper to know that here he is at one with Jean-François Lyotard, who updates the notion of language development by writing of the capitalization of language: 'The major development of the last twenty years . . . has been the transformation of language into a productive commodity. . . . The effects of the penetration of capitalism into language are just beginning to be felt.' If Lyotard is right, then critical reason is – among other things – a scarce resource. J.-F. Lyotard (1986–7) Rules and paradoxes and svelte appendix. *Cultural Critique*, 5, 217 (cited in Frow, 240).
51. Popper, 280.
52. Henry Tudor (1972) *Political Myth*. London: Macmillan, 75.
53. Tudor, 75.
54. See Umberto Eco (1987) *Travels in Hyperreality*. Trans. William Weaver. London: Picador; and Walter J. Ong (1971) Latin language study as a Renaissance puberty rite. In *Rhetoric, Romance and Technology: Studies in the Interaction of Expression and Culture*. Ithaca and London: Cornell University Press, 113–41.
55. See Frow, 268 and fn. 29.

3 *The Public Sphere*

(Liberty)

Good books imperceptibly enlightened people, and prepared the Revolution. It is by reading that those brave men were produced whom you charged to represent you and to defend your rights: it is by reading that you yourselves will learn to know your rights, and to preserve them.

La Feuille villageoise, no. 1, 1790[1]

1790s to 1990s: Plus Ça Change?

By observing the original 'big bang' of modern democracy, which happened, not least symbolically, on Tuesday, 14 July 1789, 'in four hours or so',[2] and by tracing the immediate expansion of its energies, I think it can be argued that the universe of modernity looks the way it does today not least because of journalism. Journalism was an essential element in the first few creative moments of the modern world, being one of the principal means by which its democratic energies were excited into existence and then diffused across 'the people' in whose name they occurred, giving meaning, context and shape to a whole new universe of secular popular sovereignty. Journalism was a major force for the French Revolution's progressive radicalization until 1794. It promoted new senses of national unity, popular political purpose and the possibility of improving any aspect of life by means of reason and collective will. It had its own version of tabloid or trash journalism, not to mention pornography in the service of politics, and it created a very modern 'imagined community' of readers out of the middling ranks or orders of society which it opposed to enemies and threats from above, below, and outside – an adversarial 'Wedom' with universalist aspirations, since this embattled middle was taken to represent not just the whole nation or people, but the whole of 'mankind'. In the process, the contours of what I've called the mediasphere were being created very quickly, eventually hardening into a topography that is still recognizable, even in the period of the postmodern mediasphere.

Although I shall have nothing at all to say about it in this chapter, one of the most persistent features of that topography from quite early in the French Revolution (though it was slow to start) has been the virulent, counter-revolutionary, right-wing, reactionary press of the groups who opposed popular sovereignty – king, capital, clergy – a press which has held modernizing journalism and politics in continual, denunciatory dialogue from that day to this.[3] However, despite its subsequent monopolization of whole segments of the mediasphere, I am not here concerned with reactionary journalism, for it has played no useful part in the creation, spread and popularization of modern democracy. Its significance was rather in commercializing the press, in technical capitalization, and in opposing democratic ideology by trying to create a readership which was content to be modern in terms of private comfort and public efficiency rather than popular freedom. I do not mean to include critical, investigative, satirical and oppositional journalism in this context; such interlocutors are essential participants in democratic dialogue. But my interest in this chapter is not in 'both sides of the story'; it is in the sudden flare of 'electric fire', as one contemporary called radical journalism, which applied the match of liberty to the parched rangelands of early modern popular consciousness. It might be worth pointing out that over the very long term, politics has been shifted, not without struggle, ever leftwards – the proposals of the radicals are mostly political common sense now; their radicalism consisted in wanting to get the inevitable done quickly, and in being optimistic about the future.

Russian Dolls

The notion of the public sphere has been widely discussed in relation to journalism, although not till now, as far as I know, in terms of its relations with wider cultural sense-making practices, specifically in the context of the Russian cultural semiotician Yuri Lotman's very imaginative and useful concept of the 'semiosphere', which will be discussed in more detail in Chapters 4 and 5 below.[4] I suggest that what can be called the 'mediasphere' has developed between two other spheres, connecting the public (political) sphere and the much larger semiotic (cultural) sphere, within the period of modernity. Traditionally in social analysis, both academic and journalistic, the political/economic and the textual/cultural have been studied and reported as separate domains, requiring different kinds of analysis by different discourses (at different ends of the newspaper) for different specialist readerships. But a very important *untruth* tends to arise from this otherwise very scrupulous specialization, i.e. the untrue idea that the public sphere of politics is not only detached from the cultural semiosphere of textualized meaning, but also that the political is determined not by meanings but by economics, which has priority over culture, in the same way as production is said to have a determinate or causal priority over consumption. What I intend to show in this chapter is that the political sphere is immersed in meanings, and that politics, via journalism, is fully textualized, and in constant, mutual, productive and politically significant sense-making dialogue with the other textual and semiotic systems to be found within and beyond its meaning-horizons. Arguing that politics, media and culture are contained within each other, I try to show how, in consequence of this, there's a two-way, mutually determining relationship between politics and journalism: the journalistic mediation of the public sphere has determinate effects on how political questions are acted out and realized socially; and conversely journalism as a whole, even its least political components, is a product of modernizing political energies. I'm arguing that democracy, middle classness, freedom, equality, reason, virtue, modernization, comfort, utility, secularism and popular sovereignty had a hard time establishing themselves in people's consciousness and in formal political arrangements, and that without journalism to promote possibilities and choices that had been previously unknown or unhoped for they would not have been established at all, never mind the determination of underlying socio-economic tendencies.

This chapter, along with Chapters 4 and 5, ought perhaps to be seen as describing concentric spheres, each inside the other rather like Russian dolls. The semiosphere entirely surrounds the mediasphere, inside of which is the public sphere. This neat concentrism does not describe an empirical fact but an analytical perspective, however, for the semiosphere (as we shall see) surrounds all language and culture, and therefore encompasses a lot more 'spheres' of meaning than just journalism. Similarly, the 'mediasphere' envelops more than the public sphere, important though that is, because 'the media' include music, drama and visual art as well as journalism (and of course the various media forms interact with and overlap each other). Thus a different analytical project, organized around questions of art, drama and popular entertainment, for instance, would find different spheres within each other inside the semiosphere; for instance a 'mediasphere' understood as fictional, whose characteristic form of expression is drama rather than journalism, might find within it not the public sphere but the private sphere, not truth but desire, not linear time but cyclical time, not history but myth, not the French Revolution but television.

Not that such public/private differences can ever be distinguished so easily in practice, for their very identity depends on contrast or opposition with their neighbours in the semiosphere. You can get Russian dolls with traditional peasant characters inside of one another, each like its larger container, the pleasure of discovery being repetition; or you can get Russian dolls which play political genealogy – mine is a 'Gorby doll', bought in August 1991, which contains nine Soviet and Russian leaders (Gorbachev, Brezhnev, Kruschev, Stalin, Lenin, Nicholas II, Catherine the Great, Peter the Great, Ivan the Terrible). So it is with the semiosphere; within its enabling universe of possibilities may be very different spheres of meaning, which are in opposition and 'dialogue' with each other so that, for instance, the 'Gorby doll' doesn't make sense without its playful contrast with the traditional peasant doll, since it brings together politics and folklore, linear and cyclical time, father- and mother-figures, government and children, history and myth. Similarly, the public sphere and the mediasphere (within the semiosphere) are bounded by other spheres of meaning, and in intense dialogue with them, as we shall see (Chapters 4, 5 and 6).

Ever since Aristotle it has been conventional to define humanity as '*zoon politikon*' – the political (city-dwelling) animal – thereby making politics a property of individual nature. But in practice it is only in modernity that individual people and formal politics are linked at all, since in prior constitutional arrangements the idea would have been as ludicrous as a 'Gorby doll' – a playful inversion of the divine ordering of things, as, for instance, in medieval Christendom on those surplus days called the kalends when boys became bishops for a day as play-acting took centre-stage and the world was comically turned upside down (in order to relieve and reveal its true structure). In the world of pre-modern politics, conducted in royal courts remote from the popular gaze, sovereignty belonged to the sovereign, the people were subject to it as they were subject to God, and the concept of 'popular sovereignty' was an oxymoron bordering on blasphemy. In such circumstances, the link between the people and princes, between individuals and the forces that governed their lives, was not so much political as religious – it was the Church.

While monarchs and the nobility ruled by 'sword' and 'robe' – by military force and official administration – the function identified by Michel Foucault as *governmentality* belonged largely to the Church.[5] The medieval Church assembled whole populations across an entire continent (and into several others) on a daily basis, teaching them how to construct themselves into subjectivity, and thence into obedient behaviour and belief; its institutional knowledges and procedures not only governed but also constituted the laity's sense of themselves as private individuals. At least in principle, and routinely in practice, everything people did, thought and said was tutored, disciplined, authorized, sanctified and punished by the Church. The very term 'person' is part of this apparatus of governmentality, arising as it does from a medieval opposition between the *anima* (soul) and *persona* (mask of corruptible corporeality, or bodily flesh, which covers and hides the soul, allowing the individual literally to *act* their 'I-hood'). Similarly the term 'individual' derives from the supposed indivisibility of the soul. According to this kind of knowledge, the individual, being immortal and damnable, needs to practice a certain *regime* of belief and behaviour, in private and in public, in order to sustain hope of salvation, and this regimen is required of all persons, all the time. The immense task of communicating and promoting such a pervasive regime of knowledge to each and every 'soul' around the networks and hierarchies that sustained medieval Europe, from the Pope to the poor, belonged not to the state but to the institutions and practices of the Church.

The *modern* mechanism that eventually took the place of the medieval Church as the great cultural institution of self-building and sense-making, producing private selves out of public assemblies, was the media. Since people didn't vote or participate in politics, or universally go to school, there were no institutions other than the Church to reach them one and all, every day. In the pre-modern period such a pervasive reach was oral and visual, of course, communicated from very centralized and hierarchical corporate bodies to the laity throughout the continent by the then 'mass media' of sermons and homilies, plays and pageants, songs and stories, confessions and cathedrals. The Church was the medieval mediasphere.[6]

However, all of this depended on the legitimacy of the Church as the ultimate authority (under God) over the souls of the people, and, in defence of those souls, over their personal conduct and beliefs. But once that legitimacy was overthrown in favour of new doctrines of reason and popular sovereignty, the Church *as mediasphere* was ruptured, its enveloping presence around people's lives deflated like a bursting bubble, and there was no social institution already in place to take over and secularize its great cultural-governmental and media functions. At the moment when modernity was inaugurated and the authority of the sovereign passed to the people, the authority of the Church passed to the state. However, the legitimacy of the state was grounded in the sovereignty of the people, so, for the first time, the people were literally responsible for themselves, both individually and collectively. A practical question arose: if the people as a whole were responsible for both public and private conduct, how should their will be reflected into the legislative public sphere from its myriad origins, and how should the actions of executive government and the unity of community belief be maintained simultaneously in the heads, hearts and homes of so many individuals in all their variety and distinction? How, in short, was it possible to mediate from the public sphere to the semiosphere?

From Literacy to Liberty

In fact, the only mechanism that was available to hold the two aspects of popular sovereignty together – to link the central socio-political institutions with the dispersed personal practices of private sense-making – was journalism. This was non-existent or at best underdeveloped in all countries up until the moment when sovereignty passed from monarch to the people. At that moment, as the ecclesiastical bubble deflated, the journalistic mediasphere suddenly inflated. There was a mass (though temporary) increase in newspapers, pamphlets and other forms of journalism in the period of the English Civil War and its aftermath in the seventeenth century that was not to be repeated until the decisive modernization of the British with industrialization and political reform at the beginning of the nineteenth century, when there was a second and spectacular increase in journalism and popular literacy. In France it was not until the fall of the Bastille that journalism burst with amazing energy on to the European scene: where there had been a mere half-dozen newspapers with political content at the beginning of 1789 in France, by the end of the year over 130 new newspapers had appeared. According to another estimate, 184 journals were launched in 1789, 335 in 1790, while pamphlets began appearing literally in their thousands.[7]

Modernizing political revolutions are always, among other things, journalistic; there's an outburst of literacy along with liberty. Journalism required and called into being a readership which extended at times to whole populations. Reading was the technical innovation which was destined to supplant the medieval Church, both for Reformation Protestants, for whom individual Bible-reading literally replaced the collective worship of the Roman mass, and for Revolutionary politicians, for whom people's private conduct and belief was a matter of political instruction and the ballot box, not sermons and the confessional box. This explains the extraordinary hold that notions of 'virtue' – public and private – held over politicians and journalists alike. This reforming journalism – from out of nowhere – spread like a porous membrane round the whole public sphere, enveloping it in meaning, suffusing it with new ways of understanding, and spreading its energies into the private recesses of popular reality. In addition to its role in keeping people connected with politics, journalism had to keep politics in touch with meaning – meanings which a sovereign but unleisured and often unlettered people could make sense of at a time when they were beginning to feel that 'the human condition is malleable, not fixed, and that ordinary people can make history instead of suffering it', as the historian Robert Darnton puts it.[8]

Traditionally, the common people made sense of the worlds of nature, society and personal relationships using the oral, dramatic and spectacular institutions of story, song, drama, myth, symbol, image, picture. Unfixing the monarchy meant that this whole oral semiosphere was momentarily politicized to a greater or lesser extent, and the relations between discourse, story, history, science and religion were rethought, reworked. A lot of that thinking was done 'out loud', in the journals, as the fastest available means by which the political ends of the Revolution could be communicated to the furthest reaches of the culture. The news became the *necessary* link between the public sphere of politics and the semiosphere of meanings, and *both* were transformed in the process. Just as modern citizens don't live in the same political universe as pre-modern subjects, so the contemporary semiosphere is different from the medieval one; for instance popular literacy, virtue, knowledge, or opinion were neither universal nor necessary before the Revolution, but they were afterwards.

But the mediasphere and the Revolution burst on the European scene together – they were not in a linear cause-and-effect relationship with each other, rather they were both aspects of modernization. A re-examination of some of the crucial founding moments of modernity reveals the extent to which such moments were *always* fully mediated events, with journalism in the thick of productive, political activism from the very start. Moreover, journalism did more than 'mediate' elite political events to a readership of lower orders; on the contrary, using the resources of the semiosphere, it forged a link which did not previously exist and which is still decisive – a tripartite link between politics, texts and popular readerships. In this link not only has the popular sovereignty of contemporary democracy achieved its fullest expression, but also it has proven to be one of the few effective mechanisms for applying two-way pressure (and/or communication) between the institutions of social control and the populations of modernizing countries. Journalism stands not as a derivative commentator on events decided elsewhere in the public sphere, but as a producer and shaper of those events; and it is not just a distributor of social narrative and political imagery for an audience of private consumers, but the *sine qua non* ('without that, nothing') of complex democratic modernity – without a link between the public and private spheres, between politics and readerships (audiences), between decisions and meanings, textuality and power, there would be no daily mechanism for holding such societies together; there would be *no public.*

Looking at the history of modern politics this way entails some consequences for an understanding of journalism. First, it is necessary to recognize that news itself is *cultural;* it is not exempt from features traditionally associated with the private, textual, semiosphere. Like other genres in that sphere news is characterized by image, symbol, storytelling, fiction, fantasy, propaganda and myth – all the baggage of textuality and culture which is traditionally dismissed by journalists and historians alike as epiphenomenal, subjective, unrepresentative; it is at best unavailable for empirical analysis, at worst postmodernist. Second, it is equally important to recognize that the semiosphere and the mediasphere are *determinate forces* in the historical changes associated with modernity. From the outset, it has been the socially mediated language, rhetoric, imagery, symbol and text of journalism, along with the relations built up between media and their readerships, which have both driven and stabilized political changes. Third, it is necessary to recognize that *events are semiotic,* as well as being public and political, and equally, *semiotic developments are political.* In this regard, I suggest, it is vital to expand an understanding of 'what counts' as journalism to include those neglected, disreputable, areas of the mediasphere in which 'what counts' as politics is actually being sorted out. Indeed, the decisive political developments of the day are as likely to be imagined (and imaged) in the dispersed and apparently depoliticized arenas of 'style' or 'consumer' journalism, as in the first few pages of the 'quality' daily broadsheet. Politics is privatized, just as meanings are politicized. The 'mediasphere' is where this fusion occurs, even if it is experienced sometimes by the analyst trained in academic compartmentalization as *con*fusion.

The Big Bang of Journalism

Citizens, what is the point of us [journalists] giving ourselves over to the most powerful hatreds, submerging ourselves in the most painful research, ceaselessly guarding your interests, if you read us only to satisfy a childish curiosity?   ELISÉE LOUSTALLOT, 1789[9]

If I understand him rightly, Jack Richard Censer takes the founding political moment of modernity to be a product of journalism.[10] The moment itself was when sovereignty passed from monarch to people. In France, which has been credited with the honour of inaugurating this transformation in Western history,[11] the moment occurred emblematically in one day, 14 July 1789, with the storming of the Bastille,[12] although of course constitutionally it took several years to accomplish and many decades to secure as a decisive, irreversible and globally significant change. The transfer of power from monarch to people was so decisive precisely because it was not simply a political event – its implications seeped into every area of life, pervading the semiosphere with energies that revitalized and reinvented everything from language and culture to time and space. How was such a thing a product of journalism? Because radical journalism imagined it to be literally, continuously possible, and talked it through with a readership which was also the (ever increasing) active segment of the people whose sovereignty was being established. Without the reworking of the horizons of possibility and of the whole sphere of 'popular reality' in the journalism of the time, the Revolution could not have taken the (increasingly radical) course that it did. Censer places the impetus for these developments in the work of the radical press of the early years of the Revolution.

Darnton suggests that the French Revolution involved a 'fundamental change in the tenor of everyday life'; it 'transformed life, not only for the activists trying to channel it in directions of their own choosing but for ordinary persons going about their daily business'.[13] Not only did it pervade the conduct of private life, it was also one day that shook the world, as contemporary observers were quick to recognize. In its first report of the fall of the Bastille, *The Times* in London was alarmed but accurate as to its significance. Under the heading 'Rebellion and Civil War in France', it commented: 'It cannot now be said that the present violences are the effect of a mere unlicensed mob. The concurrent voice of the nation demands a new constitution, nor do we foresee that any power can resist it.' The next day *The Times* blamed the Revolution on the 'incautious and impolitic assistance afforded to America' [by France against Britain in the American War of Independence], which sparked the 'spirit of LIBERTY' in 'all ranks of people':

> *the* vox populi *[voice of the people] had this form of argument. – 'If France gives freedom to America, why should she not unchain the arbitrary fetters which bind her own people?' . . . Such we may venture to say was the original cause of that important struggle, to the event [outcome] of which surrounding empires look with impatient anxiety – for the victory of the people must seriously affect the different interests of all Europe.*[14]

It was a simple argument, but eventually it did indeed 'affect the different interests of all Europe' – the 'surrounding empires' as well as the old order in France itself.

While such a radical transformation was obviously a complex matter with multiple determinants, from economic conditions to biographical accidents, it was in its *most* radical political aspect (which was pressed home in France rather than in America), reliant upon journalism, without which it could not have occurred.[15] This radical aspect involved extension of the 'sovereignty of the people' from a *representative concept*, where sovereignty passes from the king to the nation and is represented in national institutions like the National Assembly, to a *participatory practice*, where sovereignty passes from the king to the people as such, who retain a continuous right to exercise it over state institutions like the monarchy, the National Assembly, the judiciary, government administration, and even the armed forces. This participatory 'sovereignty of the people' was, according to Censer, an invention of radical journalists of the early years of the French Revolution; their daily discursive struggle was directed towards securing, extending, publicizing and defending this right, which was kept active in the pages of their journals, as well as in speeches to the political clubs and to the National Assembly, on those 'days' (the *journées*, which until 1794 pushed the Revolution ever leftwards) when the people were not present in their own corporeal bodies to direct legislation, juridical practice and government for themselves. The radical journalists required participatory sovereignty as an ideological weapon to discipline, in the name of the Revolution itself, the various legitimate institutions and holders of state power and constituted authority. In line with Enlightenment philosophical and governmental theories from Jean-Jacques Rousseau to Tom Paine, the journalists believed that any institution is corruptible and all government is an infringement on liberty; they also held that the people, who are endowed (by nature and adversity) with morality (*fraternité*), and endowed (by teaching and brotherhood) with reason (the desire for *liberté*), were the only collective group who could in turn be trusted to protect and advance the interests of the Revolution/nation (*égalité*).

As Robespierre's colleague Jérome Pétion argued in 1790:

> *One of the greatest benefits of press freedom is the constant surveillance of government officials, opening up their conduct of affairs to public scrutiny, exposing their intrigues and warning society of the danger; it acts like a watchful sentry, guarding the state day and night.*[16]

Meanwhile, a right-wing (but pro-Revolution) deputy, Pierre Victor Maluet, complained about the effect of such aggressive sentry duty on the state, in a famous denunciation of radical journalists (specifically Camille Desmoulins and Jean-Paul Marat) to the National Assembly:

> *What stability is there in a government when patriotic writers, friends of the people [Marat's paper was called* Ami du peuple*], are the ones who condemn the head of state to ridicule and scorn, who defame those who respect him, who denounce as infamous and consign to public vengeance any legislator who does not fall within majority opinion . . . who constantly summon people to arms; or who call for five or six hundred executions.*[17]

Marat, champion of 'public vengeance', went on to call for 10,000 or 100,000 executions, if that was what it would take to save the Revolution,[18] including all government ministers, the mayor (Bailly) and municipality of Paris, the head of the National Guard (Lafayette), and all royalist deputies in the National Assembly.[19] Camille Desmoulins celebrated the historic role of the press in more optimistic mood:

> *Here I am a journalist, and it is a rather fine role. No longer is it a wretched and mercenary profession, enslaved by the government. Today in France it is the journalist who holds the tablets, the album of the censor, and who inspects the senate, the consuls, and the dictator himself.*[20]

In order for them to cut this prophet-cum-tribune figure plausibly, as they marched to the promised land of popular freedom, the radical journalists needed not only sovereign but actual people for these important duties, and in Revolutionary Paris it wasn't hard to people the streets with the readership: there was little gap between a theory of popular participation and its practice in the centralized, metropolitan, hyper-politicized circumstances of the time, when the common people knew themselves to be simultaneously hungry, fearful and free. The model of journalism that was invented to serve this moment required a tripartite relationship between the public sphere (politics), the journalists (texts), and the people (readerships), a relationship that has characterized popular culture ever since, but which was not abstract at this stage, not even a functional division of labour, because the journalists, like the people themselves, were not impartial or passive observers, but daily actors in the whole process. Not only did most of them live and work in the left-bank Cordeliers district, the most radical section of Paris and historic home of the printing industry, but also they knew and worked with each other. Jean-Paul Marat (*Ami du peuple*, a daily) and his printer Ann-Félicité Colomb lived and operated there, as did Camille Desmoulins (*Révolutions de France et de Brabant*, a weekly, and the later four-issue *Vieux Cordelier*), Stanislas Fréron (*Orateur du peuple*, a daily), Louis-Marie Prudhomme and his most celebrated journalist Elisée Loustallot (*Les Révolutions de Paris*, a weekly with huge sales), and close by were the offices of Louise Kéralio and François Robert (*Mercure national*, a bi-weekly). Georges Jacques Danton, one of the few revolutionary stars who was *not* a journalist, lived in the same house as Desmoulins, whose speeches from a café table at the Palais-Royal had 'roused the crowds that surged through Paris' in the days before Bastille,[21] and the Cordeliers club – the most radical political party of the Revolution – was their meeting place. The club itself had a printer, Antoine Momoro, and its own radical newspapers, the *Observateur du club des Cordeliers* and the later *Journal du club des Cordeliers*. Other leading radical journalists who were also members of the club were Pierre-Jean Audouin (*Journal universal*, a daily) and Jacques-René Hébert (*Père Duchesne*, a bi-weekly). As Hugh Gough observes: 'All of them must have met each other regularly, in the Cordeliers club, on the street, at private meetings or in printers' premises, giving their existence an almost incestuous air.'[22] In return, the people recorded their thanks:

> On 21 August 1792, the Quinze-vingts Section [of Paris] naming in particular [Antoine-Joseph] Gorsas, [Jean-Louis] Carra, Prudhomme, and Desmoulins, declared that the patriotic writers had prepared the French people to take the path of liberty and equality, and that 'their writings have spread throughout France the "electric fire" that will give a constitution to a people worthy of liberty.'[23]

'Electric Fire'

One of the subtitles Marat gave to his *Ami du peuple* (originally called *Le Publiciste parisien*) was '*Journal politique et impartial*'. The impartiality of the press for such activists was real but unrecognizable to today's notions of neutrality and balance: they were impartially *for* anything that furthered the cause of popular sovereignty, and impartially *against* anything they saw as counter-revolutionary. As Censer puts it:

> These newspapermen [see note] generally saw themselves as politicians with a primary responsibility to influence the course of events and with little allegiance toward any abstract journalistic ethic. Consequently, the journalists shared the spirit, approach, practical politics, and perspective of the other radicals.[24]

The journalists were not reporters but activists, inciting and exciting the people, cajoling and educating them to action, while simultaneously providing a running critique of the institutions and individuals involved in every level of formal politics. Some of them were also elected representatives in the National Assembly or the municipalities, or organizers and leaders in the political clubs (parties) of the day, especially the Cordeliers and Jacobin clubs, and some of them, including Desmoulins, Hébert and several of Prudhomme's collaborators, were later guillotined for their journalism; Marat was murdered in his medicinal bath by a reactionary hothead while writing his *Ami du peuple*, a copy of which survives with his blood still staining it.[25]

Such radicals were unwilling to let abstract representation usurp the actual, physical sovereignty of the people – Marat wanted the meeting hall of the National Assembly to have a public gallery of 2000 seats, so that the people could exert 'direct moral and vocal pressures', and he feared that its one narrow door 'could permit a few soldiers to protect the National Assembly against the *peuple*, thwarting their salutary role as watchdog'.[26] In other words, popular sovereignty meant just that, despite the necessary existence of routine governmental institutions:

> The journalists did not mean that the peuple would exercise their control continuously – only that they had the right to do so. Although it might be desirable for the peuple to monopolize legislation and administration, this was impracticable in a country as large as France. There must be a government, but one so organized that it could never acquire sufficient power to obstruct or pervert the activities of the peuple.[27]

So much so, according to Censer, that the notion of popular sovereignty was extended not only to the root of government but also to its branches:

> The radicals wanted the peuple to have continuous active participation in all branches of government and the power of veto over all constituted bodies – legislative, judiciary, executive, and their military subordinates, the army, navy, and National Guard.[28]

Naturally, those with time on a daily basis to promote the people's interests and to discipline all these branches of the state, were not always actual people themselves (though this occurred often enough to make the system plausible), but the journalist-activists, creators of radical discourse. Hence, in the very effort of radicalizing the Revolution to the fullest extent possible, the journalists were also producing a *textualized* 'people' and a quasi-representative role for themselves, linking the institutions, practices and bodies of government to the identity of the people in whose name they operated, by a two-way process: looking 'out' from public sphere to mediasphere, in order to communicate the events of government to the citizen-readers, in order to stimulate them to collective acts of 'purification' (activism in the name of liberty); and looking 'in' from mediasphere to public sphere, in order to discipline and sway the governmental apparatus towards what the journalists saw as actions and enactments in the people's best interests. For this process, the radical journalists needed a 'people' with literally *royal* power:

> *The radical journalists had a Manichaean view of society . . . . The[y]*
> *believed in the reality of this polarization and constructed a political,*
> *economic, and cultural ideal to conform to, and influence, the outcome*
> *of the struggle. Thus . . . they gave the* peuple *full power. It was*
> *indeed the radical image of royal power – absolute despotism – that the*
> *journalists were trying to capture for the* peuple. *'Tel est notre*
> *plaisir,' said one radical newspaperman in justifying the actions of*
> *the* peuple. *No absolute monarch could have desired more.*[29]

Indeed, the radical journalists did not regard their own position as that of *media*, in the now-familiar sense of an intervening institution *mediating* between the people and their government and representatives; on the contrary, the radicals saw the National Assembly, municipalities, Church, ministers and court, as an intermediate interference in the *direct* relationship between the people and their sovereignty, a right the journalists saw incarnated in themselves, and in the Cordeliers and Jacobin clubs, which were thereby understood not as media providing information *to* the people but an intrinsic part *of* the people – the semiotic part, as it were.

It follows that for the radical journalists of the French Revolution 'the people' did not mean 'everyone alive today'. Given their Manichaeanism (division of the world into binary opposites), they were binary or polarized in their categorization of 'the people'. *In*cluded were all who were not *opposed* to the people. *Ex*cluded were all who were not *for* the people. From that day to this, journalists have constructed an *adversarial universalism* that seeks simultaneously to construct a universal 'Wedom' which cuts across traditional boundaries of class, occupation, region, religion, gender and income, to construct a universal people who are united despite such internal differences, and an adversarial 'Theydom' which comprises anyone or any group which seeks to control, corrupt, thwart or interfere with the people.[30] For the revolutionary journalists of 1789–91, this adversarial 'Theydom' was easily named as 'the aristocracy', including the royals, higher clergy, big capitalists and landowners, and the officer class. 'The people' (Wedom) were not closely defined, but included pro-revolutionaries, workers, shopkeepers, artisans and the petit-bourgeoisie, as well as peasants and working farmers. Significantly, the radical journalists were less likely to include the poor – the unemployed, destitute and lumpenproletariat – as members of the people, than to include petit-bourgeois, self-employed business owners and members of the 'knowledge class' ('*gens de lettres*').[31] In other words, their polarized society was not split down the middle into two binary halves with themselves as defenders of the 'lower' orders, but was asymmetric, comprising a 'broad spectrum of French society' from the *middle*, which was opposed to the extremities both 'above' and 'below', for while their opposition to the aristocracy could be taken for granted, they were also opposed to poor 'indigents': 'the journalists were not primarily champions of the unemployed; they considered them too susceptible to corruption'.[32]

Thus for the revolutionary radical journalists, French society – i.e. their readership – comprised all those who worked, up to and including capitalists and the bourgeoisie, under the leadership of urban Paris whose classes of literate artisans, professionals and shopkeepers included most radical journalists, in opposition to segments who could be bracketed off as corrupt or corruptible non-workers: the aristocracy above and the criminalizable classes below. Underneath the virulence and propensity for decapitation, the radicals of the French Revolution were constructing a rational model of society that is quintessentially *modern* – their readers were understood as literate, economically active, politically responsible, internally variegated, unified and national, but constantly under threat from outsiders both within and beyond the confines of metropolitan France. It was from this adversarial universal middle-ground that journalism constructed its readerships, and thence its *political imaginary* – the mediasphere.

Middling Utility

God made man in His own image, but the Public is made by Newspapers.
                                                BENJAMIN DISRAELI, 1844[33]

Meanwhile, across the English Channel, political developments were of course very different – Britain was a leading anti-Revolutionary state – but the very same process was afoot. There too *journalists* were busy constructing a public sphere, and ultimately an image of society as a whole, that conformed to the profile of their readerships. Dror Wahrman has argued on the basis of newspaper reports of parliamentary debates in the late 1790s that during this period newspapers were instrumental in *inventing* a 'middle class' in Britain, as a component and as a result of political partisanship; anti-government opposition crystallized around the concerns expressed by certain papers about the effect of war and taxes on the middle ranks of society.[34]

Wahrman points out that in this period there was no such thing as verbatim parliamentary reporting, although in Britain as in France the newspapers avidly reported parliamentary debates. Reporters were first allowed into the House of Commons in 1771, but they weren't allowed to write notes until 1783, and shorthand wasn't introduced till 1812; even then it was despised by some who thought shorthand writers were 'wholly incompetent to report a good speech. They attend to words without entering into the thoughts of the speaker.'[35] As a result, the newspapers' reports of speeches in parliament were reconstructed from journalists' notes, which according to one contemporary observer sound uncannily like students' lecture notes of a later age:

> *Far from setting down all that is said, they only take notes, to appear-*
> *ance very carelessly, one word in a hundred, to mark the leading*
> *points. It is difficult to understand how they can afterwards give the*
> *connected speeches we see in the papers, out of such slender materials,*
> *and with so little time to prepare them.*[36]

In a revealing analysis, Wahrman has found that while competition between the many newspapers kept the factual content of the reports reasonably accurate, there were significant differences in language between different newspapers, especially between those of differing political persuasion. The 'connected speeches we see in the papers', in other words, were connected not by what a given speaker had *actually said*, since there was no record of that, but 'inflected through the rhetorical and linguistic habits and practices of the reporter, editor and newspaper'.[37] Despite the suspicions of misquoted Members, such 'mediation and alteration' was not so much deliberate bias and distortion as a case of 'still waters run deep', according to Wahrman, for the differences he identifies are organized around visions of society, and specifically, the division of society into classes or ranks. Thus pro-government newspapers like *The Times*, the *Evening Mail*, *St. James's Chronicle*, *Whitehall Evening Post*, *E. Johnson's British Gazette* and the *True Briton* would tend systematically to visualize society in terms of a simple polarized division between 'rich' and 'poor', while newspapers which supported the respectable opposition, such as the *Morning Chronicle*, the *Star*, the *Morning Post* and the *Morning Herald* would visualize society via a political and social 'middle order' or 'middle class'. Neither side would promote these visions over their own signature, as it were, but put them into the mouths of parliamentary speakers: the same speaker might be reported in all of the pro-government papers as objecting to a taxation measure 'based on a social frame-work comprised only of higher and lower orders, rich and poor'; while in all of the oppositional papers his speech would persistently reiterate the 'effects of the proposed taxation scheme on the "middle orders"'.[38]

Wahrman's conclusions from his detailed analysis are startling, at least to the conventional wisdom which holds that Parliament precedes its reporting in the papers, and social realities precede their description in language. Wahrman argues that 'the influential political and cultural role of the reports of parliamentary debates in the press cannot easily be overestimated', for it is in the newspapers, not in Parliament as such (of which no single authentic image existed), that the public sphere of political contestation was constructed, a public sphere which was from the beginning a *discursive construction*:

> *To be sure, parliament did claim . . . to incorporate a* virtual repre-
> sentation of the 'middle classes', *spoken through the lips of the
> M.P.s to their own private audience in their own private sphere. But
> at the same time the 'middle classes' retaliated through* virtual repre-
> sentation of parliament, *in which they were in fact expressing their
> own opinions via the (reconstructed) lips of the M.P.s – only now
> aimed at a much less exclusive public audience, in a much broader
> public sphere.*[39]

In the newspapers' public sphere of 'virtual representation'
something new was being invented – something which did not have
a coherent referent 'out there' *until* short-term political contestation
gave an importance and a name to long-term socio-economic
circumstances. According to Wahrman:

> *Indeed it may be argued that the very presence of a "middle class" as
> a distinct social entity depended fundamentally on such choices [of
> language and of a particular conceptualization of society]. It is my
> contention that the existence of a "middle class" in a fairly complex
> society lies primarily in the eye of the beholder. . . . [T]he "middle class"
> can be seen or not seen, depending on the social scheme one chooses to
> employ, and this choice is highly political. . . . The language of "middle
> class" did not reflect social reality, but rather was a contested and often
> elaborate argument about it.*[40]

Reversing the traditional historical story, which accords causal
primacy to long-term social and economic trends, Warhman suggests:

> *we may wish to reverse the story altogether, and to see political circum-
> stances as the driving force behind choices of social schemes . . . . It
> was politics . . . that determined when and where notions of "middle
> class" appeared, and thus the purported "emergence" of this social
> class.*[41]

Wahrman concludes his study by showing that later, in the period
from Waterloo to Peterloo (1814–19), the language of the 'middle
class' was 'tamed' politically – 'associated less with a critique of the
establishment, and more with political stability and conservatism –
and thus more palatable to broader political circles'. In the late
1790s the anti-government political forces invented a middle class in
their own image – i.e. 'men of considerable standing and property
who strongly opposed what they perceived to be [British Prime
Minister William] Pitt's ruinous war [against Revolutionary France],
and who at the same time were at pains to distance themselves in
unequivocal terms from popular radicalism and its republican
tendencies':

> *In a desperate attempt to counteract the predominant trend towards
> political polarization, they were striving to maintain a legitimate space
> for political moderation between two extremes. It was this need to define
> and defend a* political *middle which led to an encomiastic [flattering]
> emphasis on the virtues of a* social *middle.*[42]

By 1832, writes Wahrman, both sides of respectable politics had bought the argument:

> *By the time it passed through parliament, the [Reform] bill was univer-*
> *sally perceived – whether in celebration or in grief – as a "middle class"*
> *triumph . . . . In the years immediately following the Reform Bill, the*
> *category "middle class", as well as the storyline of recent social trans-*
> *formation that accompanied it, became – at least for a while – univer-*
> *sally accepted as central to organizing and making sense of social and*
> *political experiences. The "middle class" as an objective existing social*
> *fact, was now appealed to as a most influential political constituency*
> *. . . . In sum, it was not so much the rising "middle class" that was*
> *the crucial factor in bringing about the Reform Bill of 1832, as it was*
> *the Reform Bill of 1832 that was the crucial factor in cementing the*
> *invention of an ever-rising "middle class".*[43]

These arguments about the determinate political role of a discursive public sphere of 'virtual representation', invented by journalists in a period of decisive agitation for modernist popular sovereignty, suggest that circumstances were similar in France and England in this respect: journalists were, for their own political purposes, identifying and producing a vision of society which *made* a 'middle' appear. The journalists used terms which were 'not as precise as the modern social historian might wish' – the French radicals were 'vague about the identity of the *peuple*', they 'never paused to explain exactly what they meant by such labels as *bourgeoisie, marchand* , or *cultivateurs*', and 'it should be evident that the journalists had no exact notion' of the *social* composition of the people whose *political* cause they championed.[44] The same was true in Britain:

> *It is important to realize that these notions of "middle class", as they*
> *were incorporated into the political debate, were far from being well-*
> *defined in terms of the social categories they encompassed. Many speak-*
> *ers did not have a clear social group in mind at all. Others had*
> *remarkably different conceptions of its identity, an identity which was*
> *often expressed in moral or educational rather than in social, occupa-*
> *tional, or economic terms.*[45]

As Wahrman suggests, 'our reverence for social categories as analytical tools should not mislead us into assuming that well-defined sociological content is a prerequisite for the meaningful deployment of social terminology, or for its rhetorical impact'.[46] On the contrary, it was necessary for the referents of such terms as 'the people' and the 'middling classes' to be imprecise in a journalism which was both partisan and seeking to appeal to a national unity at once – both adversarial (opposed to groups above and below those identified as 'we'), and universal ('we' *are* the nation [of shopkeepers]). Of course the radical journalists of France were constructing a vision of society which differed in *political purpose* from that imagined by the respectable oppositional press in England at the same time. The latter imagined not a *sovereign* but a *useful* middle order: 'the middling class of society, perhaps the most useful and efficient, as to the interior welfare of a great empire'.[47]

'Two Nations'

The theme of utility was set to become dominant in the nineteenth century. By the 1830s in both countries, a situation was established in which cross-demographic readerships with political aspirations and national self-understandings were connected to the public sphere by journalism, and journalism was undisputed leader of the mediasphere which connected the private and cultural to the public and political. But a striking feature of early journalism, along with the marvellous increase in titles, was the disloyalty of readers. Many publications lasted for one or two issues only, and during times of popular emotion it was the news and the politics people wanted, not the masthead, so if one paper didn't supply their demands they turned to another. Circulations notoriously fluctuated in line with events from a norm of 2000 to 5000 copies per issue to peaks of 200,000 copies, as people bought prodigious quantities of a paper in times of crisis.[48] All this bespeaks an active but not a disciplined readership.

Having colonized the mediasphere journalism now embarked on a long effort to convert political loyalty to brand loyalty, political campaigns to commercial campaigns, revolutionary wars to circulation wars, freedom of the press to freedom of the market. The idea was to make news and information, and the daily or weekly ritual of reading the paper, into something *useful*, which people would want routinely, even when times were quiet. In other words, having created a readership which was also the public – people who were sovereign but governed, free but hungry (for bread, comfort and information) – having created the modern mediasphere, the challenge that faced journalism was to secure the mundane loyalty of the readers, loyalty to the whole textual system of journalism, to the knowledges it created, and (hopefully) loyalty to this masthead, today. Such a task required less a public and more a consumer, albeit one with freedom of choice. The sans-culotte retired from the barricade to the parlour to read the Sunday paper, while the bourgeois activist of 1789 was by 1832 the critical *paterfamilias* who read the morning paper in thunderous silence in a ritual which reinvented the reasonable, useful, imperial citizen anew each day. In short, the 'journal' in journalism was henceforth to be located in the habits of its readers, not only in the frequency of its titles.

As is so often the case it was a lesson learned just as quickly by those who had formerly been in the opposing camp. Once *The Times* – a pro-government Pittite paper in 1797 – had cottoned on to the idea of *creating* a readership out of the middle ranks of society, there was no stopping it. Celebrating its own sesquicentenary in 1935, *The Times* claimed to have created its readership. In the house style of the day the newspaper, not a human writer, was deemed to be the author of its statements, so this is how *The Times* saw the crucial 1830s:

> *It never was the purpose of* The Times *to capture a particular kind of reader . . . . Yet it did deliberately, in the thirties of the last century, set out, not to capture, but to create a homogeneous character of that large, unattached, incoherent middle class. In carrying through so successfully a change of such importance in social and political organization it fathered also its chief support and won its dominating position in this country and abroad.*[49]

Having 'fathered' its own readership (although in the terms of this metaphor if the paper was the 'father' of its support then the 'mother' must have been the act of reading, though of course *The Times* didn't trouble to think the idea through), and having warmed to the theme of retrospective self-glorification, *The Times* could not resist going on to claim its readers as coterminous with the nation, in a gesture which is by now so commonplace that it often passes unremarked, but which has the effect of *nationalizing* the journalistically induced 'homogeneous character' (class consciousness) of the previously 'incoherent middle class', making that 'character' stand for 'England':

> *At whatever period we are afforded glimpses of the reader, he seems to be much the same in character however he varies in fortune; from the Chartist denouncing the politics of* The Times *but eagerly searching it for news; the leisured gentleman having it served at breakfast warmed and crackling like the bacon; the people at the parsonage, like the one at Haworth, where the little Brontë sisters gathered round father while he read aloud what was happening to the catholic question; to those countless homes of the seventies where crapulous Sunday newspapers were forbidden and* The Times *was prized first for its virtuous contents and second for its adaptability. A history of everyday habits and manners could be made from the letters of its readers. The reader is the omnipresent Englishman. 'This is he'; the great arbiter to whom this journal for 150 years has submitted its service so that he shall know 'elder truths, sad truths, joyful truths, fearful truths, grand truths'.*[50]

It goes without saying that despite the 'little Brontë sisters' (who may be female and budding writers but whose membership of the community of *Times* readers depends upon being 'gathered round father') the 'great arbiter' may be 'omnipresent' but is literally paternal, and so the truths are 'male truths' too. *The Times* is trying to achieve in the 'same character' of its readers what it could never achieve in demographics, for its truths were 'middle class truths' too, by its own admission. In fact *The Times* of 1935 seems to have forgotten altogether that for a century up until then (and beyond, as we shall see in Chapters 8 and 9) Britain had been characterized as '*two nations*', and the newspaper excludes altogether the truths of that other nation – the poor – from the 'character' of its 'omnipresent Englishman'. However, it was Benjamin Disraeli himself, thirty years before his major stint as imperial prime minister, who gave permanent currency to the idea of 'two nations' in his novel *Sybil: Or The Two Nations* (1845). He introduces the concept by showing in a single fictional move both what separated and what connected the two nations, in a scene set at the end of the 1830s:

> *'This is a new reign,' said Egremont, 'perhaps it is a new era'.*
> *'I think so,' said the younger stranger.*
> *'I hope so,' said the elder one.*
> *'Well, society may be in its infancy,' said Egremont slightly smiling; 'but, say what you like, our Queen [Victoria] reigns over the greatest nation that ever existed.'*
> *'Which nation?' asked the younger stranger, 'for she reigns over two.'*
> *The stranger paused; Egremont was silent, but looked inquiringly.*
> *'Yes,' resumed the younger stranger after a moment's interval. 'Two nations; between whom there is no intercourse and no sympathy; who are as ignorant of each other's habits, thoughts and feelings, as if they were dwellers in different zones, or inhabitants of different planets; who are formed by a different breeding, are fed by a different food, are ordered by different manners, and are not governed by the same laws.'*
> *'You speak of –' said Egremont, hesitatingly.*
> *'THE RICH AND THE POOR.'*[51]

This is the (hesitant) introduction of the concept of 'two nations' into British public life, via a novel. The passage is followed not by an introduction to the poor but a gothic, sublime vision of the beautiful teenage Sybil, the daughter of a Chartist 'workman at a manufactory', promising that the nations may (after the usual 500 pages) be united by mutual eroticization (marriage), since politics is clearly not up to the job. But at this point in the novel Disraeli is unable to give credit for negotiating a *connection* between the two nations to a politician like himself or to an aristocrat like the novel's hero Egremont. The 'younger stranger' who talks in capital letters of rich and poor, who knows both nations and represents one to the other, it transpires, is a *radical journalist*. As such he is in fact 'THE PEOPLE':

> *That pale man with those glittering eyes, who without affection, without pedantry, with artlessness on the contrary and a degree of earnest singleness, had glanced like a master of philosophy at the loftiest principles of political science, – was he too a workman? And are these then THE PEOPLE? If so, thought Egremont, would that I lived more amongst them!*[52]

Peace with Comfort

It is worth pausing to think about the implications of this 'thought' of Egremont (Disraeli). It seems innocuous enough, akin to the shocked discovery by certain Americans after the Gorbachev era that citizens of the former Soviet Union are people not unlike themselves. However, the fantasy desire of 'would that I lived more amongst them!' has political implications not only in the novel but for the way that union between the 'two nations' was imagined throughout the imperial period. From the perspective of the thoughtful aristocrat, the relationship is one of attraction made flesh, as it were, not by uniting the 'two nations' politically (by means of alliance with the radical journalist and his readership, for example), but by colonizing an eroticized female body (and for this kind of desire there's no real need for *mutual* attraction). The Disraelite fiction produces a pleasant enough outcome for the aristo-crat, whose warm feelings about social reform are reassuringly located next to him in bed at night; and this union is clearly presented as both positive and emblematic in *Sybil*, where Egremont stands – as hero – for the same impulse which suffused the philan-thropic, missionary and modernizing energies of the Victorian-Edwardian empire. Sustained by such images of rescue, renewal, redemption and revitalization, not to mention a warm bed at the end of the day, the 'omnipresent Englishman', like *The Times* itself, directed socially approved and *useful* energies to good works across class, gender, national and ethnic frontiers.

This is all very well for the aristocrats, but like Miriam Karlin or Peter Sellers in British class-comedies of old,[53] one is tempted to ask that perennial question of cross-demographic communication: 'What about the workers?' In fact the fantasy of modernizing union across the classes and between men and women from the 'two nations', even when it is motivated by the highest ideals of reform and progress, is not about 'THE PEOPLE' as such, but about something surprising and unsettling in the modernizing vision itself, as Rita Felski has pointed out in her book *The Gender of Modernity*. When looked at from the point of view of the supposed beneficiary (i.e. in this case, Sybil herself, as working-class woman, rather than Egremont), modernity takes on a different hue:

> One of the most striking . . . results of this rereading of the modern through the figure of woman has been the new prominence and visibil-ity of cultural expressions of yearning, dissatisfaction, and restlessness in nineteenth century culture. Rather than reiterating a confident belief in the superiority of modern Western society, most of the texts . . . rely on mechanisms of temporal or spatial displacement to locate meaning elsewhere, whether in an edenic past, a projected future, or a zone of cultural otherness.[54]

It is clear that Disraeli's literary device in *Sybil* is to overlay the 'zone of cultural otherness' (the 'other' of the 'two nations', i.e. 'the people') with both sexual longing (for Sybil) and a yearning for a 'projected future' (union between the 'two nations'). But as Felski goes on to warn, such restless dissatisfaction with the present state of things does not imply a desire for revolutionary change:

Such articulations of longing are of course not necessarily oppositional – on the contrary . . . they are tied up in complicated ways with the logics of consumerism and the politics of colonialism as well as with struggles for social change. Nevertheless, they serve to underscore the fundamental ambivalences entangled with the idea of the modern.[55]

What was understood at the time as the 'interior welfare of a great empire', then, can equally be understood now as 'the politics of colonialism'. I would only add to Felski's analysis that this colonization – of the past (edenic or otherwise), future (projected or fantastic) and of otherness (class, gender, nation, ethnicity or age) – was equally, simultaneously and continuously a *textualization* of that otherness in what amounts to a bid for power – power in if not over the semiosphere. As I've suggested earlier (in Chapter 1), following the work of Thomas Richards and Jon Klancher, the nineteenth-century middle-class reading public formed the basis for a 'knowledge class' (see Chapter 2), whose power was not territorial or economic but based on the administration of texts (bureaucracy), and on the reordering and expansion of the semiosphere by compiling the 'imperial archive' of information, classification, knowledge and communication. Disraeli's *Sybil* suggests that the desire for dominion and discipline over nature and knowledge which Richards finds in fiction about *knowledge* was also quite explicitly, in fiction about *society*, a desire for exploration and annexation of 'other' *demographic* 'nations'. Indeed I want to argue that this amounts to the *internal colonization* of the social sphere by 'that large, unattached, incoherent middle class' (*The Times*), i.e. by Wahrman's 'middling order' whose own very existence as a social formation had resulted from politicized textual strategies at the outset of the century. Once identified as a political constituency and a 'useful' social stratum, the nascent 'knowledge class' began to seize power by colonizing others within the texto-semiotic domain, just as Disraeli, longing for political modernization (and the renewal of the old fundamental class called 'the rich'), textually colonizes both what he calls 'THE PEOPLE' and what Felski calls 'the figure of woman' in his desire to overcome the opposition between the 'two nations' created by modernization itself.

It is part of my argument that textualization and the yearning it articulates should not be understood in opposition to social power, but as a crucial component of it in modernizing societies. Disraeli's attempt to imagine the union of the 'two nations' was also a form of practical politics. However, his 'one-nation' Toryism did not prevail in his own lifetime, as is poignantly suggested by the following account, from a popular biography of Disraeli, of a meeting at the end of his life (he had been elevated to the peerage with the name Lord Beaconsfield):

In 1881 Mr. Hyndman, one of the first English socialists, requested an interview with Lord Beaconsfield . . . . He had read Sybil, *and felt drawn towards the old Chief by reason of the latter's sympathy with the common people. . . . 'Lord Beaconsfield,' said Hyndman shyly, 'Peace with Honour [a phrase coined by Disraeli after the Congress of Berlin in 1875] was a dead formula. Peace with Comfort was what the people would have liked to hear.' One eyelid rose. 'Peace with Comfort is not a bad phrase . . . . You have some ideas on this subject, I suppose, Mr. Hyndman? What do you mean by Comfort, eh?' 'Plenty to eat, enough to drink, good clothes, pleasant homes, a thorough education, and sufficient leisure for all.'*[56]

The passage (which rhetorically 'feminizes' socialism itself via Hyndman's attitude to 'the old Chief') continues with Disraeli saying of this 'utopia to order': 'A fine dream, yes . . . and you think you have some chance of realizing this policy? Not with the Conservative party, I assure you'. Disraeli is here put into the same room as socialism, whose co-founder Frederick Engels had himself written about the English 'two nations' earlier in the century:

the working class has gradually become a race apart from the English bourgeoisie . . . . The workers speak other dialects, have other thoughts and ideals, other customs and moral principles, a different religion and other politics than those of the bourgeoisie.[57]

It is noteworthy that the 'utopian' socialism of the Disraeli–Hyndman meeting remained just that until after 1945; it was almost exactly the platform which was advanced by *Picture Post* (and the subsequently victorious Labour Party) during the Second World War (see Chapter 8). It is also notable that in the passage from *Disraeli* there's an explicit linkage of socialist politics with the notion of comfort. But whether modernization was seen as liberty (in the French tradition) or comfort (in the English), the attempt to cross the divisions between the 'two nations' was not destined to take the form of a Disraelite 'marriage', but rather of a full century more of 'internal colonization' of Engels's 'race apart'.

Virtual Colonization

I use the term 'internal colonization' here in a conscious echo of the work of Michael Hechter in the 1970s. His book, *Internal Colonialism*, is an interesting texto-theoretical experiment in itself, for although it comprises a study of relations between the 'Celtic fringe' (Wales, Scotland, Ireland) and the British state during several centuries of national and political development, it is not primarily interested in these matters for their own sake. As Hechter puts it himself, he came to the topic with no personal or ancestral stake in any of the Celtic countries, and he had not at that time set foot in the British Isles:

However, these regions do provide an ideal research site from which to explore some fundamental issues in sociological theory. Perhaps not entirely by coincidence, these issues also relate to problems of social change in contemporary American society.[58]

Hechter shows how the very long history of internal colonialism in the British Isles (Wales was first colonized in 1282) provides some regularities which can be used to analyse other examples of 'ethnic conflict and assimilation'. He points out that in the Celtic nations' colonization was contested by definite historical phases – *assimilationism* followed by *nationalism*. In this context 'assimilation' means 'integration', not the social Darwinist policy of 'assimilationism' in Australia up to the late 1960s, whereby Aboriginality was intended to be bred out of the community by taking Aboriginal children and adopting them to white families. But that type of 'assimilation', which is now recognized as genocide, is a chilling reminder of what 'integration' can mean if it is organized by the colonizing power, rather than by the colonized people.

But for Hechter, the 'fundamental issues' raised by 'internal colonialism' are to do with the periodization of liberatory struggle, and in this respect his work applies surprisingly directly to indigenous politics of the 1990s (particularly in New Zealand, Canada and Australia), just as he thought it applied to ethnic struggles in the USA in the 1960s and 70s. Hechter argues that like Celtic liberationists of the nineteenth century, Black political organizations in the USA moved the political struggle from an initial phase where the object was 'integration and assimilation of Blacks in American society on an incremental basis, until full equality might eventually be realized', to a second phase intended to 'increase the material prosperity and welfare of Black Americans as a separate nation within white society'.[59] In other words, ethnic liberation, whether Celtic, African-American or indigenous, is a struggle for decolonization, structured in an historical pattern moving from a Martin Luther King to a Malcolm X/Louis Farrakhan stage, from the Frantz Fanon of *Black Skin, White Masks* to that of *The Damned of the Earth*.

Internal colonization is much older than modernity – in the British Isles it reaches back to the high Middle Ages – but it is not exempt from historical currents and developments, including the democratic and imperial energies of the nineteenth century which I have tried to outline in this chapter. The French Revolution provided internally colonized peoples with a model of *national liberation* from feudal oppression; a lesson the Irish in particular learnt early and thoroughly, from Wolf Tone to Gerry Adams. Meanwhile, the other face of modernity – that of expansion, utility, knowledge and empire – drew internally colonized peoples along a different, *assimilationist* path, where their struggle for political and economic emancipation was tied to the fate of the colonizing power and its internal institutions; thus, as Hechter points out, the Welsh and Scottish people 'hoped that the rise of the new Labour Party would solve the severe problems of their respective lands'.[60] Even as he wrote, however, Welsh and Scottish nationalism experienced a popular revival, and has remained as a clear alternative strategy in these two internal colonies, whose eventual fate is still not determined.

Hechter's analysis shows that the choice between assimilation and nationalism characterizes internal colonies in general. But I would want to update his very suggestive work by suggesting that the issues of internal colonization, and of the 'alternative strategies for the liberation of oppressed minorities – assimilationism *versus* nationalism',[61] which are provoked by it, are themselves caught up in the currents I've tried to trace in this book – specifically, the trend towards virtualization of communities and deterritorialization of imperial power, substituting *readerships* and *knowledge* for people and territory. In this world, which has both democratic and imperialist tendencies, the concept of internal colonialism can be extended from territorial and ethnic 'minorities' to *demographic others*. Indeed, I would argue that the working class, women, and other internal aliens, defined for example by sexual orientation, ethno-cultural identity, or age (i.e. 'youth'), are all communities which have been subjected to *internal colonization* in the modern period, have all been explored and annexed textually, have all been subject to discipline and control by the knowledge class and classification in the imperial archive, and have all displayed that Hechterian pattern of response, the historic movement from integrationist assimilation to liberationist nationalism.

An emblematic example of what I mean is afforded by a book published in the same year as Hechter's study: Anne Summers's influential *Damned Whores and God's Police*, a history of what she calls in the book's subtitle the *'colonization* of women in Australia'.[62] In a long chapter called 'The Colonized Sex', Summers makes an explicit connection between the imperial colonization of territory and the modern colonization of women's bodies:

> *The classic colonial situation has four major components which can be described in abbreviated fashion as (1) the invasion and conquering of a territory, (2) the cultural domination of its inhabitants, (3) the securing of effective control of the inhabitants by creating divisions amongst them, thus preventing their uniting to oppose the invasion, a political tactic traditionally known as divide and rule, and (4) the extraction of profits from the colonized territory.*[63]

She sets out to demonstrate, point by point, that the history of women and that of the colonization of native peoples is the same in these four areas. In Hechter's terms, hers is the decisive move from assimilationism to nationalism – her book closes with a chapter on 'prospects for liberation' in which she rejects 'equality' (as a form of assimilation), and argues for liberation in straightforwardly nationalist terms:

> *The struggle for, and the attainment of, liberation is all about altering the most fundamental tenets of our method of social organization; it is about abolishing privilege and exploitation and concentrated power. Unless the interrelationship of all determinants of an oppressed person's existence are taken into account then we are not talking about*

liberation. We are merely concerned with juggling the levels of the exist-ing hierarchy.[64]

It is not necessary for me to point out that at the time she wrote this book Anne Summers was (among other things) a journalist, nor that her purpose was to provide a localized, timely, accessible, practical – i.e. a journalistic – account of women's oppression in Australia, to make the point that in these struggles journalism is a major player. It is the place where and the means by which the differentiated 'levels of the existing hierarchy' come to know about each other and seek to generalize rights gained elsewhere in the demographic universe. Summers herself locates women's struggles in the context of 'the liberation of women and Blacks and homosexuals'. Interestingly, in 1975 she was not willing to admit *as* liberatory what she calls the 'spurious or misguided cries for the "liberation" of animals or of groups of people (such as those who are overweight)'. Clearly the democratic ripple has moved further into the semio-sphere in the intervening twenty years – animal liberationism and the politics of bodily size are both familiar components of the public sphere.[65] In a process which began in the French Revolution and is described in the next chapter, journalism can be seen to have played a vital (if virtual) part in the alternation of those 'fundamental tenets of our social organization' that Summers requires as the condition for women's liberation. This is the very language of the French Revolution, and the extent to which its political energies eventually did 'alter fundamental tenets' not only of social hierarchies but of entire meaning-structures, is the subject of the next chapter. At this point I simply want to stress that the 'logic of democratic equiva-lence' which made such a splash on that Tuesday in July of 1789 is still rippling through the cultural, political and demographic universe, from the public sphere to the outer boundaries of the semiosphere, and journalism is riding its wave.

Notes

1. *La Feuille villageoise* 1, 30 September 1790. Quoted in John Gilchrist and W.J. Murray (1971) *The Press in the French Revolution: A Selection of Documents Taken from the Press of the Revolution for the Years 1789–1794* . Melbourne: Cheshire, and London: Ginn, 239–40.
2. 'But a victory of outstanding significance, and one which will perhaps astonish our descendants, was the taking of the Bastille, in four hours or so'. *Les Révolutions de Paris* 1, 12–18 July 1789. Quoted in Gilchrist and Murray, 54.
3. All the historians of the press seem to agree that the royalist and anti-revolutionary press was slow to get off the ground in 1789; much slower than the 'patriot' press. See for instance Gilchrist and Murray, 22–6.
4. Yuri (Iurii Mikhailovich) Lotman (1990) *Universe of the Mind: A Semiotic Theory of Culture.* Trans. Ann Shukman with an introduction by Umberto Eco. Bloomington and Indianapolis: Indiana University Press.

5. See for instance Michel Foucault (1991) Governmentality. In G. Burchell, C. Gordon and P. Miller (eds.) *The Foucault Effect: Studies in Governmentality*. Hemel Hempstead: Harvester Wheatsheaf, 102–3. Foucault writes of the 'ensemble formed by the institutions, procedures, analyses and reflections, the calculations and tactics that allow for the exercise of this very specific albeit complex form of power, which has as its target, populations'. This type of governmentality results not only in various kinds of government apparatus, but also in 'the development of a whole complex of knowledges'.

6. Umberto Eco has a good sense of this in his (1987) *Travels in Hyperreality*. Trans. William Weaver. London: Picador.

7. For the figures on newspapers, see Hugh Gough (1988) *The Newspaper Press in the French Revolution*. London: Routledge, 23–6; for those on journals, see Jeremy D. Popkin (1989) Journals: the new face of news. In Robert Darnton and Daniel Roche (eds.) *Revolution in Print: The Press in France 1775–1800*. Berkeley and LA: University of California Press, 141–64 (this citation 150); for those on pamphlets, see Antoine de Baecque (1989) Pamphlets: libel and political mythology. In Darnton and Roche (eds.), 165–76.

8. Robert Darnton (1990) *The Kiss of Lamourette: Reflections in Cultural History*. New York: W.W. Norton, 20.

9. *Les Révolutions de Paris* 13, 3–9 October 1789. Quoted in Gilchrist and Murray, 73–4.

10. Jack Richard Censer (1976) *Prelude to Power: The Parisian Radical Press 1789–1791*. Baltimore and London: Johns Hopkins University Press. See especially Chapter 3, The ideology of popular sovereignty, 37–72.

11. Ernesto Laclau and Chantal Mouffe (1985) *Hegemony and Socialist Strategy: Towards a Radical Democratic Politics*. Trans. Winston Moore and Paul Cammack. London: Verso, 155.

12. For the immediate mythical status given to this event, see Rolf Reichardt (1989) Prints: images of the Bastille. In Darnton and Roche (eds.), 223–51. See also Censer, 9, 21, 32, 42, 79, 105, 123 for the significance given to this day by the radical journalists of Revolutionary Paris.

13. Darnton, *The Kiss of Lamourette*, 4–11.

14. *The Times*, Monday, 20 July 1789, 2, col. 3–4; and Tuesday, 21 July 1789, 2, col. 4, quoted in Gilchrist and Murray, 228–9.

15. See Gough, 36, 231ff. Gough's detailed and well-documented study traces the relationship between journalism and politics from 1789 to 1799, and includes a valuable account of the production, distribution, marketing and readership of newspapers throughout this period.

16. Quoted in Gough, 47.

17. P.V. Maluet, quoted in Gough, 46. There's some confusion about the date of this speech: Gough gives it as 1791 in the text but 1789 in the accompanying footnote (77), while Censer dates the speech at July 1790 (64).

18. The passage is quoted, together with a number of other incendiary but well-reasoned and politically astute passages by Marat, in Gilchrist and Murray, 268–70.

19. Censer, 64.

20. Desmoulins (1789), quoted in Gough, 36.

21. Censer, 21.

22. Gough, 59.

23. Gilchrist and Murray, 41.

24. Censer, 4–5. While Censer uses the generics of his time, it is noteworthy that one of the six radical 'newspaper*men*' whose journals he analyses in detail was a woman, Louise Robert (née Louise Felicité Guinement de Kéralio), editor of the *Journal d'Etat et Du Citoyen* and its successor the *Mercure national.*

25. See Gough, 100–3, for an account of the executions of journalists and printers. The *Ami du peuple* with Marat's bloodstains is his no. 678 of Tuesday, 13 August 1793; it is photo-reproduced in Censer, and also in Anthony Smith (1979) *The Newspaper: An International History.* London: Thames & Hudson, 88.

26. Censer, 65–6, quoting Marat's *Ami du peuple*, 35, 25 January 1791.

27. Censer, 65.

28. Censer, 68.

29. Censer, 72. The internal quotation is from Desmoulins's *Révolutions de France et de Brabant* 18, 29 March 1790.

30. I have traced this process in more detail in *The Politics of Pictures: The Creation of the Public in the Age of Popular Media*, Chapters 7 and 8.

31. Censer, 39–41 and 49–50.

32. Censer, 40–41.

33. Benjamin Disraeli (1844) *Coningsby: Or The New Generation.* Quoted in André Maurois (1937 first published 1927) *Disraeli.* Harmondsworth: Penguin, 134.

34. Dror Wahrman (1992) Virtual representation: parliamentary reporting and languages of class in the 1790s. *Past and Present* 136, 83–113.

35. Wahrman, 86–7. The quotation is from Lord John Campbell, later Lord High Chancellor of England, who had been a parliamentary reporter in 1800–2. See also Benjamin Disraeli (1980, first published 1845) *Sybil: Or The Two Nations.* Harmondsworth: Penguin, 212, where this exchange occurs, set in the period 1837–45: '"That gallery [Strangers Gallery in the House of Commons, used by political reporters] must be tiresome. Do you use shorthand?" "A sort of shorthand of my own," said Egremont. "I trust a good deal to my memory."' From 1775 the *Parliamentary Register* was published by John Debrett, and in 1803 William Cobbett began his *Parliamentary Debates*, which later became known as Hansard. Wahrman points out that these standard sources were not verbatim either; they cannot be relied upon for the 'rhetoric and mode of argumentation of parliamentary debate', especially 'charged and contested notions', as opposed to the mere 'narrative of parliamentary proceedings' (90–1).

36. Quoted in Wahrman, 87, from a French traveller, L. Simond, who visited Parliament in 1810.

37. Wahrman, 90.

38. Wahrman, 85.

39. Wahrman, 110–11.

40. Wahrman, 111.

41. Wahrman, 112.

42. Wahrman, 91.

43. Wahrman, 113.

44. Censer, 39–42.

45. Wahrman, 93.

46. Wahrman, 93.

47. *Parliamentary Register* (1798) quoted in Wahrman, 101.

48. See Gilchrist and Murray, 9, also Gough.

49. *The Times* (1935) *A Newspaper History 1785-1935: Reprinted from the 150th Anniversary Number of* The Times, *January 1 1935*. London: The Times Publishing, 10.
50. *The Times*, 11. Like *The Times*, the internal quotation is not authored, so presumably *The Times* is quoting itself, or perhaps it is self-creating, like a god.
51. Benjamin Disraeli (1980, first published 1845) *Sybil: Or The Two Nations*. Ed. Thom Braun. Harmondsworth: Penguin, 96. It is worth mentioning that 'one-nation Tories' lasted from Disraeli himself right up to Thatcherism, and this edition of *Sybil* is introduced by one of them, R.A. Butler, who gave his own name to a peculiar brand of consensual welfare-conservatism that rejoiced in the name of 'Butskellism' in the 1950s – combining Butler's name with that of Hugh Gaitskell, social democratic leader of the Labour party before Harold Wilson.
52. Disraeli, 169.
53. The TV series *The Rag Trade* and the movie *I'm Alright Jack* respectively.
54. Rita Felski (1995) *The Gender of Modernity*. Cambridge, Mass.: Harvard University Press, 210.
55. Felski, 210.
56. André Maurois (1937, first published 1927) *Disraeli*. Harmondsworth: Penguin, 263–4.
57. Frederick Engels, *The Condition of the Working Class in England*, quoted in J.V. Stalin (1972, first published 1954) *Marxism and Problems of Linguistics*. Peking: Foreign Languages Press, 13.
58. Michael Hechter (1975) *Internal Colonialism: The Celtic Fringe in British National Development, 1536–1966*. London: Routledge & Kegan Paul, xiv.
59. Hechter, xiv-xv.
60. Hechter, xvii.
61. Hechter, xvii.
62. Anne Summers (1975) *Damned Whores and God's Police: The Colonization of Women in Australia*. Ringwood, Vic.: Penguin Books. A second edition of this celebrated book was published in 1994.
63. Summers, 198.
64. Summers, 464–5.
65. Summers, 462.

CHAPTER

4 *The Semiosphere*

(Fraternity)

This image of the universe can be better danced than told . . .

YURI LOTMAN[1]

The term 'semiosphere', coined by the Russian cultural semiotician Yuri Lotman (on the model of biologist V.I. Vernadsky's concept of the 'biosphere'), is a way of describing 'semiotic space', specifically 'the semiotic space necessary for the existence and functioning of languages, not the sum total of different languages; in a sense the semiosphere has a prior existence and is in constant interaction with languages'. Lotman argues, against the grain of semiotic and communication theory, that 'the unit of semiosis, the smallest functioning mechanism, is not the separate language but the whole semiotic space of the culture in question'.[2] In other words, and as Umberto Eco puts it in the introduction to Lotman's book:

> If we put together many branches and great quantity of leaves, we still cannot understand the forest. But if we know how to walk through the forest of culture with our eyes open, confidently following the numerous paths which criss-cross it, not only shall we be able to understand better the vastness and complexity of the forest, but we shall also be able to discover the nature and branches of every single tree.[3]

Like the forest, there is more than one level at which one might identify a semiosphere – at the level of a single national or linguistic culture, for instance, or of a larger unity such as 'the West', right up to 'the species'. This flexibility is useful, for it makes it possible to discuss, for example, the relations between the public sphere and the semiosphere of a particular country or period, while retaining a sense of even more 'universal' unities within which such relations, already large-scale and complex, can be understood. Hence 'rainforest' is a larger unity than 'Australian rainforest' or 'tropical rainforest', and both are larger than 'the Daintree rainforest', but at all these levels the term 'rainforest' has meaning and utility. So it is with the term 'semiosphere', as I take it from Lotman.

Lotman characterizes the semiosphere as follows. It is a condition which precedes any actual semiotic act or text; like 'the wood' it is a precondition for 'the trees'. Within it, all sorts of languages co-exist, natural and artificial, marked by heterogeneity, difference and diversity that increases towards the borders of the particular sphere. The system is governed by laws of 'binarism and asymmetry'. Binarism is the principle of multiple subdivision by means of progressive and pluralized opposition within a system of overall unity. It is, as has been noted above, a fundamental characteristic of journalism, which has since 1789 shown a marked tendency to Manichaeanism, from the binary opposition of the people and the aristocrats to that of the cold war. Journalism both creates and exists within a semiotic space that I've called 'Theydom' and 'Wedom'. This 'Wedom' then becomes the quotidian semiosphere of popular culture – the 'popular reality' of my title, into and out of which all significant events, meanings, actions and characters must be trans-lated. Naturally, while it constitutes the known universe, Wedom cannot exist alone, without its adversarial opposite Theydom, whether this takes the form of a threat, a (potential) lover, or an absence.

What Lotman calls 'asymmetry' is the degree of mutual trans-latability (difference) between different semiotic structures and languages, and also the alternating turn-taking of reception and transmission (dialogue). Without some degree of difference (but not absolute difference) there will be no semiosis, which is dialogue. The cultural function of journalism is to interrogate difference, to conduct a dialogue with whatever anomalies, deviances, ups and downs it discovers in the semiosphere, especially along what Lotman calls the 'hottest spots for semioticizing processes', the boundaries of the semiosphere.[4] Journalism is the cultural mechanism in modern societies for translating texts of an alien semiotics (literally, culturally or politically foreign) into 'our' language, the language of central, ordered, stratified, regular, mythic common sense.

Lotman shows that dialogue is collective as well as individual, characterized in both cases by alternating periods of 'reception' and 'transmission' (reading and writing). At any one time, certain national cultures will be intensive semiotic producers, transmitting widely across the semiosphere; at other times they will be relatively quiet, taking in influences from outside, slowly transforming what is 'read' from strangeness to translation and transformation of the 'home' culture, eventually to provoke a change of the 'receiving culture' back into a 'transmitting culture', which 'issues forth a flood of texts directed to other, peripheral areas of the semiosphere'. Lotman suggests that Enlightenment France can be seen this way:

France had absorbed cultural currents from the whole of Europe: the ideas of the Reformation from Holland, Germany and Switzerland, the empiricism of Bacon and Locke and Newtonian mechanics, the Latinism of the Italian Humanists, and the Mannerism of the Spanish and Italian Baroque; but in the age of Enlightenment she made all Europe speak her language . . . . In the eighteenth century there was a choice: either to be a follower or an opponent of the ideas of the Enlightenment, namely, religious toleration, the cult of Nature and Reason, and the eradication of age-old superstition in the name of the freedom of Man. Paris became the capital of European thought, and innumerable texts poured out of France to all the corners of Europe. Compare this period with the pause which followed . . . [1810]: France 'became a receiver' again and opened itself to English culture from Shakespeare to Byron, to German culture – Schiller, Goethe – and to the Romantic writers of northern Europe from Kant to Walter Scott.[5]

Difference, opposition, dialogue, asymmetry – the semiosphere is characterized by boundaries, between inside and out, home and foreign, Wedom and Theydom; boundaries which are constantly being policed, renegotiated, moved and dissolved. Lotman argues that the elementary act of thinking is translation; this is most intensive at the margin or periphery of a given semiotic space, even though law-formation takes place at the centre. Thus there is constant to-ing and fro-ing (dialogue) between centre and periphery, until the relative positions are reversed and new centres are established.

One such form of to-ing and fro-ing, according to Lotman, is the opposition between what he calls the 'central cyclical text-engendering mechanism' which produces texts which classify, stratify and order, according to a cyclical time, and a 'text-producing mechanism organized according to linear time'. Linear texts include 'oral tales about "surprises," "news," various happy and unhappy occurrences'. Such texts record anomalies not regularities, events not principles, and histories, chronicles and records rather than 'law-affirming texts both sacred and scientific'. While mythic or cyclical texts are a 'structural model of the world', anecdotal or linear texts are 'a special archive of anomalies'.[6] Clearly the latter is a typology for journalism in a literate (modern) culture, albeit a journalism whose stories are frequently replete with mythical elements. Thus journalism is the dialogic go-between within a given semiosphere as well as policing its boundaries – it is in journalism that the dialogue between law-formation in the centre and 'surprises' at the periphery is in fact conducted.

Democratic Equivalence

Thus, returning to the period of the French Revolution as discussed in Chapter 3, it is now time to show how the strictly political and journalistic production of news, of a readership for political participation, and of fully socialized concepts of liberty, fraternity and equality, co-existed with (*within*) and interacted vigorously with the existing semiosphere(s) of Parisian, French, European and human culture which were active and available at the time. Furthermore, it was at once the function of the journalism of the period to translate, make known, and explain different sites of language, culture and meaning-creation within the semiosphere to each other – a function journalism retains to this day, which accounts for its voracious appetite for stories from the margins, from outlandish, deviant, specialist and extreme areas of life. Certainly there was a lot to translate, make known and explain. The logic of the Revolution politicized and transformed every aspect of the semiosphere, and it worked both diachronically (through time) and synchronically (across (semiotic) space).

Diachronically, the 'sovereignty of the people' (liberty) proved to be a truly revolutionary concept, since it set in train a logic of democratic equivalence through time, whereby groups who were not liberated in 1789 could demand (or in some cases be offered) emancipation. This 'logic of equivalence' is theorized by Ernesto Laclau and Chantal Mouffe as follows. They argue that there's a crucial difference between subordination and oppression – the difference being that subordination (a relationship) can only be seen as *oppression* when there is 'a discursive "exterior" from which the discourse of subordination can be interrupted'. They say:

> *Our thesis is that it is only from the moment when the democratic discourse becomes available to articulate the different forms of resistance to subordination that the conditions will exist to make possible the struggle against different types of inequality.*[7]

They give the example of women's subordination, which was not experienced as oppression in Europe until the seventeenth century, and so feminism 'as a movement of struggle against women's subordination could not emerge'. But in the revolutionary period it became possible to see women's subordination from the outside – from the perspective of the Revolution – and thus to shift democratic discourses from the civic to the sexual arena (what's sauce for the gander is sauce for the goose). Laclau and Mouffe give the example from England of Mary Wollstonecraft:

> *whose book* Vindication of the Rights of Women, *published in 1792, determined the birth of feminism through the use made of it in the democratic discourse, which was thus displaced from the field of political equality between citizens to the field of equality between the sexes.*[8]

While it is Laclau and Mouffe's thesis that it was only from the moment when democratic discourse 'becomes available' to different parts of the semiosphere that struggle against previously fixed and naturalized relations of subordination could begin, it is my thesis that journalism is *the* necessary mechanism for *making* these discourses generally available, and also for *articulating* the different forms of resistance. Political philosophy such as that of Wollstonecraft is also crucial, especially in published form, but it is not the case that journalism simply popularized existing philosophical ideas; some of the Revolution's best ideas *were* journalism. The teaching of new political philosophy to millions of non-philosophers, making the 'logic of democratic equivalence' *available*, is a job for journalism.

A striking example of this logic from the French Revolution is in the republican journal *La Bouche de Fer* ('suggestion box') which reported a speech to the confederation of the 'Friends of Truth' by Etta Palm d'Aelder in 1791:

> *Justice must be the first virtue of free men, and justice demands that the laws be common to all beings as the air and the sun; and yet everywhere the laws are in favour of men, at the expense of women, because everywhere power is in your hands . . . . Would that our sacred Revolution which is due to the progress of philosophy, would work a second revolution in our morals: that the instruments of severity so weighted against us, and which true philosophy condemns, would give place to the sweet, just and natural law; that your love, your friendship, your approbation would be henceforth the recompense of virtuous citizenesses; that civic gowns replace on these attractive heads the wretched pompons, symbols of frivolity and shameful signs of our servitude.*[9]

Not surprisingly, perhaps, Palm's argument rings a contemporary note, for the logic of democratic equivalence is *diachronic* – a logic which has taken the best part of two hundred years to produce the emancipation it desired, and is still in struggle in the area of shifting men's actions from 'nature' to 'culture'. As Palm says:

> *The prejudices that have surrounded our sex are based on unjust laws, which grant us only a secondary role in society, and often force us to the humiliating necessity of conquering the wicked nature or savage character of a man, who, having become our master through the greed of our parents, has caused to change for us the sweetest, the most sacred of duties, that of spouse and mother, into a painful slavery. Yes, Messieurs, there is nothing more humiliating than to demand as a right what it would be glorious to obtain by choice; . . . to acquire your heart, your hand, the association of a companion for life, of another self, by a pose that is not our own . . . for, I must tell you, Messieurs, that it is more often by simpering, by trifles, and the beauty-box, I almost said even by vice, that we win your approval and affection rather than for a lofty mind, a great genius, a heart both truly feeling as well as delicate and virtuous.*[10]

Bringing the politics of the ballot-box to the relations of the beauty-box, and making the 'rights of Man' equivalent from the bed to the boulevard, has proved historically to be not only a 'glorious' but a protracted process, in which eventually ground was given on both sides – not only is it necessary to 'read' sexual relations in terms of political choices, freedoms and justice, but conversely it is now possible to 'read' political relations in terms of what Palm identifies as 'love, friendship, and approbation', a 'heart truly feeling' as well as virtuous (as we shall see in Chapter 5). Palm's speech and its publication is a good example of the feminist public sphere in action, at the very beginning of both feminism and of modernity; though it is noteworthy that in 1791 at least there was no sense (as there is in Felski's formulation discussed in Chapter 2) of this journalistic extension of feminism being distanced from the thing itself – the speech and the report in the paper are both aspects of a feminist public sphere which is clearly addressed both internally to women, with a view to 'remedying [injustice] by education and by laws in our favour'; and externally to men and to the society as a whole, to warn them that the traditional femininity of compliance is 'painful slavery', and sexual relations are based on a lie, where women make 'a special study of coquetry in order to soften our captivity'.[11]

Laclau and Mouffe are quite definite about the timing of the moment when this logic of democratic equivalence – and with it feminism and the feminist public sphere – was first promulgated. They say: 'The key moment in the beginnings of the democratic revolution can be found in the French Revolution since . . . its affirmation of the absolute power of its people introduced something truly new at the level of the social imaginary':

> *But in order to be mobilized in this way, the democratic principle of liberty and equality had first to impose itself as the new matrix of the social imaginary; or, in our terminology, to constitute a fundamental nodal point in the construction of the political. This decisive mutation in the political imaginary of Western societies took place two hundred years ago and can be defined in these terms: the logic of equivalence was transformed into the fundamental instrument of production of the social.*[12]

It was the French Revolution – the moment when sovereignty passed to the people – that made it 'possible to propose the different forms of inequality as illegitimate and anti-natural, and thus make them equivalent as forms of oppression'. And it was *journalism* which made these proposals, and transmitted them throughout the Republic, the continent, the world and the ensuing two centuries. The radical journalists of the early years of the Revolution were quick to follow the dictates of logic, and argue for the emancipation, not only of women, but also of 'Jews, actors and hangmen';[13] slaves and colonized peoples; peasants; and citizens of little education.[14] (It seems only gypsies and children remain. . .)

Sans-culottizing the Universe

Synchronically, the revolution of reason spread like the wild 'electric fire' of the journalism which carried its message. The displacement of a monarchical legitimacy based on divine anointment and seminal heredity provoked a fundamental crisis in accepted realities, and every aspect of life that could be subjected to criticism in the name of reason was indeed transformed. Time's customary counting beads were restrung in 1793: the seven-day week was abolished in favour of a metric *décade*, whose day-names were:

Primidi	Sextidi
Duodi	Septidi
Tridi	Octodi
Quartidi	Nonodi
Quintidi	Décadi

The months were renamed too, following the seasons (of Paris):

January Nivôse (snows)	*July* Messidor (harvest)
February Ventôse (winds)	*August* Fervidor [Thermidor] (warmth)
March Pluviôse (rain)	*September* Fructidor (fruits)
April Germinal (sap)	*October* Vendémiaire (vintage)
May Floréal (flowers)	*November* Brumaire (fogs)
June Prairial (meadows)	*December* Frimaire (frosts)

And the years were renumbered to count not from the Christian year dot but from the day the monarchy ended: 22 September 1792, i.e. 1st Vendémiaire, Year I. Since a ten-day week and a three-week month produce a 360-day year, five patriotic holidays were inserted to celebrate the Virtues, Genius, Work, Opinion, Rewards, thereby giving journalism (*L'Opinion*) a civic feast of its own. Leap years would have an extra feast of the people, or 'sans-culottide', called the *jour bissextillaire* (this calendar lasted till 1805). The radical *Révolutions de Paris* disliked the names of the months, calling them a 'barbarous nomenclature', and accusing their authors of not having 'sufficient respect for people's reason'. The paper suggested a '"political" calendar':

> to call the month of January that of the Justice of the People, because of the punishment of Capet; July, the month of the Bastille; September, the month of the Republic, and so on. We cannot hope to familiarise too much the coming generation with the epochs of our Revolution.[15]

Having reinvented time and restarted the calendar, the Revolutionaries dissolved space: the provinces of France were abolished in favour of symmetrical departments, and all the complex feudal divisions were dissolved into the unity of the nation – the 'Republic, one and indivisible'. Paris was reformed into sections, 1400 street names were changed, Montmartre became Mont Marat, 6000 towns changed their name, 30 of them to Marat. Nothing was exempt: crockery, furniture, chess pieces, 'queen' bees, playing cards (kings, queens, jacks became liberties, equalities, fraternities). Naturally, along with legal and religious codes, dress codes were revolutionized; the *sans-culotte* being the emblem of radical militancy and the Liberty cap (Phrygian bonnet) being the emblem of the

Republic itself. Revolutionaries tried to reform the language too, especially to replace the formal *vous* form by the fraternal *tu*.[16] And the spirit of freedom was called orally as well as by print: two of the most famous compositions of the Revolution were songs – the *ça ira* ('things will work out', 1790) and the *Marseillaise* (written by Rouget de Lisle in 1792). However, both of these songs achieved their prodigious popularity with the help of journalism, for they were printed, pirated (and parodied) all over France, partly to promote national unity, partly to counteract what was thought to be the tendency of the muse of song towards aristocratic corruption.[17]

Science was yoked to revolution via modernization, popularization and the pursuit of comfort. Jean Dhombres notes that in a race to write textbooks about the latest discoveries, 'popularization was held to coincide with organization and also with modernization. All branches of scientific knowledge, and the very ways such knowledge was disseminated, were being restructured.'[18] He points to the 'considerable increase ... in the production of "useful" books devoted to explaining particular skills', and to the tendency in the journals to mix revolutionary politics with 'the dissemination of techniques for more comfortable living, which arose naturally from progress'. Thus the *Feuille villageoise*, the biggest-selling rural paper of the Revolution, announced that in the service of enlightenment it would 'lay before you all those useful discoveries which may improve your lot, enrich your leisure and lighten your labors . . .'.[19] Dhombres says: 'without a doubt ... the meter came into the world with a sans-culotte pedigree', while one Citizen Decremps published from his home in the rue des Droits de l'Homme a textbook called *La Science Sansculotisée*, beginning with an essay on astronomy which was directed to amateurs, 'gens de lettres' and especially to mariners, under the banner headline of the 'REVOLUTION IN LESSONS'; the essay opens with 'the utility of Astronomy' and concludes 'avec les remarques satyriques'.[20]

Thus the logic of popular sovereignty, once proclaimed, could not be confined to government, but must extend to every field of discursive creativity across the semiosphere and even to the celestial spheres. As the *Mercure national* put it as early as 1790:

> *In spite of its imperfections, our language will soon be one of the most noble, the richest, the most sonorous, and the most expressive of the living languages, if we wish to study it, purify it at the fire of liberty, and render it finally dignified for a* peuple roi.[21]

Meanwhile, upon the ground of this language purified with liberty, art too must submit to popular sovereignty, as the *Journal universel* chorused in 1791: 'The public, the public, there is the great judge, the impartial judge, the incorruptible judge of productions of all types'.[22]

These cultural invocations of popular sovereignty are interesting for their retention of the language of *ancien régime* hierarchy in the actions of the people: the Manichaean people take on the qualities

of their adversaries – the 'noble richness' of a language fit for a
'*peuple roi*' who are the 'great judge'. Thus while the radicals wanted
actual physical people to inhabit their concept of popular sovereignty, it was still an abstract concept delineated with characteristics
drawn not from the nature of the people as such but from their
adversaries. The people were imagined as having taken over the
absolutist, dictatorial powers of their adversaries (although unlike
real nobles, kings and judges, the people were seen as incorruptible
and impartial). Journalism took it upon itself not only to communicate the judgement of the people back and forth across the range
of modern, progressive, useful, comfort-enhancing and political
innovations in the semiosphere, but also to construct a character for
the people to whom and on whose behalf the journalists addressed
those judgements.

Hard-core Philosophy, X-rated Politics

> *Life can little else supply*
> *But a few good fucks and then we die.* JOHN WILKES[23]

Since journalism is the textual system of modernity, it is important
to indicate how this textual system interacts with and is differentiated from others. Journalism is recognizable for being daily, factual,
in prose, scripted, about public events. But such terms are *not* a
description of an internal property of the 'nature' of journalism, for
each is part of a system of oppositions – journalism is, then, not one-
off (like book publishing), not fictional, not poetic, not oral, not
about mythical events. In short, journalism takes its form from its
position in relation to other textual systems in the semiosphere, a
position which changes over time. This section will look at some of
the boundaries between journalism and its dialogic opposites –
pamphlets, philosophy, pornography – to show how it occupied and
differentiated its specific space in the semiosphere.

In any process of cultural contact, before a dialogue can begin in
which new knowledge and information is produced out of the intensive process of mutual translation between two asymmetric textual
systems, Yuri Lotman says that 'a situation of mutual attraction must
precede the actual contact'.[24] Just as the semiosphere *as a whole*
precedes any semiotic act or system, so 'the need for dialogue, *the
dialogic situation,* precedes both real dialogue and even the existence
of a language in which to conduct it: the semiotic situation precedes
the instruments of semiosis'.[25] He illustrates this idea by describing a
fundamental dialogic encounter: the 'dialogic situation of a mother
who is breastfeeding and her infant'. He comments: 'however strange
this may sound in this kind of textbook – a necessary condition for
dialogue is love, the mutual attraction of the participants'. He notes
that 'in the search for a common language each of the participants
tries to use the other's language' (i.e. the mother burbles while the

baby matches her facial expressions). This dialogue includes sequences of transmission and reception (turn-taking):

> *For instance, and this is something many people will have observed, there is an 'exchange of laughter' between mother and baby, that 'language of smiles' which Rousseau thought was the only conversation guaranteed to be free of falsehood.*[26]

Lotman suggests that this is 'an exceptionally good [choice of subject] for understanding the general mechanisms of dialogue'. It so happens that it describes exactly the situation of mutual attraction and turn-taking that existed between philosophy, pornography and journalism in the period leading up to and into the French Revolution. The 'language of smiles' also accounts for the characteristic form taken by contemporary electronic journalism, which I have previously identified as one of the contemporary 'smiling professions',[27] and also for the existence since the Enlightenment (at least) of conditions of mutual attraction, dialogue, translation, and turn-taking between sex and politics in the popular press; tabloid journalism, it transpires, is founded not on falsehood but love.

Around 1789 journalism exploded into the French semiosphere with astonishing rapidity. But it was not alone; pamphlets, for example, were perhaps its nearest neighbour (as they had been in the English Civil War 150 years earlier). Today the function of the pamphlet is integrated into the institutional repertoire of newspapers, in the form of the comment column and in-depth feature, especially in weekend papers; also, something of their political function survives in the electronic media in radio talks and talk-back, and in TV 'positioned' documentaries. But in revolutionary France the pamphlet shared the stage with journals as a protagonist in the production of modernity. To show how their numbers ballooned Antoine de Baecque lists the numbers of political pamphlets published throughout the revolutionary period:[28]

Year	Number of pamphlets
1774–86 (12 years)	(averaging 26 a year) 312
1787	217
1788	819
1789	3,305
1790	3,121
1791	1,923
1792	1,286
1793	663
1794	601
1795	569
1796	182
1797	245
1798	154
1799	211
Total	13,608

Baecque points out that the major categories of such pamphlets were: reflections on government and institutions; political essays; comment on current affairs (the largest group); political polemic (i.e. pamphlets engaged in dialogue with *other* pamphlets by a counterpoint of praise and denunciation). However Baecque selects for discussion an important subcategory – the 'ribald and anonymous' so-called pornographic pamphlet, which is 'tendentious . . . politically committed . . . defamatory' – and which, he suggests, constitutes a fair sample of ephemeral writing in general across the whole range of pamphlet categories:

> *Herein resides the fascinating value of these little books, playing their part in the creation of a new political mythology, stamped by a strange, frenetic Manichaeanism that contrasts the degenerate aristocrat of the dark with the new revolutionary man of the light. We are forced to ask ourselves how inflammatory language and mythologizing can offer a legitimate exegesis on the politics of the day.*[29]

Indeed, writing of the pre-revolutionary period, Robert Darnton has argued that because of the censorship of news, it fell to scandal, gossip and obscene stories about royalty, nobles and courtiers to take the place of political journalism:

> *It is easy to underestimate the importance of personal slander in eighteenth-century French politics, because it is difficult to appreciate that politics took place at court, where personalities counted more than policies. Defamation was a standard weapon of court cabales. And then as now, names made news, although news did not make the newspapers. Rigorously excluded from legal periodicals, it circulated in pamphlets,* nouvelles à la main, *and by* nouvellistes de bouche – *the real sources from which political journalism originated in France.*[30]

Darnton also makes the interesting observation that the royal censorship of libels of this sort made pornography the strange bedfellow of the Enlightenment in a very literal sense: the booksellers and dealers who traded in illegal publications used the euphemism '*livres philosophiques*' – 'philosophical books' – to describe pornographic publications, but this appellation also of course applied to the equally dangerous works of the *philosophes*, the blueprint for the Enlightenment, written by such as Rousseau, Montesquieu, Voltaire, Diderot. The idea of hard-core philosophy, X-rated politics, is not easy to imagine in these latter days of functional divisions of labour in the knowledge class, but in pre-1789 France the category 'philosophical books' helped not only to protect booksellers, dealers and smugglers, but also to tutor a reading public in the realities of the Revolution, not least because the philosophers wrote personal or bawdy works themselves, just as the pornography had political as well as erotic import:

> *We consider the* Social Contract *[Rousseau] literature and* Histoire de Dom B*****, Portier des Chartreux *pornography . . . . But the bookmen of the eighteenth century lumped them together as*

*'philosophical books.' If we try to look at their material in their way,
the seemingly self-evident distinction between pornography and philosophy begins to break down. We are ready to perceive a philosophical
element in the prurient – from* Thérèse philosophe *to* Philosophe
dans le boudoir *– and to reexamine the erotic works of the
philosophes: Montesquieu's* Lettres persanes, *Voltaire's* Pucelle
d'Orléans, *Diderot's* Bijoux indiscrets. *It no longer seems puzzling
that Mirabeau, the embodiment of the spirit of 1789, should have
written the rawest pornography and the boldest political tracts of the
previous decade. Liberty and libertinism appear to be linked.*[31]

Certainly they were linked in the Revolutionary period itself. As
Baecque points out, titles such as *The Austrian Woman on the Loose,
or the Royal Orgy, The Secret Relations of the Queen with Cardinal de Rohan
After His Appearance at the Estates General, Dom Pederast [Bougre] at the
Estates General, The Fires of Sodomy in the National Assembly* and *The Abbé
Maury Among the Girls,* all served a Parisian public which was 'more
and more openly being offered a new literature, explicitly sexual in
its terminology, and using sexual sensationalism above all in a
tireless effort to prove that the old ruling classes were unfit to survive
into the new age'.[32] Baecque goes on to show how philosophy (or
at least political theory, which in this period is the same thing) and
pornography are indeed coterminous:

> *Impotent, riddled with venereal disease, wholly given over to distem-
> pered, narcissistic pleasures, the aristocrat was depicted as irrevocably
> destined for the dustbin of history. The literary 'invention' of the degen-
> erate aristocrat was a masterpiece of propagandistic moral destabiliza-
> tion; he became the symbol of a society the pamphlets presented as worn
> out. In contrast are the 'patriotic sexual practices' trumpeted by the
> pamphlets . . . . This 'political' Manichaeanism is a paramount device
> in the pamphleteering of the period. The lewdness of political pornog-
> raphy (it put things very bluntly) offers us an interesting approach to
> the study of this duality in the politics of the day.*[33]

Such duality bespeaks the collision of different languages in the
semiosphere and a transformation in the configuration of the whole;
pornography was a 'patriotic energy' needed to overcome (as it
were) a royal mythology which was itself founded on semen:

> *The ridiculing of Louis XVI must have done a great deal of damage
> at a time when nobility was still identified with 'seminal fluid' and
> when the Salic law still required that the royal 'race' be transmitted
> through an unbroken chain of males.*[34]

In such circumstances, sex and politics are neighbours not only in
the semiosphere but also in the public sphere. To accuse the king
of impotence and having a penis comparable to a match-stick, 'no
bigger than a straw, always limp and always curved', or the queen of
adultery (with all sorts, up to and including a cardinal), of masturbation and lesbian practices, or to accuse aristocrats of orgies, of

homosexuality, venereal diseases and low sex-drive (except when fantasizing about cuckolding patriotic politicians), especially when such sexual traits are contrasted with the vigour and simple sexual tastes of the revolutionaries, is to make sexual politics was not only scandalous but also insurrectionary.[35]

Love–Hate Politics

It seems that these sexualized scandals were communicated across demographic lines, not least by a wonderful character called the 'Armour-Plated Journalist' – the *Gazetier Cuirasse*, whose 'scandalous anecdotes of the Court of France' (published 'A hundred Leagues from the Bastille') was 'an extremely illicit book' dating from 1771.[36] Such 'journalism' united very different classes in the common cause of undermining the authority of the court. Darnton quotes a contemporary pamphlet which 'pretended to defend the queen, and various courtiers and ministers as well, by refuting the calumnies against her in minute, scabrous detail'. This document gives the following account of how its own gossip gets around:

> *A vile courtesan puts these infamies in rhyming couplets and through the intermediary of flunkeys distributes them all the way to the market place. From the markets they reach artisans, who in turn transmit them back to the noblemen who first wrought them and who, without wasting a minute, go to the royal chambers in Versailles and whisper from ear to ear in a tone of consummate hypocrisy, 'Have you read them? Here they are. This is what is circulating among the common people of Paris.'*[37]

The consummation of the union of pornographic language and radical politics was achieved most conspicuously by Jacques-Réné Hébert in the notorious *Père Duchesne*. This was the voice of the sans-culottes (i.e. people who wore workers' trousers rather than aristocratic breeches), the most radical popular movement of the Revolution. Famous for peppering his 'great angers' and 'great joys' with great obscenities, Hébert was clear about the politics of so doing:

> *Hébert himself claimed that 'You must swear with those who swear'.* . . . *'Anyone who appreciates frankness and probity,' he said, 'will not blush at the* foutres *[fucks] and* bougres *[buggers] that I insert here and there with my joys and my angers.'* . . . *Hébert had one goal before him – to make himself understood by the people. Above all, the people wanted someone who spoke their own language. In Hébert they recognized themselves.*[38]

This proletarianism paid dividends; *Père Duchesne* was one of the most successful journals of the Revolution, lurching leftwards, somewhat in advance of the government, as it provoked and praised the sans-culottes: 'it can be said that at the height of its fame it was the best-known paper in France', whose circulation was 'said to have reached a million when it was subsidised and distributed to the army in 1793'.[39] Hébert's pleasure at the death of the Queen, now known as 'Madame Veto' or the 'Austrian bitch', and guillotined in October 1793 a few months after ex-king 'Capet' or the 'fat cuckold' had been executed, can be gauged by the subheading in the next issue of *Le Père Duchesne* (bearing in mind that subheadings in newspapers at this time were largely for the benefit of street hawkers, or *colporteurs*, to give them something to shout about):[40] it read: 'The head of Female Veto separated from her fucking neck.'[41]

Just as hate was sexualized in the Revolution, so love was politicized. Robert Darnton offers two symbolic anecdotes to show how these binary opposites of human emotion enter into dialogue at times of the highest political emotion. The first event took place right at the start of the Revolution, on 23 July 1789, a week after the fall of the Bastille. The intendant of Paris, Berthier de Sauvigny, and his father-in-law Foullon de Doué, were lynched in the street in Paris by separate crowds. After the murder of Foullon, his head was paraded on a pikestaff, mouth stuffed full of hay to symbolize what he had apparently suggested the hungry people should eat. This crowd approached the other, which had captured but not yet killed his son-in-law Berthier. This is what happens, as Darnton tells it:

> *The two crowds merge in a single wave of violence, carrying Bertier [sic] on its crest. He stares in horror through the pikes and sees the head of his father-in-law, coming closer and closer, until it is thrust into his face: 'Kiss papa! Kiss papa!' chants the crowd.*[42]

The next issue of Prudhomme's *Les Révolutions de Paris* commented on the popular emotions which inspired this 'terrible and shocking spectacle':

> *Frenchmen . . . your hate is frightening; it is shocking . . . But you will be free! . . . O my fellow citizens . . . think, finally, of what good, what satisfaction, what happiness awaits you, you and your children and your descendants, when august and blessed liberty will have set its temple among you! Yet do not forget these proscriptions outrage humanity and make nature tremble.*[43]

Hate and happiness, the kiss of death and the kiss of life, were in such intimate mutual embrace at this time that perhaps they were one and the same thing. 'Kiss papa!' was possibly the most cruel slogan personally, but most liberating politically, in a polity where sovereignty was based on paternity (male succession to the throne) and paternalism (the king as 'father' to his people), and where the people's loyalty (the kiss of fealty) was still owed, even as the first death blow had already been struck to the monarchy itself. Such is the love of liberty.

The second emblematic kiss mentioned by Darnton, the 'kiss of Lamourette', took place in one of the Revolution's most dangerous moments, in July 1792, when its very survival was in doubt. War, treachery, defections, popular violence, counter-revolutionary plots and agitation, fear and dearth were crowding in on the National Assembly:

> On July 7, 1792, A.-A. Lamourette, a deputy from Rhône-et-Loire, told the Assembly's members that their troubles all arose from a single source: factionalism. They needed more fraternity. Whereupon the deputies, who had been at each other's throats moments earlier, rose to their feet and started hugging and kissing each other as if their political divisions could be swept away in a wave of brotherly love.[44]

Love and kissing have pretty much absented themselves from the public sphere these days, but they're still a major feature of the mediasphere. And sometimes, as the next chapter will show, the kiss of 'brotherly love', carried to the far corners of the global semiosphere by the 'electric fire' of journalism, can stop the world in its tracks and change the course of history.

Notes

1. Yuri (Iurii Mikhailovich) Lotman (1990) *Universe of the Mind: A Semiotic Theory of Culture*. Trans. Ann Shukman with an introduction by Umberto Eco. Bloomington and Indianapolis: Indiana University Press, 203.
2. Lotman, 124–5.
3. Umberto Eco, Introduction to Lotman, xiii.
4. Lotman, 136.
5. Lotman, 146.
6. Lotman, 153, 162.
7. Ernesto Laclau and Chantal Mouffe (1985) *Hegemony and Socialist Strategy: Towards a Radical Democratic Politics*. Trans. Winston Moore and Paul Cammack. London: Verso, 154.
8. Laclau and Mouffe, 154.
9. *La Bouche de Fer*, 3 January 1791, quoted in John Gilchrist and W.J. Murray (1971) *The Press in the French Revolution: A Selection of Documents Taken from the Press of the Revolution for the Years 1789–1794*. Melbourne: Cheshire, and London: Ginn, 238–9. See also Hugh Gough (1988) *The Newspaper Press in the French Revolution*. London: Routledge, 201, who notes that the famous writer-philosopher the Marquis de Condorcet, who was associated with the *Bouche de fer*, argued for women's suffrage in the *Journal de la société de 1789*. Gough says twenty-three journals aimed specifically at women appeared in the revolutionary decade, including the directly political *Feuille du jour* (January 1790) which was published by 'une société des femmes de lettres'.
10. Gilchrist and Murray, 237.
11. Quoted in Gilchrist and Murray, 237.
12. Laclau and Mouffe, 154–5.
13. This strange articulation was the subject of a debate in the National Assembly. See Gilchrist and Murray, 93–4. Protestants were also emancipated in the Revolution.
14. See Gilchrist and Murray, 238–9, 259–60 (slaves and colonists), 237–8 (women), 239 (peasants), 45–6, 173–4, 240–1 (education).

15. Gilchrist and Murray, 264–5, quoting from the radical *Révolutions de Paris* of septidi Brumaire, an II.

16. Robert Darnton (1990) *The Kiss of Lamourette: Reflections in Cultural History.* New York: W.W. Norton, 6–11.

17. See Laura Mason (1989) Songs: mixing media. In Robert Darnton and Daniel Roche (eds.) *Revolution in Print: The Press in France 1775–1800.* Berkeley and LA: University of California Press, 252–69.

18. Jean Dhombres (1989) Books: reshaping science. In Darnton and Roche (eds.), 177–202, this quotation 199.

19. Dhombres, 200–1.

20. Reproduction of the opening page of Henri Decremps's *Sans-culotte science . . .* in Dhombres, 192.

21. *Mercure National*, 47, 14 December 1790, quoted in Jack Richard Censer (1976) *Prelude to Power: The Parisian Radical Press 1789–1791.* Baltimore and London: Johns Hopkins University Press, 71.

22. *Journal universel*, 488, 25 March 1791, quoted in Censer, 72.

23. John Wilkes, the 'father' of British press freedom, quoted in Ronal Hyam (1990) *Empire and Sexuality: The British Experience.* Manchester and New York: Manchester University Press, 56.

24. Lotman, 147.

25. Lotman, 143–4.

26. Lotman, 144.

27. John Hartley (1992) *The Politics of Pictures: The Creation of the Public in the Age of Popular Media.* London and New York: Routledge, Chapter 5.

28. Antoine de Baecque (1989) Pamphlets: libel and political mythology. In Darnton and Roche (eds.), 165–76. The pamphlets are listed in the *Catalogue de l'histoire de France* in the Bibliothèque Nationale in Paris.

29. Baecque, 168.

30. Robert Darnton (1982) *The Literary Underground of the Old Regime.* Cambridge, Mass.: Harvard University Press, 203.

31. Robert Darnton (1989) Philosophy under the cloak. In Darnton and Roche (eds.), 27–49, this quotation 49.

32. Baecque, 169.

33. Baecque, 169.

34. Darnton, *Literary Underground*, 205. He cites Pierre Goubert (1969) *L'Ancien Régime*, Paris, I, 152, for the 'seminal fluid'.

35. See Darnton, *Literary Underground*, 200–1, and Baecque, 170–2.

36. See Darnton, Philosophy under the cloak, 30.

37. Darnton, *Literary Underground*, 201. He is quoting from *Le portefeuille d'un talon rouge contenant des anecdotes galantes et secrètes de la cour de France.*

38. Gilchrist and Murray, 21.

39. Gilchrist and Murray, 9.

40. See Jeremy D. Popkin (1989) Journals: the new face of news. In Darnton and Roche (eds.), 141–64; for street vendors and subheadings, 154. See also Gough's index on *colporteurs*.

41. Quoted in Darnton, *Literary Underground*, 205.

42. Darnton, *The Kiss of Lamourette*, xii.

43. *Les Révolutions de Paris*, 2, 18–25 July 1789, quoted in Gilchrist and Murray, 5–56. They give the date as 22 July.

44. Darnton, *The Kiss of Lamourette*, 17.

5 *The Mediasphere*

(Equality)

Where we would wish to reform we must not reproach. THOMAS PAINE[1]

Cultural Synchrony

The *mediasphere* is the world of the readership. Yuri Lotman has pointed out that cultural history is quite different from biological evolution, so that (for example) a sense of literary or cultural 'evolution' that is founded on analogy with biological evolution is very misleading. A biologist, says Lotman, 'finds only living creatures contemporary with him' or her, and once a species is as dead as a dodo it can never play any further part in the contemporary biosphere. But in culture, on the contrary, 'works which come down to us from remote cultural periods continue to play a part in cultural development as living factors'. Hence, 'what "works" is not the most recent temporal section, but the whole packed history of cultural texts'.[2] But still there is a tendency to assess a culture by what is published at a given moment, not what is circulating among its readers and audiences:

> With this approach the state of literature at any one time is judged by
> the list of works written *in that year*, instead of works being read *in
> that year* – which would produce a very different picture.[3]

The picture that would be produced if readerships were analysed, can be called the *mediasphere*. 'In fact,' continues Lotman, 'everything contained in the actual memory of culture is directly or indirectly part of that culture's synchrony.' I would suggest that one of the major mechanisms for keeping cultural memory synchronous, for interconnecting the various languages and sub-languages of the semiosphere, for translating marginal and peripheral semioses into central, hegemonic ones, for marking cultural frontiers and alienating Theydom from Wedom, is journalism.

While what Lotman describes as 'the most recent temporal section' is in one sense the essence of journalism, whose subject is recency, it is nevertheless the case that journalism too obeys the law of *cultural* rather than biological 'evolution'. The mediasphere is the very place where those 'works which come down to us from remote periods' *can* 'continue to play a part in cultural development as living factors'. Indeed, the dialogue between recent and remote, relating present and past, the emergent with the residual, new imperatives with old structures, is the *plot* of journalism; its time structure. However, the mediasphere, being the sphere of readership, has a temporal dimension in addition to the time-lines of a story; it has the 'cultural synchrony' of the readership to take into account as well – the 'here and now' of the readership's 'whole packed history' at a given moment. This very peculiar and unstraightforward matter of timing in the mediasphere is intensified by politics, which in this respect is the art of timing – of making to appear now things that the opposition would delay, of fitting new circumstances into existing structures of meaning and opinion, of sensing the exact moment when change is possible. Journalism, like politics, requires timing and tact in relation to the public/readership whose semiosphere is, as Lotman says, temporally and spatially 'packed':

> *Every normal person has these (and many other) layers which form a heterogeneous mixture which functions as a whole. In the mind of modern man [see note] there mingles Newtonian, Einsteinian (and even post-Einsteinian) ideas with deeply mythological images as well as persistent habits of seeing the world in its everyday sense. Against this substratum can be seen images created by art or deeper scientific ideas and also the constant transcoding of spatial images into the language of other models. The result is the complex semiotic mechanism which is always in motion.*[4]

One of my favourite heroes of journalism is Tom Paine, whose residence in a house in Sandwich, Kent, was celebrated by a plaque which I passed every day on my way to school for five years, and who was to that extent a real neighbour, a 'living factor' during my own explorations of the 'whole packed history' of textualized culture. But there is another more general justification for seeing Tom Paine as culturally and politically synchronous with the current age. As a *global democrat* whose political journalism extended the modern doctrine of popular sovereignty to a transnational popular readership, Paine has been hailed as a hero of postmodernity's own technology:

> *An article in the May 1995 edition of the American digital culture magazine* Wired *describes Tom Paine as 'the moral father of the Internet. His ideas about communications, media ethics, the example*

he set of free expression, are being resuscitated via the blinking cursors, clacking keyboards, hissing modems, bits and bytes of another revolution, the digital one,' writes Jon Katz, Wired*'s media critic. 'If his ideas no longer have much relevance to conventional journalism, they fit the Net like a glove.'*[5]

The distinction made here between 'conventional journalism' and 'digital culture' should not be overstated, for as I pointed out in the Introduction to this book, the technology of journalism is less important than the ideas it communicates and their popular reach. The internet uses new digital technology to communicate old democratic ideas, while 'conventional journalism' is itself a fully paid-up member of the global digital age, as the passage above amply demonstrates in itself – it is an Australian newspaper review of a British book, quoting an American magazine. It was published in a week when the global reach of 'conventional journalism' extended to a deal on the supply of new digital technology between Rupert Murdoch, owner of the paper in which this Painite review was published, and the *People's Daily*, official organ of the Communist Party of the Peoples' Republic of China; in the same week the Prime Minister of Australia announced his plans for making Australia a republic by the year 2001, a modernization which would bring the Commonwealth of Australia up to Painite speed after two hundred years. In short, Paine and postmodernity are in synch with each other, taking journalism into 'digital culture' (and vice versa) with the same agenda that inaugurated the modern era.

But Tom Paine is unique in modernity; he played a decisive role in the American Declaration and War of Independence, he wrote a book which was indicted for high treason for its revolutionary potential in his native England, and he was elected a deputy in the National Assembly (and also imprisoned) in Revolutionary France. He was a journalist *par excellence*, transcoding the experiences of continental Europe, Britain and the New World to each other in a career of undefeated commitment to political reason and popular sovereignty. In the second part of *Rights of Man* he addresses a preface to Lafayette (himself a hero of the American and the early part of the French Revolution), in which he ties politics to readership via timing:

For my own part I think it equally as injurious to good principles [of government] to permit them to linger, as to push them on too fast. That which you suppose accomplishable in fourteen or fifteen years I may believe practicable in a much shorter period. Mankind, as it appears to me, are always ripe enough to understand their true interest, provided it be presented clearly to their understanding, and that in a manner not to create suspicion by anything like self-design, nor offend by assuming too much. Where we would wish to reform we must not reproach.[6]

This wonderful tact in relation to a readership is 'cashed in' politically a few pages on, when Paine writes:

Mankind are not now to be told they shall not think or they shall not read; and publications that go no further than to investigate principles of government, to invite men to reason and to reflect and to shew the errors and excellences of different systems, have a right to appear. If they do not excite attention, they are not worth the trouble of a prosecution, and if they do [excite attention] the prosecution will amount to nothing, since it cannot amount to a prohibition of reading. This would be a sentence on the public instead of on the author, and would also be the most effectual mode of making or hastening revolutions.[7]

This conflation of nation, public and 'mankind' with *readership* is an inescapably modern gesture. Threatened with the criminal prosecution of his book, Paine argues that 'the only effectual jury in such cases would be the whole nation fairly elected', and adds that even the so-called 'prejudices' of education and habit would not 'stand the test of reason and reflection'. No one, says Paine, is 'prejudiced in favour of a thing knowing it to be wrong. He is attached to it on the belief of its being right and when he sees it is not so, the prejudice will be gone.' In short, the people, if they were ever 'fairly and candidly dealt by', would choose freedom (rather than poverty and high taxes!), but the mechanism by which they come to choose is *reading*. At such a point, change can be both rapid and done 'without convulsion or revenge'.

The Aestheticization of Revolution

It behoves journalists, then, not only to understand the true 'principles of government' but also to present them clearly, fairly and candidly to the national readership. This insight is two hundred years old, exactly the same age as political modernity, and yet it is rarely considered a part of political science. However, journalism itself is well up to speed, in some cases at least, as I hope to illustrate in the remainder of this chapter, by focusing on a much more recent example of journalism that was sensitive to its readership, to the political importance of the story, and to the transcodings of time, space and subject-matter that characterize a public sphere that is inside a mediasphere inside the semiosphere. I refer to the election of Nelson Mandela to the state presidency, and the ANC to power, in the Republic of South Africa in April 1994.

One aspect of the 'packed history' of this event was its revitalization of the founding slogan of modernity: 'liberty, equality, fraternity!', and of a number of echoes, some more audible than others, of the French Revolution. These were most noticeable in France, of course, whose most recognized name in contemporary journalism is *Vogue* – one of France's most successful semiotic and commercial exports to the world. *Vogue* decided to devote a whole issue to Nelson Mandela just before the election took place. *Vogue par Nelson Mandela* was, and remains, an extraordinary document.[8] To begin with, it fulfils a prediction of the French Revolution itself: here's Prudhomme's *Les Révolutions de Paris*, the biggest selling radical newspaper in the French Revolution, in 1790:

> *As for the slave trade and negro slavery, the European governments will find it useless to oppose the cries of philosophy, the principles of universal liberty that germinate and spread throughout nations. Let them learn that it is never in vain that peoples are shown the truth; once the impulse is given, it must absolutely give way to the flood that is going to sweep away the ancient abuses, and the new order of things will raise itself despite all precautions that have been taken to prevent its establishment. Yes! we dare to forecast with confidence that the time will come, and that day is not far off, when you will see an African, with frizzy hair, with no other recommendation than his good sense and his virtues, come to take part in the legislation at the heart of our national assemblies.*[9]

And, in *Vogue*, with no other recommendation than his good sense and his virtues, this is what Nelson Mandela himself has to say in response to a reporter's question on this very issue:

> – What does it mean to 'be black'?
> *It is not a goal in itself in our struggle, for we have always aimed at building a nation that will include us all, whites and blacks. We have suffered the cruellest form of oppression. People have been killed for the simple reason that they were black. We want to put the past behind us, but justice must prevail, for segregation denied the very existence of blacks. We have a democratic culture, a democratic tradition. The ideas of Voltaire, Rousseau and Montesquieu are not mere academic notions. We stand by the principle of liberty, fraternity and equality for all ethnic groups.*[10]

Certainly, I'm proposing a direct, culturally synchronous relationship between Nelson Mandela and the French Revolution: as he says, his 'democratic culture, democratic tradition' *is* the French Revolution, while the radicals among the French Revolutionaries predicted his eventual triumph (though they would have been appalled that it took 204 years). Mandela says that the ANC 'stands by' the principles of the Enlightenment, thereby agreeing with Lotman, for whom 'everything contained in the actual memory of culture is directly or indirectly part of that culture's synchrony'.[11]

But there is more to *Vogue by Nelson Mandela* than semiotic synchronicity, for I believe that this publication marks a decisive shift from modernist to postmodern journalism. Readers may wish to know what is meant by postmodernism in this context; in answer to that question I strongly recommend them to read Robert B. Ray's wonderful essay of the same name. It's a wise and witty piece, and among its little nuggets are these:

> *In French,* poste *means 'television set.' Postmodernism is really* poste- *modernism, what happened when modernism met TV . . . . While*

> *England perfected industrial production France anticipated post-indus-*
> *trial marketing, fostering desire through its inventions: the department*
> *store, the commercial daily press, the photograph. Only this site could*
> *occasion modernism, a reactionary movement, founded on nervous*
> *hostility to the democratization of taste.*[12]

Postmodern journalism is capitalized cultural studies, semiotics with funding, a carefully controlled textualization of politics for a popular readership which is highly literate in a mediasphere where scholarship has scarcely ventured. It's an unfamiliar *mélange* if you come to it speaking the language of modernist rationalism, but, as I've tried to show above, that modernism was always also semioti- cized, full of desire, emotion, visuality, kissing. When *Vogue* decides to cover one of the two most important contemporary political events in the world (the other was Mikhail Gorbachev's amazing, world-shaking attempt to restructure and open the USSR), it's not surprising to find that the traditional binary oppositions of politics are *in play*. But whereas front-page journalism insists on valuing one side of a binary opposition over the other, postmodern *Vogue* does something much more dialogic (in Lotman's sense): the public sphere is represented in terms of things that traditionally belong to the private, personal sphere – not least style, fashion, personality, sensuality, beauty.

At this point alarm bells should be ringing furiously for all those brought up in the context of a social theory based on the Frankfurt School's denunciation of the demagogic 'aestheticization of politics' which was so ably exploited by the Nazis in the 1930s, and so cogently criticized by writers like Theodor Adorno, Max Horkheimer, Hannah Arendt, Walter Benjamin and Bertolt Brecht: surely a commercial fashion magazine is going to feature the *look* of politics, substituting glamour for glasnost, frocks for freedom, looks for liberty? Well, yes, and nobody does it better than *Vogue*, but the net effect in this case is not at all obviously to throw freedom to fascism, as Walter Benjamin feared:

> *Fascism attempts to organize the newly created proletarian masses*
> *without affecting the property structure which the masses strive to elimi-*
> *nate. Fascism sees its salvation in giving these masses not their right,*
> *but instead a chance to express themselves. The masses have a right to*
> *change property relations; fascism seeks to give them an expression*
> *while preserving property. The logical result of fascism is the intro-*
> *duction of aesthetics into political life.*[13]

Benjamin, writing in the light of European politics, and of the then new technologies of mass communication like radio, cinema and the mass media, before and up to the Second World War, correctly discerned the political danger of Nazi mass mobilizations of the people:

> *All efforts to render politics aesthetic culminate in one thing: war. War*
> *and only war can set a goal for mass movements on the largest scale*

while respecting the traditional property system. This is the political formula for the situation. The technological formula may be stated as follows: Only war makes it possible to mobilize all of today's technical resources while maintaining the property system.[14]

This is powerful critique, not to be dismissed lightly. Whether it was so inevitable even in Benjamin's day is an open question, but certainly this critique, which has spawned a generation of Left pessimism that is not only burdened by the rhetoric of inescapable logic but also prone to presenting itself to its constituency with the least possible aestheticization (Michael Foot!), does not explain the situation confronted by and in *Vogue by Nelson Mandela*. Here we have an aestheticization of *revolutionary* politics, done in the name of a dispossessed people who are about to assume property rights for the first time; here we have an aestheticization of politics which is determined to *avoid* war, to mobilize today's technical resources to maintain the system so that the hitherto disenfranchised 'masses' can *enjoy* it. And here we have an aestheticization of politics where the outcome of mass mobilization (the election of an ANC-led government) is a foregone conclusion, and where the readership of *Vogue*, for whom all this aestheticization is done, represents the very wealthiest of the existing propertied classes, who are however being encouraged to approve, applaud, and alter their whole perspective on politics, but who don't even have a vote. Some new configuration of meaning-relations, if not property relations, is afoot in the mediasphere, and the obsessive binarization of public life into politics *versus* aesthetics, a move which confines 'politics' to talking heads and endless pictures of professional politicians entering and leaving doorways to the endless questions of professional political journalists, while confining 'aesthetics' to the women's page, is clearly – as John Wilkes, icon of press freedom, would say – fucked.

Voguing with Postmodernity

Postmodern political journalism, as evidenced by *Vogue by Nelson Mandela* (Fig. 5.1), seems to raise new questions about a new configuration of forces in the mediasphere. However, as I've been arguing all along, I think these forces are not so much new as newly noticed; they're a continuation of modernity by other means, as it were.

Here then is some of the topography of a mediasphere which takes as its opening theme not the *logic* of critique but the *beauty* of Nelson Mandela. It is as much about style (as befits *Vogue*), as about politics. But still it is about politics, since the issue is given over to a man who was seeking election to head a government; a man who, like the rest of his people, had never been allowed to vote in an election himself, and who had only recently been set free from 27 years in gaol for treason. It features a photo-essay of his first election rally, without mentioning the campaigns of the rival parties; in this

Fig. 5.1 Vogue by Nelson Mandela. Portrait by Tommy Motswai
(© French *Vogue* December 1993–January 1994)

sense it is 'biased' in traditional terms, but of course this is the politics of a whole people's freedom, and a moment of global hope and calm, where the usual politics of compromise is certainly happening, but is not the *point*.

But still it is about style. Relying on the *Vogue* reader's literacy in how to read *Vogue*, the 'signature' section is both tactful and shocking; following the conventional layout, sequence and form of *Vogue*, it builds from image and interview to politics and education (of the reader, about South Africa, but also of South Africa itself) in some of the most imaginative design and heart-stopping photojournalism I've ever seen. It does what *Vogue* does so well – it ravishes the eye, but this is exactly why it is so shocking, for the images that do so are from some other part of the semiosphere entirely; the part usually signified by the tradition of the victim in documentary photography and filming.

It marks the aestheticization of *radical* politics in a magazine read by the crowned (certainly the tiara'd) heads of Europe, not to mention the most upscale readership of all the 'glossy' magazines. It is therefore communicating (putting into the symbolic equivalence of dialogue) the politics of a person and organization whose constituency is the 70 per cent of South Africans who can simply be described as *poor*, to a readership which is *rich*, but nevertheless encouraged to approve, to participate, albeit not to vote.

It appears in a magazine the bulk of whose primary readers are women, in a part of the mediasphere where women readers tend to have the default-setting on literacy (though the politics of style is now respectable and commercially viable men's fare too, since *The Face*). Women are very prominent in both the production of the magazine and in its stories; the principal photography was done by Louise Gubb, and many of the stories and images from South Africa foreground women, not just as stylists but as activists. There's a piece on freedom of writing by Nadine Gordimer, South African novelist, while senior Paris *Vogue* editors Colombe Pringle and Brigitte Paulino-Netto write much of the copy and do the major interviews. Winnie Mandela, however, is not mentioned.

Vogue is a French monthly, but one which has global sales, and can be picked up at ordinary newsagents from Heathrow airport to Fremantle, which is where I bought it, without ceremony or fanfare, off the shelf, as just another consumer item alongside the groceries. In this planetary mediasphere the politics of South Africa is here and now, personal, and important to the globally dispersed 'citizens of media' – not of course with the practical imperatives experienced by voters in the RSA itself, but this is still powerful politics, providing post-national identifications to readerships whose allegiances are no longer defined by their territoriality.

Vogue's global permeability is also a matter of marketing, opening up trade lines along the songlines of the contemporary semiosphere. The French have literally capitalized their 'cultural capital' in style. Even if you don't speak French, or your local newsagent isn't as well stocked as mine, you can still get *Vogue*: there are versions for national markets in the USA, UK, France, Italy, Germany, Spain and Australia; and there are men's *Vogues* in France, Italy and Germany, children's *Vogue* in Italy (*Vogue Bambini*) and Spain, and specialist *Vogues* for house, garden, lifestyle, travel, wine, architecture, automobile. The parent Condé Nast Group also owns such stablemate magazines as *GQ, Brides, Glamor, Mademoiselle, Allure, Vanity Fair, Tatler* and *Details* in the USA, UK and Europe.

Like most 'glossy' magazines *Vogue* is astonishingly cheap per unit, considering the extreme capitalization of word, image, design and style that has gone into its production: in Australia the *Vogue by Nelson Mandela* issue cost A\$5.95 for nearly 300 pages (original price 40 French francs, which was F10 more than the then standard Paris *Vogue* cover price): six dollars in a town where at the time an espresso cost \$2, a book \$25, and cinema entrance \$20 for two, making *Vogue* the collectible bargain of 1994 in style journalism, photo-art and instant history.

Vogue by Nelson Mandela contains 30 pages (plus the back cover), of full-page colour advertising for jewellery; much of it featuring diamonds. There are 18 pages of editorial connected with jewellery, including a four-page publisher's promotion for South African diamonds (De Beers does not advertise in its own name). Is this just the normal hype for a pre-Christmas issue? Or is this whole issue of *Vogue* a bid to keep up demand for De Beers among the diamond-buying classes by personalizing and glamorizing the soon-to-be-elected communist-backed ANC government of South Africa? Is this journalism or sponsorship? – an open (but not necessarily a burning) question at the best of times in *Vogue*, which habitually runs brand-name promotions, and astute readers are used to seeing prominent ads for labels which feature in the fashion pages. It's all part of *couture* culture. For instance there's an ad for the South African Tourist Office and SAA airways. . . . In *Vogue*, it's not always clear who is the addresser, but readers know this already, and may choose simply to flip past the promotions to the more obvious propaganda.

This takes the form of 88 pages of the special Nelson Mandela 'signature' *Vogue* (plus the front cover), containing 20 different features. This section is sandwiched between two others which are dedicated to the same theme but not 'signed': a series of 22 news pages containing 16 stories under the overall heading of 'At the Heart of South Africa'; and a 27-page fashion section which takes into fashion itself the theme of peace and ethnic reconciliation, mixing black and white, north and south, tribal and chic, fashion and South African diamonds. The latter section opens with a four-page fold-out showing fifteen of the world's most celebrated and expensive fashion models spelling the name NELSON MANDELA a letter at a time on their T-shirts (Fig. 15.2). They are gathered to pay homage to Nelson Mandela's Nobel Peace Prize, although no mention is made of co-winner State President F.W. de Klerk. *Vogue* notoriously refuses to name fashion models, but makes an exception this time.

Égéries venues de tous les pays
pour présenter les collections à Paris, elles
se sont donné la main le temps d'écrire
son nom : Nelson Mandela. En hommage
au prix Nobel de la paix.

Fig. 5.2 *Hommage to Nelson Mandela.* Photograph by Ellen von Unwerth (© French *Vogue* December 1993–January 1994)

N = Nadja Auermann
E = Claudia Schiffer
L = Yasmeen Ghauri
S = Claudia Mason
O = Helena Christensen
N = Vera Atcholl
    'space' (sans T-shirt) = Naomi Campbell
M = Patricia Hartmann
A = Karen Mulder
N = N'Goné Sy
D = Georgianna Robertson
E = Heather Stewart-Whyte
L = Brandi Quinones
A = Yasmin Lebon
    'full stop' (singlet) = Stephanie Roberts[15]

che à droite : Nadja Auermann,
...fer, Yasmeen Ghauri, Claudia Mason,
...n, Vera Atcholl, Naomi Campbell, Patricia
...ren Mulder, N'Goné Sy, Georgianna
...ther Stewart-Whyte, Brandi Quinones,
...n Lebon, Stephanie Roberts.

Considering the reputed daily earnings of these top supermodels (five-figure sums in US dollars), and bearing in mind the production costs of getting all fifteen of them into the same photo-frame, their inhabitation of each letter represents the most extreme capitalization of language yet seen, I think (I doubt whether this shot, taken by Ellen von Unwerth, was commercially charged, but from the reader's point of view that is irrelevant, since the *value* is there on the page). All the models are giving the sign for victory (four months before the election), and the caption claims that 'Fashion is universal. Liberty is its name.'

Liberty, Fraternity, Irony?

The slogan of the French Revolution, on the lips of Nelson Mandela, is 'liberty, fraternity and equality for all ethnic groups'. The fashion

Fig. 5.3 'Liberty'. Photograph by Colin Paterson Jones (© French *Vogue* December 1993–January 1994)

Fig. 5.4 'Fraternity'. Photograph by Derek Hudson (© French *Vogue* December 1993–January 1994)

section of *Vogue* always begins with 'Vogue's Eye View' (and there's always a Gianni Versace ad on the facing page). Within such generic familiarity, there is room for maximum surprise. 'Vogue's Eye View' in *Vogue by Nelson Mandela* presents us with:

> *a man who has never submitted to the inadmissible. He is a man whose very existence is the living proof that one* is *beyond what one endures. He is a man who allows us to be proud of belonging to the human kind. . . . In the heart of South Africa resounds his name. While in the heart of our pages beats his love of freedom.*[16]

Time to turn the page; here's where *Vogue*'s opening fashion spread (fashion statement of the month) is to be expected. Instead, three double-page pictures, each captioned by a saying of Nelson Mandela. The first (Fig. 5.3): – LIBERTÉ: '"Let us speak of FREEDOM," says Nelson Mandela.' The picture is a blue seascape, with distant cliffs (Robben Island?), swooping gulls. Turn the page – as expected: FRATERNITÉ (Fig. 5.4). '"It was at Oliver Tambo's funeral, a time of great fraternal feeling. He was an admirable man, the head of the ANC in exile; he kept the world's attention focused on our people's suffering," says Nelson Mandela.' The picture shows part of the funeral crowd, many mourners hold pictures of Tambo (a busy, polychromatic picture to contrast with the serenity of 'Liberty'.). Turn the page – the expectation of 'ÉGALITÉ', by now fully in place, is thwarted. The caption reads 'DOULEUR' – 'PAIN' (Fig. 5.5). '"Pain has two faces: physical and psychological. But it should not be seen at the individual level only. It is a collective problem," says Nelson Mandela.'

Fig. 5.5 'Pain'. Photograph by Derek Hudson (© French *Vogue* December 1993– January 1994)

Douleur

"La douleur a deux visages: physique et psychologique. Mais elle ne doit pas être considérée d'une façon uniquement individuelle. C'est un problème collectif", dit Nelson Mandela.

The picture shows a weeping woman being assisted by two others – individualizing and collectivizing by the most effective visualization, transcoding her personal grief into the history of a nation. At this point, it is clear that politics has not abandoned *Vogue*: this is an active, not an archival, invocation of the French Revolution, differentiating the South African Revolution from the French by 'mistranslating' (in Lotman's sense) the two in order to produce a productive, dialogic asymmetry which is creative of meaning for readers on both sides of the conversation. Turning the page, it is less surprising to see the sequence continue with an Africanization of Mandela: IMPALA (Mandela's favourite animal, for its grace in getting out of difficult situations); LIMPOPO (the river where archaeological evidence of ancient African civilizations is to be found); LION (who respects anyone with self-confidence). And then the sequence moves into a standard interview with Mandela, where he declares his cultural synchronicity with the Enlightenment.[17]

There follows a sequence which is not to my taste at all – several features which emphasize tribal and ritual aspects of Xhosa and Zulu life; which make too much of Mandela's royal and tribal lineage; which show one or two more pictures than curiosity demands of half-unclothed Zulu women and full-frontal tribal initiates (male). However, even in this sequence the pictures maintain an asymmetric dialogue with the absent fashion shots that they both resemble and refuse; the costumes are clearly ceremonial and stylish, they are on that voguish cusp between youthful vigour and mannerism that suggests where some of the wellsprings of fashion iconography come from (racist rhetoric of the primitive, plundered for the ornamentation of the *jeunesse dorée* of Paris), rather than offering readers documentary truths about South Africans. This sequence ends with a description of the various ethnic groups in the 'Promised Land' of South Africa, over which Mahatma Mandela, a 'modern-day black Moses', presides as 'the man who would unite ethnic groups of every tongue and colour into a single mosaic, which will at long last constitute the people of South Africa, the first truly non-racial population on this earth'. In other words, against its own mystification of Mandela, the copy has to concede that he 'committed himself to all-out modernity, not to become a kinglet for his great Xhosa tribe', so by their own admission *Vogue*'s enthusiasm for tribalism flatly contradicts the purposes of the man they're lionizing, saying more about French 'taste' (or at least its most fashionable arbiter) than his 'destiny'.[18]

These 20 pages of ancestry and tribal wisdom are, as it happens, printed between portraits of the *modernist* Mandela – the shots accompanying his interview, and then at an ANC rally in Cape Town (both sets by Louise Gubb, to whom all praise). The interleaving of the tribal Mandela between vibrant shots of the political Mandela has a rhythm to it; sequentially the intervening pages are like a slow movement, letting the reader contemplate other motifs than the main theme, and tactfully indulging a not fully post-racist European

Dans le township l'Elsies River : rendez-vous au stade l'Avenwood. Au meeting de Mandela, les femmes viennent en famille et en costumes.

Fig. 5.6 Women come to ANC rally *'en famille* and in costume'. Photograph by Louise Gubb (© French *Vogue* December 1993– January 1994)

curiosity about the nature of tribal mysteries, so that turning the page at last to the first days of the election campaign in Cape Province comes as a shock – an aestheticization of politics which exceeds and contradicts the pessimism of those for whom reason and modernity cannot cope with beauty and emotion.

Fig. 5.6 of a woman wearing a large hat, however, shows that there is one more difference from the aestheticized politics which so alarmed the Frankfurt School; in South Africa the sartorial appropriation of political choice is done by the *public*, not by the politician (Mandela dresses in a conservative business suit). Here, it's the *crowd* that aestheticizes politics, wearing their most liberated costumes, making political rallies into all-singing, all-dancing, as well as all-voting affairs; linking joy and power, love and revolution, style and modernity, in a semiosphere where the united colours of the ANC, party of the most oppressed people on the planet, become the fashion statement of the season for the 'hautest' haute couture on the planet.[19]

There's a slip, unworthy of the impala-like grace which *Vogue* has so far shown in negotiating this tricky ideological terrain, but a slip that reveals what power and impact pictures can have in postmodern politics. Louise Gubb's pictures clearly and exultantly do a lot more than merely record the event; they are memorable images, and they show trust between the photographer and the people pictured, focusing on the iconography of the ANC, and on the engagement of the people present at the rally. There's not a hint of tribalism in them, but they are introduced with an editorial blurb by a senior *Vogue* staffer from Paris, who delivers herself of this:

> *From the depths of Africa's immemorial past they [a group of poetesses] invoke Mandela's ancestor king Sabata for proof of this illustrious candidate's royal blood. Tribal spirits are summoned forth in protection of their country and their chief.*[20]

Now this is the sort of nonsense to which the French Revolution was intended to put a stop, and *Vogue*'s editor-in-chief (copy) would have done better to promote Mandela as Prudhomme had suggested, 200 years earlier, on the recommendation of his 'good sense and virtues', not those of blood and spirits, which certainly don't play an official part in French presidential elections, as far as I know. Perhaps this is where caution about the aestheticization of politics is well placed, for it translates politics into nature, as Bertolt Brecht argued long ago:

> *It is precisely in the so-called poetical forms that 'the people' are represented in a superstitious fashion, or, better, in a fashion that encourages superstition. They endow the people with unchanging characteristics, hallowed traditions, art forms, habits and customs, religiosity, hereditary enemies, invincible power and so on.*[21]

This essentializing 'representation of the people' is given the racist tribal twist in the *Vogue* copy, but my point is that the picture-essay clearly and confidently contradicts all that mystical mumbo-jumbo, which equally clearly comes from Paris not Africa. And so I think it is not this poetic mystification which needs analysis, but the position of the discourse. Aestheticization isn't the problem, but presuming that the 'nature' of others belongs to them and not to the imaginary space of the speaker is a problem, a problem which doesn't need psychoanalysis to explain on the theoretical plane, even if Brigitte Paulino-Netto does do auto-therapy as journalism. Indeed, as Lotman has put it, and as can easily be corroborated by reading the first chapter of Freud's *Totem and Taboo*:[22]

No matter whether the given culture sees the 'barbarian' as saviour or enemy, as a healthy moral influence or perverted cannibal, it is dealing with a construct made in its own inverted image. It is entirely to be expected, for instance, that the rational positivistic society of nineteenth-century Europe should create images of the 'pre-logical savage', or of the irrational subconscious as anti-spheres lying beyond the rational space of culture.[23]

There's a great deal more in *Vogue by Nelson Mandela*, about which a great deal more could be said. However, since style journalism has not yet achieved the status of archive truth, and is not kept in scholarly or other libraries, it is doubtful that you can get hold of a copy to compare this analysis with your own readings; an addresser–addressee dialogue which is fundamental in cinema and literary studies. 'Popular reality' is not the common currency of scholarly writing, which means writers cannot take for granted that their readers will have seen, or at least have access to, the texts under discussion. Much as I'd like to offer a free back copy of *Vogue* with every copy of this book, I can do little more than list the contents before moving on for fear of overburdening this analysis with description. Not dealt with, then, are these features in *Vogue by Nelson Mandela*: an interview with Desmond Tutu; features on oppression; the pass-card; the history of the ANC; SOLIDARITY, VIOLENCE, and JOY in a format to recall and extend the opening 'liberty, equality, and pain', except that these are black and white, documentary photographs, and while SOLIDARITY and VIOLENCE feature women, JOY features a musician with a trumpet given to him by Louis Armstrong. There's a 'hymn' to Mandela's freedom, a feature on Willie Bester (artist), Johnny Clegg (singer), indigenous women's art and costumery, ritual objects, clothing decorated with safety pins, an article on 'a writer's freedom' by Nadine Gordimer (South African Nobel laureate for literature), and a feature on the future of schooling in the townships. In the (non-signature) 'At the Heart of South Africa' part of the magazine there are features on safaris, wines, Miss South Africa, trains, women athletes, personalities, Sun City, museums, galleries, the ANC's publicity agency, media, music, night life, Paul Simon, and literature. In the (non-signature) 'Point de Vue de Vogue' fashion section, in addition to the models' homage, there is a feature on 'Totems without Taboo' – fashion which mixes 'north/south' with 'east/west' motifs, the new '*enfants sauvages*' with dreadlocks, a fire-queen outfit with ivory bracelets from Burkina Fasso, and a 'soirée in the jungle' with that ultimate image of postmodernity, a photograph of a smell – the perfume on the skin of the model, named as 'Tribu' by, naturally, United Colours of Benetton.

Yannick Noah, a French tennis and singing star (who is black), and his girlfriend, the 'top top model' Heather Stewart-Whyte (who is white – and the 'E' in MANDELA in the models' homage), pose together 'for the first time' (i.e. newsworthily), out of 'love for

YANNICK ET HEATHER

LUI, C'EST YANNICK NOAH. DU TOP DU TENNIS, IL EST PASSÉ À LA MUSIQUE. DANS SON TOUT DERNIER ALBUM "URBAN TRIBU", UNE CHANSON, "HOT'N SPICY", DÉDIÉE À CELLE QU'IL AIME: HEATHER STEWART-WHYTE, 25 ANS, ANGLAISE ET TOP TOP MODEL.

Pour la première fois et "par amour pour la paix", ils posent ensemble.

Double Mixte

"Je suis un étranger au Cameroun,
le pays de mon père: je suis un "café au lait".
Je suis un étranger en France: là, je suis noir
dans la patrie de ma mère blanche.
Suivant le continent dans lequel je me trouve,
je suis ou blanc ou bien noir..."

PAR MARTINE DE MENTHON, PHOTOS DOMINIQUE ISSERMANN

Fig. 5.7 Yannick Noah and Heather Stewart-Whyte – 'mixed doubles'. Photographs by Dominique Isserman (© French *Vogue* December 1993– January 1994)

peace'. Their set shows not clothing but skin; interracial embrace, hands, eyes, and a kiss (Fig. 5.7).

Nelson Mandela himself literally signs off his 'signature' *Vogue* with a 'Message to Vogue Magazine', which is reproduced visually showing the ANC notepaper on which it is written, opposite a life-sized, in-your-face picture of the Nobel peace laureate, wagging his finger directly at you, reader, saying:

The promotion of peace and happiness throughout the world is one of the greatest challenges of the time. It is a goal we cannot achieve as long as millions continue to be ravaged by poverty, hunger, illiteracy, disease and other socio-economic problems. It is the obligation of all of us, the rich nations included, to help fight these evils, and to bring peace to the world. N.Mandela. 14-10-93.[24] (Fig. 5.8).

Chic Happens

Claudia Schiffer (the 'E' in 'NELSON') euphoricizes democracy in *Vogue*; like the other supermodels she is herself symptomatic of the democratization of fashion, and of its consequently increasing tendency to cross into the public domain of news-journalism – for example Schiffer is one of the few models (or Germans) ever to make the cover of *Time* (17 April 1995), on the occasion of New York opening of her Fashion Café (a joint venture with British model Naomi Campbell and Australian Elle Macpherson), for which she wore a new look by Italian designer Gianni Versace. Claudia Schiffer sublimates postmodern democracy, just as Friedrich Schiller once democratized the sublime in his 'Ode to Joy', a paean to universal fraternity which (via Beethoven's Ninth Symphony) now provides the European Union with its super-national anthem:

> *Seid umschlungen, Millionen!* I embrace thee, O ye millions,
> *Diesen kuss der ganzen Welt!* Here's a kiss for all the world.

This is the founding sentiment of modernity: the universal kiss.

Another of the founding moments of modernity, as we've seen in Chapter 4, was the so-called 'kiss of Lamourette', named after the deputy (whose own name translates as 'little love'), who caused battling members of the French National Assembly to kiss and embrace in 1792, momentarily delaying the more usual and more sanguinary resolution of political conflict.[25] And, as we've seen in this chapter, '*l'amour*' is still a powerful political force, the kiss a serious instrument in the initiation of political dialogue. It is a neglected component of the semiosphere, some of whose energies it clearly realizes. As Lotman so eloquently writes:

> *The semiosphere, the space of culture, is not something that acts according to mapped out and pre-calculated plans. It seethes like the sun, centres of activity boil up in different places, in the depths and on the surface, irradiating relatively peaceful areas with its immense energy. But unlike that of the sun, the energy of the semiosphere is the energy of information, the energy of Thought.*[26]

So it is with the kiss, and with the love that irradiates *Vogue by Nelson Mandela*. This media kiss bespeaks the seething energy of 'Thought' in the moment of its most intense cross-border dialogue, linking public and private, personal and national, the genders, strangers, races, and erstwhile enemies in fruitful difference and passionate translation, which like the lovers' kiss can be productive of radical changes, and whole new knowledges can be created that reconfigure the horizons of possibility for all who are bathed in its 'immense energy'.

But it is quite uncommon for the kiss, or '*l'amour*', to be considered analytically as part of the universe of 'Thought', not only because it is conventionally binarized in social theory as the *opposite* of thought (emotion, personalization, aestheticization, sensation, eroticization), but also because one of the things it provokes is a quite proper scepticism which is the birthright of every reader (I'll say nothing of lovers): doubt and distance unsettling desire even as lips meet. Perhaps this is why the contemporary political symbolic embrace often degenerates into a mere embarrassed handshake: Arafat and Rabin, Gorbachev and Reagan, Mandela and de Klerk. Certainly in cultural (not to mention political) studies the kiss is exiled to fiction, downgraded to the status of the cultural B-movie, where it flourishes but does not disturb. Meanwhile, the political kiss is more likely to be found credible if it belongs to the 'Kiss papa!

Fig. 5.8 Nelson Mandela talks to Vogue readers. Photograph by Louise Gubb (© French *Vogue* December 1993–January 1994)

Message To Vogue Magazine.

The promotion of peace and happiness throughout the world is one of the greatest challenges of the time. It is a goal we cannot achieve as long as millions continue to be ravaged by poverty, hunger, illiteracy, disease and other socio-economic problems. It is the obligation of all of us, the rich nations included, to help fight these evils, and to bring peace to the world.

MMandela   14. 10. 93

Promouvoir la paix et la joie à travers le monde est un des plus grands défis de notre époque.
C'est un but inaccessible tant que des millions d'entre nous sont encore dévastés par la pauvreté,
la faim, l'illettrisme, la maladie et tous les autres problèmes socio-économiques. Il est de
notre devoir à tous, pays riches compris, d'aider à vaincre ces démons, et d'apporter la paix au monde.
Nelson Mandela, le 14.10.93.

Le lendemain, le prix Nobel de la paix était attribué à Nelson Mandela.

Kiss papa!' genre of hatred and terrorism,[27] readable only as its opposite simply because 'reading politics' has developed into a NO KISSING zone, and it is part of journalistic literacy, understood by producers and readers alike, that kissing is confined to teenage magazines aimed at girls but not boys; there's a great deal about kissing in *Dolly* and *Girlfriend*, not very much in the *Australian Financial Review* (or whatever it is the boys read). For instance the April 1995 *Dolly* has a four-page feature on 'The Perfect Kiss'. It gives an eight-point guide on how to do it, celebrity first-kisses, guys to avoid, 'The Meaning of a Kiss' (anthropological, psychological, romantic), and 'weird and wonderful kiss facts'. It also offers these current teenage synonyms for kissing: 'tongue samba, sucking face, tonsil hockey, pashing off, swapping spit, lip locking, snogging, tonguie, smooching, frenchie, face mashing'.[28] While this specialization has left the way clear for a romanticization of the kiss, smothering it with hormones and giggles, the separation of '*l'amour*' from life, the public kiss from public affairs, has provoked in the adult press a characteristic response: *irony*.

Thus, in the same month that Paris *Vogue* published *Vogue by Nelson Mandela* (January 1994), its stable-mate *Australian Vogue* also published its own first-ever 'signature issue'. This one, however, chose a different location in the global semiosphere – the fictional, performative, dream-factory zone of the movies, opera, theatre, dance, and heaped irony on kitsch on joke on mannerist copy; in short, *Vogue by Baz Luhrmann, Catherine Martin and Bill Marron* camps it up like there's no tomorrow. Nancy Pilcher, *Vogue Australia*'s editor, explains:

> *What better way to begin a new year than with the inspiration of Australia's most creative team? That was our thought in inviting Baz Luhrmann, the director of* Strictly Ballroom, *and his design team Catherine Martin and Bill Marron to guest edit our first issue of the year.*[29]

The emphasis, then, is on Australia and creativity, specifically 'the creativity that makes us distinctly Australian and has the world sitting up and taking notice'. *Strictly Ballroom* was the international film success of 1992 for Australia, reinventing 'Australian' cinema as high camp (after it had toyed with high culture for a few years), inaugurating the 'Ballroom' age of *Priscilla, Queen of the Desert* and *Muriel's Wedding*. But before we turn to the page where 'Vogue's Eye View' should be expected, and discover someone there called 'Judy Lamour', a word or two on irony.

If political modernity begins with the irruption of 'The People!' into the public sphere with the storming of the Bastille in July 1789, then postmodernity is modernism with the private sphere of domesticity and the personal sphere of desire, Lotman's (and Rousseau's) 'language of smiles', put back in. By 1841 the philosopher Søren Kierkegaard was able to suggest that this postmodern connection between personal life and truth (science, philosophy) had a name: he called it irony.

In our age there has been much talk about the importance of doubt for science and scholarship, but what doubt is to science, irony is to personal life. Just as scientists maintain that there is no true science without doubt, so it may be maintained with the same right that no genuinely human life is possible without irony. . . . Irony limits, finitizes, and circumscribes and thereby yields truth, actuality, content; it disciplines and punishes and thereby yields balance and consistency.[30]

So for present purposes postmodernity is truth humanized with irony:

Particularly in our age, irony must be commended. In our age, scientific scholarship has come into possession of such prodigious achievements that there must be something wrong somewhere. . . . Furthermore, if our generation has any task at all, it must be to translate the achievement of scientific scholarship into personal life, to appropriate it personally.[31]

Hence the task of 'our generation' is to bring things together:

politics	*the kiss*	*journalism*
public sphere	mediasphere	semiosphere
science, philosophy	irony	personal life
intellectuals	readers, audiences	communities
Liberté	Égalité	Fraternité

The crowd that stormed the Bastille was transformed into the people by journalism, and 'The People!' of postmodernity are now, as ever, the readers and audiences of media – but today it's the journalism of the private sphere, of desire and the domestic, fashion and love, that calls the political public into being, and into certain kinds of action. The old-fashioned divisions between the public and the private sphere, male and female cultural domains, politics and fashion, news and entertainment, have to be rethought in the context of the postmodern media. The traditional political sphere of politics has progressively been privatized, feminized, suburbanized and consumerized over the present century, while the most important new political movements – e.g. environment, ethnic, gender, peace and youth movements – all originate in what used to be seen as the private sphere.

An argument about what this might mean would have to start by taking seriously places where desire and truth are recombined, using the cement of irony; where the personal, political, visual, sexual and domestic coalesce and kiss. Whether this coalition is in fact a new sort of political practice or even a new kind of textualized community, that scholars ought to try to understand, is a question that remains (for *you*, dear reader). But one thing is certain. The practice of irony, as a method of analysis which seeks to connect what is true to what is human, turns out to be quintessentially an *Australian* activity. Here's Kierkegaard again:

Anyone who does not understand irony at all, who has no ear for its whispering, lacks eo ipso [precisely thereby] what could be called the absolute beginning of personal life . . . He does not know the refreshment and strengthening that come with undressing when the air gets too hot and heavy and diving into the sea of irony, not in order to stay there, of course, but in order to come out healthy, happy, and buoyant and to dress again.[32]

Irony, then, the 'absolute beginning' of personal life, is undressing and surfing. And so, as Meaghan Morris has already done in *Ecstasy and Economics*, which combines a reading of Paul Keating (then Treasurer, later Prime Minister of Australia) with an essay on cultural studies, called 'On the Beach', we have solved the problem of method in cultural studies, with a symptomatic Australian gesture.[33]

Tongue in Chic

But what of Liberty, Fraternity, Equality? Here's Karl Marx on the events in Paris in 1848, after the overthrow of a restored French monarchy and the installation of a bourgeois-led provisional government. The slogans that liberated a nation in the revolution 60 years earlier return as farce, bringing to the body politic not the kiss but bitter irony:

But the workers were determined this time not to put up with any bamboozlement. . . . They were ready to take up the fight anew and to get a republic by force of arms. With this message, Raspail betook himself to the Hotel de Ville. *In the name of the Paris proletariat he commanded the Provisional Government to proclaim a republic; if this order of the people were not fulfilled within two hours, he would return at the head of 200,000 men. . . . Under these circumstances the doubts born of considerations of state policy and the juristic scruples of conscience entertained by the Provisional Government suddenly vanished. The time limit of two hours had not yet expired when all the walls of Paris were resplendent with the gigantesque historical words:*

République française! Liberté, Égalité, Fraternité!

. . . Only its defeat convinced [the Paris proletariat] of the truth that the slightest improvement in its position remains a utopia within the bourgeois republic, a utopia that becomes a crime as soon as it wants to become a reality.[34]

So continued a century of struggle based on opposing classes, opposing ideologies, and a Manichaean politics that was exported from Europe around the world, wherein those in power (such as the recently enfranchised bourgeoisie in France) set about criminalizing the *act* if not the desire for liberation among the popular classes. This division of the body politic into the most extreme 'Wedom' and 'Theydom' achieved its ultimate expression in the theories of a

VOGUE goes to the movies

Agnès B. cotton top, $145. Scarf from Twentieth Century-Fox. All prices approximate; details last pages. Hair by Max Pinnell for Bumble + Bumble, NYC. Additional hair by Mitch Stone and Dena Greene. Make-up by Francesca Tolot for Cloutier.

Baz Luhrmann, Catherine Martin and the *Vogue* Australia team flew to Los Angeles with Cathay Pacific, and stayed at the Hotel Nikko, Beverly Hills.

He captured Marilyn Monroe on film, shortly before her death, in a series that came to be known as The Last Sitting. Now, legendary photographer Bert Stern focuses his lens on Kylie Minogue in the classic rags-to-riches story of a Hollywood hopeful

JANUARY 1, 1969 **20** CENTS

Fig. 5.9 Kylie Minogue as Judy Lamour. Photograph by Bert Stern (© *Vogue Australia*)

professor of sociology called Dr Geoff Croisé, whose academic fantasies of racial binarization became known to the world as apartheid, which became state policy in South Africa in 1948–49, 100 years after Europe's 'year of revolutions'. The utopia of liberty, equality, fraternity, in the name of the French Revolution, was criminalized for non-whites, and in this context even to desire freedom was treason, resulting in death, exile and decades of imprisonment for those who expressed it.

Judy Lamour is a fictional character who 'began her life as Muriel Burrows, a girl from suburban nowhere'. Instead of 'Vogue's Eye View', *Vogue by Baz Luhrmann et al.* gives us a fake *Vogue*, dated 1 January 1969, containing 22 pages and 53 photographs of the 'lifestory' of Miss Lamour, shot by Bert Stern, the 'legendary photographer' who 'captured Marilyn Monroe on film, shortly before her

Both pages, Angus Strathie made-to-measure velvet jacket, cotton shirt, velvet pants and hat all in fabric from Linecraft. Skin Deep tie. Cane from The Vintage Clothing Shop. Chanel boots from the Chanel boutique.

ROCKY SCHENCK

Fig. 5.10 Nicole Kidman in Vogue-a-Vision. Photograph by Rocky Schenck (© *Vogue Australia*)

death, in a series that came to be known as 'The Last Sitting'.[35] This much, then, is true. As for Australian creativity, this Hollywood myth (rags to riches, triumph to tragedy) is not only an Australian dream in itself, since Australia belongs to the global semiosphere of English-language (American) cultural production, but also it does have a direct connection to Down Under, since 'Judy Lamour' is played by expatriate Australian singer and actor Kylie Minogue (for it is she) (Fig. 5.9).

And politics is not forgotten: the sequence showing the fictional Lamour at the height of her fame ('the dance sequences alone were a triumph'), has it that:

> *She would always remember her early years, particularly these scenes with comedian Hal Holiday, although she was never to work with him*

Fig. 5.11 Annita
Keating, Baz Luhrmann
and Paul Keating –
'Leading men'.
Photograph courtesy of
Baz Lurhmann (© *Vogue
Australia*)

*again. (Not long after the film opened, he quit acting to join the
Communist Party.)*[36]

Without pausing to think about Zero Mostel or Frank Hardy or Paul
Robeson, we race on to marvel at the way the team have transformed
Kylie Minogue from a Norma-Jean lookalike into a intriguingly
passable Judy Garland, and then into an ageing Joan Crawford, only
to find that they've done exactly the same to Nicole Kidman later
on in the magazine, using her world-renowned but Australian frame
to showcase clothes designed by 'the acclaimed Australian designer'
Richard Tyler, who now works exclusively in the USA.[37] This twenty-
four-page extravaganza in *Vogue-a-Vision* also gives the team their
front cover – a close-up of Ms Kidman in MGM musical costume,
blowing a kiss to the reader, who may well not recognize her, given
the unwontedly straight hair (Fig. 5.10). The kiss, however, is
undeniable.

In the news pages of *Vogue by Baz Luhrmann et al.* Baz descends
to his anecdotage in pursuit of stories about the 'leading men' with
whom he has worked (Fig. 5.11). One such is Paul Keating, Prime
Minister of Australia. It turns out that the Labor victory in the 1993
federal election was not only staged, but was a production directed
by Baz Luhrmann. Baz explains:

> '*After travelling around the world, I realised how much I loved it here,
> so I wanted to be involved in the 1993 election. At the opening of*

Fig. 5.12 Elena Meyer (South Africa) 'in the arms of her rival' Deratu Tuluy (Ethiopia) (Photograph Agence Vandystad, © French *Vogue* December 1993–January 1994)

Strictly *in Sydney, Keating had made a funny, warm speech . . . and of course he had learnt ballroom dancing. He was also the first person I had heard talk about the republic, which is something I've always wanted, even as a child. . .'. Following clandestine meetings in Canberra, Baz agreed that the team would help with the Labor campaign. 'It wasn't about creating a more glamorous image, it was about making him look more like his real self on television. It was one of the greatest opening nights of my life,' says Baz. Later, after victory was secure, the prime minister and Mrs Keating, Catherine Martin,*

A Report to the Nation from the Council for Aboriginal Reconciliation at the end of its first three years

A Council for Aboriginal Reconciliation Publication

Together we can't Lose

Cathy Freeman [right] and Melinda Gainsford lived up to Australia's best sporting traditions when Cathy won the gold medal and Melinda the bronze in the Women's 200 metres at the Commonwealth Games in Canada last year.

And they showed us how to win in other ways when they carried both the Australian and Aboriginal flags on their victory lap: as one nation proud of our diverse heritage.

This special feature is about how many other Australians are also winning as they work together to make their communities better.

Fig. 5.13 Cathy Freeman and Melinda Gainsford. Photograph taken by Fairfax Photography for the Council for Aboriginal Reconciliation. © Fairfax Photography

Craig [?] and Tara [Morice] and I went to a very small cafe in King's Cross to eat and read the papers quietly at dawn. It was like reading the reviews after the first night.[38]

Irony notwithstanding, then, it seems that parliamentary democracy is a theatrical production, and luckily for the rest of us Australia was bathed in the energies of *Strictly Labor* for long enough thereafter to produce a return to the politics of the kiss. It's also a return to *Vogue by Nelson Mandela*, not to mention the revolutionary 'kiss of

Lamourette', where what seems to be a generic image of the politics of ethnic reconciliation can be found. In the section of that *Vogue* entitled 'At the Heart of South Africa', one of the news pages is devoted to women athletes. It is illustrated by a striking photograph of Elena Meyer, (white) silver-medallist for South Africa at the Barcelona Olympics, 'in the arms of her rival, the Ethiopian Deratu Tuluy'.[39]

The two women are on the point of a kiss, which symbolically unites not only Africa black and white, but women the world over. In the same vein, the Council for Aboriginal Reconciliation, an office within the Prime Minister's portfolio in Australia, assisting in one of the Keating government's major political priorities, released its first 'Report to the Nation'. Characteristically of postmodern journalism, this was not a bureaucratic document but a zip-out insert in the *Australian Women's Weekly*.[40] The twelve-page document tag-lined 'A Council for Aboriginal Reconciliation Promotion', is an 'advertorial', promoting not diamonds but democracy, sponsored by the public purse in a magazine owned by Australia's richest man. It is headed 'Together we can't Lose', and among its stories is one about how sixteen journalists were taken to the remote Dhanaya outstation in far-north Arnhem Land to learn first-hand about Aboriginal life and culture. One of them comments, as if to illustrate Lotman's concepts of asymmetry and dialogue on the bound-aries of different cultural semiospheres, where the positions of 'receiver' and 'transmitter' of language alternate and mutual mistranslations eventually produce new meanings:

> We learned to be quiet . . . we learned humility. We learned to listen
> . . . we were taken, step by step, into another culture, another history.
> All of us found this new, confronting, alien, complex and compelling.
> During the final session, local Aboriginal people said they were
> dismayed that journalists were often ignorant of cultural differences,
> failed to seek Aboriginal opinions, and sensationalised and distorted
> issues.[41]

Thus it is journalists who occupy the position of Mr Interlocutor between the Aboriginal and the non-Aboriginal semiospheres, and it follows that the Council's aim of promoting the Mandelan utopia of 'justice and equity for all' demands that 'all of us need to get involved, particularly at grassroots level'. Significantly, the vehicle chosen to reach the grassroots of citizen readers, 'the Nation', is popular ('women's') journalism, and, incidentally, a marvel of Painite tact.

The image chosen to entice the *Australian Women's Weekly*'s reader's interest in the report on reconciliation is a large colour photograph of Aboriginal athlete Cathy Freeman, famous at the time throughout the Australian mediasphere not only for having won a gold medal at the 1994 Commonwealth Games in Canada, but also for having run her victory lap waving the Aboriginal as well as the Australian flag; a gesture of inclusion of Aboriginal people into the symbolic domain of national euphoria that was controversial at the time, though widely applauded, not least by the Prime Minister himself, who sent her a well-publicized fax to that effect. In the Council for Aboriginal Reconciliation's Report to the Nation, nothing seems to signify their purpose so well as a reminder of that day; but the image they choose is not just of Cathy Freeman winning, nor even of her victory lap. It is a picture showing her arm-in-arm with her Australian rival, Melinda Gainsford, who had come third in the same race in Canada (Fig. 5.13). The two smiling women, black and white Australians, are not only in each other's arms but also draped with their 'respective' national flags. As Nelson Mandela puts it, 'liberty, fraternity and equality for all ethnic groups': it's *Strictly Politics*.

Notes

1. Thomas Paine (1937, first published 1792) *Rights of Man: Being an Answer to Mr. Burke's Attack on the French Revolution*. Ed. Hypatia Bradlaugh Bonner. London: Watts, 121.
2. Yuri (Iurii Mikhailovich) Lotman (1990) *Universe of the Mind: A Semiotic Theory of Culture*. Trans. Ann Shukman with an introduction by Umberto Eco. Bloomington and Indianapolis: Indiana University Press, 127.
3. Lotman, 127.
4. Lotman, 203. Those who share my discomfort at the masculine generic name for humanity might wish to note that this translation is by Ann Shukman.
5. David Rollison (1995) Citizen Paine. *The Weekend Australian*, 10–11 June, Review section, 8. Rollison is reviewing John Keane (1995) *Tom Paine: A Political Life*. London: Bloomsbury.
6. Paine, 121.
7. Paine, 127–9.
8. *Vogue par Nelson Mandela: Paris Vogue*, 742, December 1993–January 1994. Subsequent references to this magazine are to '*Vogue* 742'. English translations of the 'signature section' are published as an insert in the same edition, opposite page 272.
9. *Les Révolutions de Paris* 63, 18–25 September 1790, 523–4. Quoted in John Gilchrist and W.J. Murray (1971) *The Press in the French Revolution: A Selection of Documents Taken from the Press of the Revolution for the Years 1789–1794*. Melbourne: Cheshire, and London: Ginn, 238.
10. Nelson Mandela, interviewed by Colombe Pringle in *Vogue* 742, 150–3.
11. Lotman, 127.
12. Robert B. Ray (1990) Postmodernism. In Martin Coyle, Peter Garside, Malcolm Kelsall, John Peck (eds.) *Encyclopedia of Literature and Culture*. London: Routledge, 131–47 (these quotations 137, 143).
13. Walter Benjamin (1973) The work of art in the age of mechanical reproduction. In *Illuminations*. Ed. Hannah Arendt, trans. H. Zohn. London: Fontana, 219–53, this quotation 243.
14. Benjamin, 243.
15. Hommage à Nelson Mandela, *Vogue* 742, 228–31.
16. Colombe Pringle, Point of view of Vogue, *Vogue* 724, 139.
17. *Vogue* 742, 140–9.

18. Promised land, by Alexandre Adler. *Vogue* 742, 172–3. This section also contains features on 'the wisdom of the tribe' (anthropology and costume), 'Madiba, fils de chef' (Mandela as a Xhosa child), and initiation ceremonies, which gives *Vogue* the excuse for three pages of photographs of naked young men.
19. Cape Town, Septembre 1993. Photos by Louise Gubb, copy by 'B.P.-N'. (Brigitte Paulino-Netto). *Vogue* 742, 175-81.
20. 'B.P.-N'. in *Vogue* 742, 175.
21. Bertolt Brecht (1977) Against Georg Lukacs. In E. Bloch *et al.*, *Aesthetics and Politics.* Trans. and ed. R. Taylor. London: New Left Books, 68–85, this quotation 80.
22. Sigmund Freud (1938, first published 1919) *Totem and Taboo: Resemblances between the Psychic Lives of Savages and Neurotics.* Harmondsworth: Penguin, Chapter 1, The savage's dread of incest, 15–40.
23. Lotman, 142.
24. Message to Vogue Magazine (handwritten) by Nelson Mandela. *Vogue* 742, 226–7.
25. See Robert Darnton (1990) *The Kiss of Lamourette: Reflections in Cultural History.* New York: W.W. Norton, xi–xiv and 17–18.
26. Lotman, 150.
27. See Darnton, frontispiece, xi and 13.
28. Alex Brooks, The perfect kiss. *Dolly*, April 1995, 67–9.
29. *Vogue Australia*, January 1994, 13.
30. Søren Kierkegaard (1989, first published 1841) *The Concept of Irony: With Continual Reference to Socrates.* Ed. and trans. Howard V. Hong and Edna H. Hong. Princeton: Princeton University Press, 326.
31. Kierkegaard, 327–8.
32. Kierkegaard, 326–7.
33. Meaghan Morris (1992) *Ecstasy and Economics.* Sydney: EMPress.
34. Karl Marx (1978) *Karl Marx: Selected Writings.* Ed. David McLellan. Oxford: OUP, 291.
35. *Vogue Australia*, 123–44.
36. *Vogue Australia*, 137.
37. *Vogue Australia*, 170–93.
38. 'Leading Men'. *Vogue Australia,* 78.
39. *Vogue* 742, 104.
40. Together we can't lose: a report to the nation from the Council for Aboriginal Reconciliation at the end of its first three years. Inserted in *Australian Women's Weekly* (which is a monthly, despite its title), February 1995.
41. Journalists go bush to listen and learn. CAR Report to the Nation, 7.

6 *The Postmodern Public Sphere*

(Suburbia)

Beyond the castle gates dinner was shared, as was love.[1]

Virtual Suburbia

I thought about the dear old telly, and what an education it has been to one and all. I mean, until the TV thing got swinging, all we uncultured cats knew next to nothing about art, and fashion, and archaeology, and long-haired music, and all those sorts of thing.   COLIN MACINNES[2]

This chapter is an account of the diffusion, suburbanization and sexualization of knowledge in a world of popular media. It is concerned with the knowledges that pertain to the development of what can be called the 'postmodern public sphere'; not so much knowledge of public affairs as traditionally defined, but new modes of knowledge which bespeak new ways of forming the public, and of communicating and sustaining what it means to be the public, in communities whose major public functions – the classical functions of teaching, dramatizing and participating in the public sphere – are increasingly functions of popular media, and whose members are political animals not in the urban forum but on the suburban couch; citizen readers, citizens of media.

In the twentieth century knowledge has dispersed and diffused, escaping and exceeding traditional distinctions such as these:

formal	informal
intra-mural	extra-mural
public	private
universal	particular
factual	fictional
real	illusory

The nineteenth-century fantasy of being able to collect all the facts, data and information from the world into a vast but ultimately coherent 'imperial archive', in Thomas Richards's phrase,[3] is no longer an incentive to revolutionary practices of scientific and literary innovation, but by now a nostalgic, reactionary, impediment to understanding what's going on (however, it is still a fantasy encrypted into the rhetoric and practices of a good deal of modernist intellectual and academic work).

At stake in this chapter is the question of what has happened to the public sphere in a world of private media during this period of diffusion. My argument is that like the imperial archive of knowledge, the public sphere is more real as fantasy, an ideal type, than as historical achievement; where it does exist it is in the virtual sphere of media, not the physical centre of town. The critical pessimism of twentieth-century social theorists who lament the passing of an informed, rational public sphere and the rise of popular entertainment media, has simultaneously overplayed the extent to which the Enlightenment public sphere was achieved as an institutional and socially pervasive reality, and it has also proven to be an impediment to understanding the role that the popular media do play in producing and distributing knowledge, visualizing and teaching public issues in the midst of private consumption, writing the truths of our time on the bodies of those image-saturated 'telebrities' whose cultural function is to embody, circulate, dramatize and teach certain public virtues within a suburban cultural context. The virtues in question are feminized, private, personal, 'consumeral' (not consumer*ist* for there's no formal ideology involved); I think that between them they are not only the virtues of suburbia, but also the future of democracy, for good or ill. However, they are hard to recognize within an intellectual tradition that tends, often unwittingly, to favour:

origins over destinations
producers over consumers
urban over suburban
male over female
the voice of authority over the *vox populi*
truth over desire
word over image
printed archive over popular screen

Contemporary suburbia is the physical location of popular reality, a newly privatized, feminized, suburban, consumerized public sphere. But suburbia is itself a diffused and dis-located phenomenon (i.e. not tied to a regional location but generalizable even across continents). Nevertheless the home and suburb, together with their associated institutions (shopping centre, family, media) and practices (dressing and congregating; looking, listening and talking), constitute the place where and the means by which public, political knowledges are not only circulated and consumed but recreated, generalized and personalized. The postmodern (media) public sphere, which like suburbia itself is not a place at all, is the locus for the development of new political agendas based on comfort, privacy and self-building. I would argue that the major contemporary political issues, including environmental, ethnic, sexual and youth movements, were all generated *outside* the classic public sphere, but that they were (and are) informed, shaped, developed and contested within the privatized public sphere of suburban media consumerism. And so suburbia emerges from this discussion not as a place you can walk into (an oft-noted 'problem' of actual suburbs), but as an image-saturated space which is both intensely personal (inside peoples' homes and heads) and extensively abstract (pervading the planet). It's where personal, family, political and cultural meanings are reproduced – a place where people make themselves out of the semiotic and other resources to hand.

There is clearly a problem of method associated with the investigation of such a phenomenon, given both the irreducible particularity of certain images and places, and the abstract or 'virtual' character of the mediated public sphere of contemporary suburban citizenship. The problem is compounded by the poor reputation enjoyed by both suburbia and the media in Western intellectual traditions. But whether pessimism about popular culture is in fact inspired by a fear of losing control of the teaching, preaching and speeching functions enjoyed by the 'knowledge class'[4] since at least medieval times, and whether popular disengagement from regular politics is evidence of the demise of democracy, or instead, of its extension into areas previously hidden from what Ernesto Laclau and Chantal Mouffe have identified as its own 'logic of equivalence'[5] – these strike me as empirical questions, requiring observation and assessment of evidence.

However, the form that 'empirical evidence' takes in this media-saturated, textualized 'semiosphere' is itself discursive and textual, and it is personal as well as public life that needs to be explored. Of course this chapter doesn't pretend to solve these problems of method, but it does address them – from a 'textualist' perspective. *En route* it will tend to wobble without warning (but not without purpose) between two of this planet's most suburbanized cultures, Britain and Australia. It is part of my argument that the cultural boundaries of contemporary society are no longer confined, if they ever were, to the physical and territorial frontiers of localities like suburbs, or of spatial entities like nations. On the contrary, the cultural 'universe', and suburbia within it, is much better conceptualized using Yuri Lotman's concept of *semiotic* space, the 'semiosphere', which (like its twin concept of 'the biosphere') signifies a whole planetary unit within which all the immense variety and difference of meaning is organized, differentiated, cross-fertilized, and related.[6] Lotman says of the semiosphere:

Humanity, immersed in its cultural space, always creates around itself an organized spatial sphere. This sphere includes both ideas and semiotic models and people's recreative activity, since the world which people artificially create (agricultural, architectural and technological) correlates with their semiotic models. There is a two-way connection: on the one hand, architectural buildings copy the spatial image of the universe and, on the other hand, this image of the universe is constructed on an analogy with the world of cultural constructs which mankind creates.[7]

Dialogue or translation between asymmetrical and binarily opposed spatialized areas, such as urban and suburban space, intellectual and popular knowledge, 'high' and media culture, even British and Australian suburbia, is incessant and creative, according to Lotman, who says that there is 'constant transcoding of spatial images into the language of other models. The result is the complex semiotic mechanism which is in constant motion.'[8] Such a dynamic, dialogic concept of meaning requires attention not only to the way suburbia appears in itself, but how it is connected to other semiotic, spatial, intellectual and architectural spheres; how meaning generates spatial arrangements (like actual suburbs), which then impinge on meaning; and how the virtual, semiotic sphere of culture both generates and cohabits within the physical, architectural space of suburbia.

Hedgemony

The most successful suburb was the one that possessed the highest concentration of anti-urban qualities: solitude, dullness, uniformity, social homogeneity, barely adequate public transportation, the proximity of similar neighbourhoods – remoteness, both physical and psychological, from what is mistakenly regarded as the Real World. . . . The suburban experience, with its pattern of commuting, its jealously tended gardens and its separating hedges, its tedium and its isolation, its cosiness and its dominating domesticity would become the normal mode of existence for the Londoner and the Englishman at large.

DONALD J. OLSEN[9]

Like the imperial archive of knowledge, and the media that popularize(d) it, suburbia is a Victorian, and therefore also an imperial invention,[10] leaving its mark from Poona to Purley, often in the apt domesticated-imperial form of the *bungalow*. As Georges Duby has noted, 'the idea of *privacy* . . . first emerged in the nineteenth century in England, at the time the society that had progressed furthest in the establishment of a "bourgeois" culture'.[11] Suburbia is therefore a phenomenon of modernism and realism, developed to solve the problem of what to do with the large numbers of white-collar workers needed for petty control functions and professional, technical and clerical labour in the imperial capital of London, while providing (and providing for) a positive/progressive value system which put privacy, comfort, family life, self-development and stability above the attractions of urban or collective culture. From the start suburbia attracted hostile comment from all the usual sources, ranging from journalism to high theory:[12] social theorists, cultural commentators, professional planners, architects, aesthetes, philosophers, environmentalists, economists – no one seems to have had a good word for suburbia.

Politically, suburbia has been blamed for creating an apathetic, reactionary, conservative, conformist, status-conscious, petit-bourgeois class whose members are incapable of organizing anything for themselves, but who are prey to demagogues, propaganda and media influence, forming the bedrock of passive support for authoritarian, anti-democratic, even fascist politics.

Economically, suburbia is reckoned wasteful – an unproductive domain of pure consumption which contributes nothing to His Majesty The Economy (Althusser's phrase), or to the wealth of nations (Adam Smith's phrase), except the cost of housing itself, which formal economics dismisses as a non-productive sector anyway, unlike the macho sectors of manufacturing and primary industry.

Environmentally, the suburbs are vilified for sprawling all over the countryside, filling it up with tarmac, cars and concrete while encouraging its inhabitants to live lifestyles oozing with garbage, plastic, toxins and tins.

Socially, suburbia is the place where society falls apart into atomized individualist nuclear families, isolated from each other and from community co-operation.[13] As Thomas Sharp put it in 1940: 'Now, Suburbia . . . is socially sterile. . . . It involves its inhabitants in a great waste of time and money and energy in journeying to and fro. . . . And especially . . . its spreading means the eating up of great areas of valuable agricultural land and the banishment of the countryside. Suburbia is essentially selfish and anti-social in this respect.'[14]

Sexually, suburbia is where women's subjugation to the 'feminine career' is secured, tying them to housework, child rearing, and abuse;[15] it's also the site of sexual perversity, domestic violence, incest and anorexia.[16] Colin MacInnes put the case in 1959: 'In Soho, all the things they say happen, do. . . . And what's more, although the pavement's thick with tearaways, provided you don't meddle it's really a much safer area than the respectable suburban fringe. It's not in Soho a sex-maniac leaps out of a hedge on to your back and violates you. It's in the dormitory sections.'[17] Suburbia is also where patriarchal men subside into boozy stupor in front of the TV, never lifting a finger to cook, clean, or do childcare, doing a bit of DIY on a weekend, trimming the hedges to keep up appearances.

Aesthetically, suburbia is unstylish, twee, naff, genteel, dull, desolate, ugly, and getting more so, it seems. In 1925 P.G.

Wodehouse wrote of 'the early morning patois of Suburbia, which is the English language filtered through toast and marmalade', while in 1967 McLuhan and Fiore wrote of 'darkest suburbia and its lasting symbol: the lawnmower' (*OED*). In 1992 Graeme Turner, who calls it 'Suburbia verité', says that *Sylvania Waters* (of which, more later) 'is often just plain ugly, because the ideologies which surface in "private" conversations and behaviours are unrepentantly consumerist, racist, xenophobic, homophobic, and sexist'.[18]

Spiritually, Walter Murdoch, after whom Murdoch University is named, pronounced 'the suburban spirit' the 'everlasting enemy'. In 1921 (while living in Suburban Road, South Perth) he described 'the awful sameness of Melbourne's suburban streets, with their red-tiled houses, neat lawns, gravel paths, *Pittosporum* hedges, reflecting a uniformity of spirit, a complacency, a positive fear of originality or difference'.[19] Or, as T.W.H. Crosland put it in 1905, 'Man was born a little lower than the angels, and has been descending into suburbanism ever since.'[20]

Dramatically (yes!), here's the town-and-country planner Thomas Sharp again:

> *In any case, even if Suburbia had not the fatal faults that it so obviously has in its social sterility, its aesthetic emptiness, its economic wastefulness, where is the point in sacrificing the invaluable dramatic contrast of the two old utilities [of town and country] for one simple neutrality?*[21]

Philosophically, in the best (i.e. classical) tradition of binary thinking – which (no matter how often it is criticized by professional philosophers) is still widely used in ordinary conversation, in media representations and popular social criticism alike to classify the world and thus make sense of it – the suburbs ought not to be there at all. They are an offence to binary logic, being neither city nor country. They're an in-between, both urban and not urban at once, a logical impossibility, being a third term in a two-term universe. As Lewis Mumford put it in 1922, suburbia is made of 'dormitories where . . . life is carried on without the discipline of rural occupations and without the cultural resources that the Central District of the city still retains' (*OED*).

Bereft of both 'discipline' and 'cultural resources', if suburbia does figure in any binary system of thought with wide currency and respectability in intellectual traditions, it is on the wrong side of the fence in a *hedgemonic* system of oppositions (if I may put it that way) which serve to separate the field of knowledge-production and social actions understood as 'free', from the field of information consumption and social existence understood as 'manipulated', or at best 'produced'; for example, using some of the key terms of this chapter:

imperial archive	(mass) media
public sphere	suburbia
good repute	no repute

Suburbia is also, historically, the habitat of the social class with the lowest reputation in the entire history of class theory, the social class that attracts no love, support, advocacy or self-conscious organization: the petit bourgeoisie, the lower middle class, the class for whom it seems hardest (certainly it's very rare!) to claim pride of membership. Scholars scarcely venture into suburbia except to pathologize it, despite the fact that by some accounts intellectuals themselves occupy a petit-bourgeois speaking position.[22]

Diversion: A Suburban Bus Trip

Even more unusual has been the development in London of what are perhaps the only really loved buses in the world.[23]

While suburbia hasn't fared well in formal intellectual and academic thinking, it has sometimes done better in government policy discourses. In Australia for instance it is a generation since Gough Whitlam was elected to office to lead a government which owed some of its electoral success and continuing reputation to the fact that Whitlam had developed policies specifically addressed to the suburbs – housing, education, health, infrastructure, sexual equality. An especially able academic theorist of suburban development is Hugh Stretton, whose radio Boyer Lectures in 1974 were entitled *Housing and Government*. Stretton argues for the importance of the domestic economy (unwaged work) as well as the commercial one, and points out that not only do people use their homes for all sorts of productive and creative activities which are recognizably 'suburban', but also that 'formal culture' often originates in suburbia – writers, composers, painters and so on do their work at home, and their followers do much of the work of enjoying culture in the same place. 'That's where most people now hear most music, read most books, see and hear most drama, read and see and hear most of the world's news and most of the analysis and commentary on it.' Furthermore, Stretton points out that such energetic engagement in public culture does not confine people to their homes but propels them out, into the city and the country, where 'public community and city life' continues, supported by those whose interest is stimulated by home consumption.[24] These ABC radio talks (the Australian equivalent of the BBC's Reith Lectures) were addressed directly to the Whitlam government while simultaneously broadcasting their message to an electorate listening at home – a good example of the mediated public domain at work – making suburban policy a matter of 'high' political debate at a critical period of cultural change. But somewhere along the line the plot was lost, and 'high' political commitment to fully theorized suburban culture slowly ebbed away.

However, the traffic may again be increasing, and it comes from rather an unexpected place. In Australia, as in other countries in the

English-speaking intellectual semiosphere, there has been a continuing debate about the politics and utility of theoretical work in the humanities area of the academy, and specifically in cultural studies. One of the turns that this controversy has taken in the decade of the late 1980s and early 1990s is known in Australia at least as the 'cultural policy debate', associated with the work of Tony Bennett in particular. One aspect of this debate has been for those who are interested in the *utility* of cultural analysis to turn away from 'high theory', textual criticism, political critique of state apparatuses, and instead to analyse governmentality in its cultural mode, with a view to making theoretically informed but practical and pragmatic interventions in the development of social policy within the sphere of culture. Meanwhile, some writers, notably Ian Hunter, have focused a powerful critique on the ethics of academic humanities work itself, contesting the assumption of the mantle of the 'universal intellectual' by cultural critics, and suggesting more modest, bureaucratic aims and procedures for those of us who work in what are after all state/cultural institutions (universities). Others involved in the 'cultural policy debate' began to conduct an intense dialogue with the 'ideological state apparatuses', becoming involved in the formulation of official policies in relation to broadcasting, the arts, multiculturalism, Aboriginal reconciliation, and so on. It is in this rather superheated context, for the cultural-policy-wallahs were by no means uncontested within the intellectual community, that a new interest in suburbia began to develop among certain followers of the 'policy' camp. Colin Mercer, for example, Director of the Institute for Cultural Policy Studies which had been founded by Tony Bennett as the spearhead of the 'policy push', acted as a consultant for the new city of Joondalup in Western Australia to help it develop a cultural policy in relation to the design and orientation of its civic buildings (i.e. which way should a shopping centre face: *inwards* to the malls, or *outwards* to the street?). Suddenly, Foucauldian theories of governmentality met practical questions about where suburban developers should put the lamp-posts.

Such an encounter was bound to end in bathos. But on the way, suburbia re-entered intellectual debate in the humanities. The 'policy moment' provoked Denise Meredyth for instance, to lambaste what she saw as the hegemonic regime of 'universal intellectuals' in relation to academic cultural studies, and to argue for 'the mundane, laborious and often boring investigation of the actual composition' of the 'zones of social administration':

> *This kind of investigation may involve a descent from the peak of cultural critique and a willingness to explore the social spaces surrounding the arts faculty at ground level. It might also involve admitting that these areas stretch beyond the horizon of 'critical vision' and into the sprawling areas of public administration, social welfare, popular schooling and citizenship. Still, even if it may not suit the urbane tastes of the universal intellectual, there is a lot to look at on a bus trip to the suburbs.*[25]

Her 'bus trip to the suburbs', then, is not a tourist but a works bus, taking planners, service-providers, and the odd protesting cultural critic to those 'sprawling areas' of public administration, social welfare, popular schooling and citizenship. Despite her aim to redress the historic prejudice of 'critical vision' against everyday life, however, Meredyth's project retains a half-apologetic, half-truculent tone which does little to suggest why anyone *other* than bureaucrats would want to get on the bus in the first place. In fact, her purported attempt to retheorize suburbia in relation to cultural studies adds up to a desire to reinstate purely sociological categories and social-work priorities, and to cause 'universal intellectuals' to see the error of their ways from the vantage point of the 'bus trip to the suburbs'. That such a 'universal' critic as Meaghan Morris (to name but one) has been theorizing culture from the perspective of feminized subur-bia and ordinary life during her entire career seems to have escaped Meredyth's attention.[26]

But this encounter between cultural studies, cultural policy and suburbia is important, and of more than locally Australian signifi-cance (though of course any specific policy debates are bound to be localized), because what is at stake here is not only the future of suburbia itself as a policy object, but also the future of cultural analy-sis. It is indeed important for cultural critics to take account of ordinary life, but equally it is vital that the agenda for such an account is not monopolized by the existing concerns of social planners and service-providers. One of the things that cultural studies can claim to have taken seriously is the existence and nuances of *popular culture* in all its amazing textual and performative variety, and this of course is the very culture that thrives so vigor-ously in suburbia. In short, cultural studies has been 'exploring the social spaces surrounding the arts faculty at ground level' for thirty years. In the context of a newly burgeoning 'policy' interest in subur-bia in the humanities, then, it is important not to forget all this as we peer out of the window on our dreary bus ride with the running commentary of 'public administration, social welfare, popular schooling and citizenship' dinning in our ears.

In fact I would propose not this fictional daytrip but a *virtual* one, not 'a bus trip to the suburbs', because that would only show the front gardens (an experience I can only describe as *lawnnui*), whereas, as everyone knows, the interesting bits of suburbia are round the back or inside the house, well out of sight of busloads of tourists, which is why such buses never go there. We need a differ-ent means of communication, one that might provide the sightseer with better visual evidence of the internal life therein, a means of communication which Terence Hawkes is bold enough to call *art*:

> *This is to see art as one of the major activities through which a society 'means'. . . . What, for instance, do we mean by 'man', by 'woman', by 'duty', by 'justice', by 'nation', by 'honour', by 'marriage', by 'love'? These are far from simple issues, yet our whole way of life depends on*

our answers to such questions: they give our culture its distinctive identity at a particular historical juncture.[27]

The art Hawkes himself investigates is popular drama, but such questions are posed by and within other media, both factual and fictional, especially popular journalism. To study the art of popular culture and the communications media is, in this view, to pose questions which are at once mundane (of everyday life) and of a high order of importance at the intersection of the personal (man, woman, marriage, love) and the social (duty, justice, nation, honour). The challenge to this position is of course its person-centred humanism (its questions about 'man . . . woman'), and so even to ask such questions has been seen as inappropriate. For instance, Ian Hunter argues that the 'humanist' tendency to ask questions about the essence of the self in the tradition of the universal intellectual 'takes the principles of modern humanism far too seriously', resulting in a 'Kantian' defence of 'the humanities academy' as a 'timeless bastion of ultimate principles . . . as the voice of humanity demanding that the state live up to the principles on which it should be founded'. Instead of treating the humanities as the seat of 'principled opposition to the state', says Hunter, we should avoid 'moral grandiloquence' and 'resist the temptation to see further or deeper than the institutional forms'.[28] Instead, 'moral competence' for the job is, Hunter recommends, demonstrated by 'self-abnegation, strict adherence to procedure, and dedication to professional expertise'.[29]

Such an adherence to procedure may offer some guidance on the ethics of bureaucratic provision for suburbia, but it is hopeless as a means of finding out what suburban culture 'means' from the inside, and useless as a means to discipline the chorus of critics whose pejorative views on suburbia I have catalogued earlier. The no-nonsense, common-sense, down-to-earth approach is also quite unsuited to academic research where the object of the exercise is not to take suburbia at face value, or as a self-evident reproach to the wankers from the arts faculty, but to see whether something is going on there that we (academic cultural studies) *don't* already know about, something for which we *don't* have an existing 'procedure' or 'expertise' (a bus trip won't show us the semiosphere); in short whether the 'sprawling areas of social administration' have anything to offer academic intellectual inquiry in relation to Hawkes's questions about art. Meredyth and Hunter leave media, culture, even commerce entirely out of account in this 'zone', which is a pity, for considering what '*a society*' means by such questions as those posed by Hawkes may turn out to be something quite different from residual Renaissance humanism, for the critical theorization of art since the 1960s (conducted by those much-maligned universal intellectuals) has radically destabilized any ideology of 'the essence of the self'. What's sauce for Derrida is sauce for suburbia, for it is here that media, culture, commerce and communication *produce* selves, and here that what contemporary 'society "means" by . . . man . . . woman . . . duty . . . justice . . . nation . . . honour . . . marriage . . . love' gets sorted out, or not, on a daily basis.

My alternative tour of suburbia, then, via popular media and images that are designed for suburban readerships, is a *virtual* voyage of exploration, looking for evidence of meaning-formation that may previously have escaped the attention of cultural critics, be they universal or bureaucratic. I think I've found it too, and present it in Chapter 7 – evidence that, welling up within the medium of suburban popular culture itself, there is a different kind of public sphere (media readership), with a different kind of logic (the glance), with a surprising but simple mechanism for calling the public together (which I will emblematize as 'the frock' to signify the means by which meanings are conveyed through semiotic systems which are visual, bodily, social, and manufactured rather than personal), and a secret weapon to overcome the prejudice of respectable critics (sexualization). This is the subject of the next chapter.

Frocking Suburbia

At the outset of our trip, though, let it be said that none of this may be new; the convergence of sex and suburbia was noted right from the start, in the nineteenth century, though naturally only to be denounced:

> *The* Building News *in 1875 condemned the 'want of taste and frequent extravagance' in the architecture of the London suburbs: . . . 'It is the pushing to extreme the more sensuous elements of our architectural styles . . . We see the same tendency in women's attire, and among the less educated tastes of every class of society.'* [30]

After more than a century, in the place where houses are frocks and the 'tastes of every class' have escaped the discipline of education, it may be timely to look at things from the point of view of the 'more sensuous elements', whence it may be possible to glimpse the internal meanings and knowledges of suburbia. However, it has to be noted in advance that such internal knowledges and meanings are already translated into the ironic, kitsch, joking, camp, self-referential parts of the semiosphere, where suburban archetypes which display the *most* 'want of taste and frequent extravagance' already enjoy a curious inversion of their poor repute. Now that style is a form of cultural politics, the style police have begun to pay suburbia the compliment of the send-up, taking on board some of its internal meanings and knowledges by overcoding them (making 'less educated', unselfconscious styles self-reflexive and foregrounded).

But in order to get suburbia out of the specialized *Building News* (which is of course already a translation of suburbia into journalism), and into the generalized semiosphere, a crucial change has to be effected: these meanings have to be *personalized* and *performed*, translated from their position as the objects and surroundings of everyday life into human characters and actions which can be transmitted through the mediasphere. Personalization and performance can be (and is) done across the whole range of popular culture, especially in the entertainment media of pop music, dance, TV shows and fashion, but a crucial role is played by journalism in translating the 'meaning' of a particular singer, show or style into the 'mores' of the season. This is where the 'tendencies in women's attire', noted by *Building News* in the nineteenth century, connect not only with 'architectural styles' as such but also with questions of 'sensuousness', 'taste' and 'education' across 'every class of society'. Only journalism can make such far-flung, cross-demographic, crossdisciplinary connections as these; for while fiction, fantasy and crossdressing are all active in the same area, they do not have the property enjoyed by journalism of counting as true, nor do they have the accepted cultural function of translating and explaining the different parts of the semiosphere to each other. Thus, to pursue the question of 'suburban taste' it is necessary to venture into the social imaginary, not the suburbs, and there to look for the persons and performances that journalism latches on to in order to visualize and verbalize what is going on.

One British icon of feminized suburbanism is the so-called 'Essex girl'. Essex girls won pride of place – a cover-mention – in *The Face*'s review of 1991. That year 'Essex girl' jokes were all the rage, as were their clothing choices and favourite pop stars. Their contribution to fashion for the season was given the thumbs-down by *The Face*: 'shell suit Shauns and Lycra Lindas' were relegated to its 'Best We Forget' column.[31] As (in its own estimation) the world's greatest style magazine, *The Face* could hardly bring itself to share Essex girl jokes with its readers, but in the year of the coup against the President of the Soviet Union it gestured to the genre with this: 'Q – What do Gorby and an Essex girl have in common? A – They both went on holiday and got (that's enough, *Ed*).'[32]

'Essex girl' is a taste/class category, denoting lack of both, applied to young working women from outer metropolitan suburbs (in Australia they'd be 'Westies'), who became culturally visible as their spending power began to outstrip the readiness of urban(e) stylesetters to accept their purchasing choices. Notorious for what they do in cars – the sort of naff cars travelling salesmen and company reps drive – Essex girls get fucked, literally, or (like Gorby on holiday) metaphorically. 1991 was not only the year of their joke (which was also generic – outside Britain they circulated as 'blonde jokes'), but also their sitcom, *Birds of a Feather* (pron. 'fevvah'), which explored the domestic space between petit-bourgeois suburban respectable Essex girls and crime, petty or otherwise, as the two sisters cope with the vicissitudes of a comfortable lifestyle while their blokes are in the nick, banged up (to rights) for armed robbery.[33]

Meanwhile, in a revenge of the Essex girls of the world, 'one of the most bizarre phenomena to have struck the cities of Australia for quite a few years' was noticed on other pages of the same review-of-1991 issue of *The Face*, and it's another form of petty larceny – taking without consent the sound, songs, looks, style *and audiences* of various musical acts whose members may or may not still be alive. The so-called 'tribute acts', pictured frolicking on Bondi Beach, Kierkegaard-style (see Chapter 5) include Rosemary 'Madonna', camped-up 'Village Girls' (Village People) and a trio of cross-dressing, six-foot male Kylie Minogues. Other well-known (internationally successful) Australian tribute acts include Australian Cure and Bjorn Again (Abba). These acts, already full of ironic overstatement, on the cusp between homage and horror, are of course denounced by observers as contemptible: '"I think it's a sad crappy idea, but criticizing them is like picking on little fluffy animals – they're just giving the public what it wants"',[34] . . . but then these young contemptibles also turn out to be the ultimate reality: they make money (they can fill aircraft hangars, while 'real' groups can't get an audience at all). The *Face* article closes with this ironic tribute to 'freeze-dried nostalgia': '"It's just giving the public what they want, love," says Glen, the six-foot bloke who is the mastermind and star of the Kylie show. And who can do better than that?'

The tribute groups excel, however, in the very areas of pop style that are already the most exuberantly faked. Madonna fakes femininity in a kind of critique by flaunting; the Village People celebrate he-man stereotypes by camping them up. But then they're refaked by the Village Girls, and Rosemary fakes Madonna's most made-up metonymic attributes.

During this same period (mid-1991) the real Kylie Minogue, already an accepted journalistic style icon of Australian suburbanality, revamped her own image. Just as Madonna's self-worshipping *In Bed With Madonna* was doing the rounds, so the authentic 'little fluffy animal' of the pre-teen pop market pupated into a vamp, becoming a fake in the process. 'Raunchy Kylie', squealed the cover of *TV Week*, 'I'm not trying to do a Madonna!'[35] 'Kylie Remade', cooed the cover of *The Face*, 'too sexy!' Translation was complete: 'In bed with Kylie: Miss Minogue reveals more. . .'.[36] 'Nothing is original', sighed Kylie Minogue. And didn't *The Face* know it; the first item of copy in this issue was a reader's letter berating the magazine for a previous cover picture of actor Patsy Kensit, and wondering sarcastically whether the next unworthy covergirl would be Kylie Minogue (clearly understood as the limit-case of absurdity), but of course it was indeed her face on the cover.

Even the status of her photo-set was blurred, being art, fashion, celebrity and irony all at once. It was a nine-page celebrity spread with full (and curiously positive) interview by Chris Heath, but it was not mere publicity. The pictures were taken by Andrew Macpherson, a photographer whose long set on New York drag queens was featured in the same issue, a theme whose exuberant sex-fakery carried over to his pix of the singer in the baby doll dress on the hotel bed. . . . Art or publicity, the set was also fashion – all the clothes she wore were labelled and priced in standard fashion captions. Kylie Minogue's status as a singer, however, was barely hinted at, by something she was doing with a hairbrush on the bed; this was as near as she got to a microphone, but it seemed to have as much to do with sex as singing.

The Face was thus one of the first trend-setting journalistic outlets to take seriously the translation of Kylie Minogue from suburban to general cultural status; to 'read' the Australian actor and singer as English *telebrity* and Essex girl *extraordinaire*, thus to personalize in the metropolitan consciousness the otherwise wide and featureless plains of suburban, feminized, consumerist ordinariness. In short, Kylie Minogue became for a while a visualization of 'the people' – not a 'vox pop' but a 'frocks pop' (see next chapter) – in the continuing contemplation of the meaning of the social which is the cultural function of the postmodern public sphere.

Notes

1. Caption to an illustration of the *Psalter* of Odbert, abbot of Saint-Bertin, 1000 AD, in Boulogne Library. In Georges Duby (ed.) (1988) *A History of Private Life. Vol. II: Revelations of the Medieval World*. Trans. Arthur Goldhammer. Cambridge, Mass.: Harvard University Press, 32.
2. Colin MacInnes (1959) *Absolute Beginners*. London: Allison & Busby, 143. After calling TV a 'sort of non-university education', the passage continues on a more cautionary note: 'The only catch – and of course, there always is one – is that when they do put on a programme about something I really know about – which I admit is little, but I mean jazz, or teenagers, or juvenile delinquency – the whole dam things [*sic*] seems utterly unreal. Cooked up in a hurry, and made to sound simpler than it is. Those programmes about kiddos, for example! Boy! I dare say they send the tax-payers, who think the veil's being lifted on the teenage orgies, but honestly, for anyone who knows the actual scene, they're crap. And maybe, in the things we don't know about, like all that art and culture, it's the same, but I can't judge.' Apart from being an unusually early (1958) example of *plus ça change* in the world of TV, it's also a clear instance of popular fiction performing a pedagogic function for its presumed readers, both teenage and otherwise; teaching the former that TV is not all positive and the latter the reverse.
3. Thomas Richards (1993) *The Imperial Archive: Knowledge and the Fantasy of Empire*. London: Verso.
4. John Frow (1993) Knowledge and class. *Cultural Studies* 7(2), 240–82.
5. Ernesto Laclau and Chantal Mouffe (1985) *Hegemony and Socialist Strategy: Towards a Radical Democratic Politics*. Trans. Winston Moore and Paul Cammack. London: Verso.
6. Yuri Lotman (1990) *Universe of the Mind: A Semiotic Theory of Culture*. Trans. Ann Shukman. Indiana: Indiana University Press, Part Two, The semiosphere, 121–214.
7. Lotman, 203.

8. Lotman, 203.
9. Donald J. Olsen (1979) *The Growth of Victorian London*. Harmondsworth: Peregrine Books, 263, 297. First published 1976 by B.T. Batsford.
10. See Olsen, especially Chapter 5, The villa and the new suburb.
11. Duby (ed.), xi.
12. For Australian perspectives (apart from Meaghan Morris), see Diane Powell (1993) *Out West: Perceptions of Sydney's Western Suburbs*. Sydney: Allen & Unwin; Katherine Gibson and Sophie Watson (eds.) (1994) *Metropolis Now: Planning and the Urban in Contemporary Australia*. Sydney: Pluto Press; John Fiske, Bob Hodge and Graeme Turner (1987) *Myths of Oz: Reading Australian Popular Culture*. Sydney: Allen & Unwin, Chapter 2. See also Craig McGregor (1984) *Pop Goes the Culture*. London: Pluto Press. For historical comparison, and a British perspective, see Geoffrey Crossick (ed.) (1977) *The Lower Middle Class in Britain*. London: Croom Helm; and, for an unusual and tolerant insight into the original London suburbia (among other places) when it's really under stress, based on the data of Mass Observation and written by that organization's co-founder, see Tom Harrisson (1978) *Living Through the Blitz*. Harmondsworth: Penguin. As for links between British and Australian suburbias, how about this unguarded aside from Donald J. Olsen: '(King's Cross, the one significant specialized neighbourhood in all Australia, may arguably be a less important centre of Australian culture than Earl's Court.)' Olsen, 28.
13. See Deborah Chambers (1992) Women and suburban culture: investigating women's experiences of the transition from rural to suburban living. In Brian Musgrove and Rebecca Snow-McLean (eds.) *Signifying Others: Selected Papers from the Second Cultural Studies Association of Australia Conference*. Toowoomba: USQ Press, 121–9.
14. Thomas Sharp (1940) *Town Planning*. Harmondsworth: Pelican Books, 53.
15. On the 'cult of domesticity' for suburban women, and how it prepared the way for broadcast media, see Lynn Spigel (1992) *Make Room for TV: Television and the Family Ideal in Postwar America*. Chicago: University of Chicago Press.
16. On media/anorexia see Abigail Bray (1994) The 'edible woman': reading/eating disorders and femininity, *Media Information Australia*, 72, 4–10.
17. Colin MacInnes, 60. It may be appropriate that one of the most sustained and telling analyses of this aspect of suburban life in recent times is not only written by a man but is also a novel – Peter Carey (1991) *The Tax Inspector*. Brisbane: University of Queensland Press.
18. Graeme Turner (1992) Suburbia verité, *Australian Left Review*, October, 37–9.
19. John La Nauze (1977) *Walter Murdoch: A Biographical Memoir*. Melbourne: Melbourne University Press, 122.
20. T.W.H. Crosland (1905) *The Suburbans*. London: John Long, 80–3.
21. Sharp, 54–5.
22. See especially Meaghan Morris (1988) Politics now: anxieties of a petty-bourgeois intellectual. In *The Pirate's Fiancée: Feminism, Reading, Postmodernism*. London and New York: Verso, 173–86; and Meaghan Morris (1988) Things to do with shopping centres, *Working Paper No. 1*, Center for Twentieth Century Studies, University of Wisconsin-Milwaukee.
23. Olsen, 321. (This sentence can only have been written without an eye on the buses of South Asia, from Afghanistan to the Philippines.)

24. Hugh Stretton (1974) *Housing and Government.* Sydney: ABC, 41.
25. Denise Meredyth (1992) Changing minds: cultural criticism and the problem of principle. *Meanjin* 51(3), 491–504.
26. Meaghan Morris's work is, as she says, 'unrepentantly practised' as a 'theoretically specialized criticism' (i.e. she's a 'universal intellectual' in Hunter/Meredyth's terms), while at the same time she's centrally concerned with the realities – the culture – of petit bourgeois, suburban and family life. Meaghan Morris (1992) A gadfly bites back. *Meanjin* 51(3), 545–51. See also Morris's (1988) Things to do with shopping centres; Morris (January 1988) At Henry Parkes Motel, *Cultural Studies* 2(1), 1–47; Morris (1992) *Ecstasy and Economics: American Essays for John Forbes.* Sydney: EMPress. The second essay in this book, 'On the beach', contains a discussion of Hunter's position.
27. Terence Hawkes (1992) *Meaning by Shakespeare.* London and New York: Routledge, 5.
28. Ian Hunter (1992) The humanities without humanism. *Meanjin* 51 (3), 479–90.
29. Hunter, 488.
30. Olsen, 224.
31. Among the list of 'Best We Forget' phenomena of 1991: 1991 in Review. *The Face* 40, January 1992, 86.
32. *The Face* 40, January 1992, 82 (The phrase 'that's enough, *Ed*' is a homage to *Private Eye*).
33. *Birds of a Feather* was shown in Australia on ABC TV in May 1993. Subsequent series were also screened.
34. *The Face* 40, 62–6. This comment is attributed to 'Jon Casmir, a leading Sydney music journalist who has written about these groups himself'.
35. *TV Week*, 16 November 1991, cover.
36. *The Face* 37, October 1991, cover, contents page, letters page and feature.

7 *The Frock of the New*

(Sexualization and Telebrity)

My discussion aims to retain an awareness of the discursive possibilities that were available at a given historical moment and to assess the political implications of particular representations of women and modernity in that light. This historical tightrope of empathy and critique is a difficult one to negotiate skillfully: it remains for the reader to decide how successfully this negotiation has been achieved.   RITA FELSKI[1]

PhiloSophie

Why do you ask me about Killee Minog?
I don't care about Killee Minog.   VANESSA PARADIS[2]

During 1991–92 two rather different images of Australian suburban culture suffused Australian suburban TV screens, both of them factual but neither journalistic in the standard sense. They were *Sylvania Waters* (ABC/BBC) and *Sex (with Sophie Lee)* (Channel 9). Both were documentary series, and they both illustrate a continuing dissolution of the supposedly rigid line between fact and fiction on TV: *Sylvania Waters* was *generically* 'dirty' as a 'soapumentary' (and all the more engrossing for that); while *Sex* was formally much more straightforward, taking its place in the burgeoning 'lifestyle' genre (gardening, home, holiday . . . sex).[3]

Suburbia is quite common on TV, but sex is not. TV sex is almost exclusively confined to fiction (and, until the shortlived *Chances* at any rate, restricted to movies rather than soapies), although even fictional sex is traditionally signified by its absence.[4] Actual sex involving non-fictional people – e.g. a *documentary* sexual encounter (even kissing, if done with passion) between ordinary suburban citizens – is very rare on TV, and it is literally subversive, generically risky, because it undermines the division between fact and fiction,

SOPHIE S
SHOCK US

THERE'S sex, sex ... and then there's Sophie Lee! Three months ago, you couldn't mention one without the other.

The sultry 23-year-old actress was everywhere — talking about sex, arguing about sex, presenting a high-rating TV documentary called *Sex*.

It was exhausting work that brought her to the brink of physical collapse.

It also changed the way men react to her. Instead of whistling and catcalling in the street — as they did in her *Bugs Bunny Show* days — they now take her seriously.

While Sophie is happy about that, she says it has a downside.

"I go out on a date with a boy and he thinks I am a sex expert," she says, rolling her eyes. "How uncomfortable to be sitting opposite someone at dinner and have them thinking, 'Oh my God, she's a sex counsellor'.

"It embarrasses me. I'm by no means a spokesperson for sex or anything like an expert."

But that hasn't stopped Sophie saying yes to a follow-up six-part series, exploring the topic in greater depth. The first episode is due to air nationally on the Nine Network shortly.

"I want to tackle issues like abortion and condoms — topics that affect teenagers," she says. "It wasn't so long ago that I was a teenager, and I know how confusing those years can be.

"I'm not a journalist and I'm certainly no Jana Wendt. But I thought that a documentary could do some good. These issues need to be talked about.

"I'm worried about AIDS. Who isn't? And if I can do something to heighten awareness — good."

Sophie's huge teenage following will undoubtedly be thrilled by the new series, and morals crusader Reverend Fred Nile — an outspoken Sophie critic — is sure to be outraged.

Sophie shrugs. She didn't set out to become a spokesperson on sex for her generation. But she does have firm ideas on how the series will be handled. She will decide the topics, interview the experts, then take the cameras out on the street to talk to young people.

The former *Bugs Bunny* host is back – with a new six-part series on sex

Sophie, whose baby-doll beauty conceals a smart and determined young woman, insists that she doesn't want to make a career out of sex.

She hopes all this talking about it won't harm her credibility as an actress, which is her first priority.

"It's a struggle not to be typecast. Like the psycho killer in a soapie who always gets offered psycho roles, the person who does documentaries on sex is associated only with sex," she says.

She hopes to counterbalance the sex with a starring role in the new *Flying Doctors*. It's a spin-off series, set in Broken Hill three years after the Royal Flying Doctors Service in Coopers Crossing is forced to close.

Sophie, Val Jellay and Maurie Fields are the only cast originals to go into the new show.

To concentrate on her TV projects, Sophie is taking time out from '60s-style band *Freaked Out Flower Children*.

Last year, she tried to juggle performances with her television work, and the stress nearly put her in hospital. She was working six days and three nights a week, and life became a nightmare.

"I averaged five hours' sleep a night all last year. I spent days wishing I could grab an hour's nap; just put my head down on a pillow for a moment. You can't keep going like that," she says.

Sophie kept it up — against doctors' advice — until early this year, when she finished the documentary. Then she collapsed and was unable to get out of bed for a week.

When she recovered, she made some important decisions. Rest and relaxation were vital for her health. So was having fun. Last year, whenever the pressure was getting too much, she would

threaten to go walkabout in the des even going as far as booking pla tickets to Alice Springs.

This time she was definitely going friend who has experience camping the Outback volunteered to take h They packed the car with jerry cans water and petrol, and an ice box of fo

It was the realisation of a dre Sophie had cherished since growing in the industrial city of Newcastle, the central coast of NSW.

"I don't know many people w would want to go with me to t Outback and I couldn't really go myself. I suppose I could pay somec to take me, but you can't pay somec to be your friend," she says.

Sophie and her companion — who s says is just a good mate — spent tv weeks driving through the Simps Desert. They notified the real-life Flyi Doctors of their route and kept in tou as they visited remote homesteads a Aboriginal settlements.

Often they drove for days in 42-degr heat without seeing another person. F Sophie, it was bliss.

She looks fit and happy, and h simplified her personal life. Eig months ago she broke up with *Freak Out Flower Children* guitarist Gum Phillips and is revelling in her freedo

"I live on my own, I go out with n girlfriend and we hang out with o friends. Somehow, it's easier to be on n own right now," she says candidly.

Sophie says she has no room in h life for drugs. Allegations of cocaine a LSD use, she says with a heavy sigh, a completely unfounded.

"I don't have time to do drugs," s says emphatically. "Drugs are very ba for people who want to work. In n position I have to be on the ball all t time. It's that simple."

Sophie does admit to one weaknes though – beer.

"In the Outback, I drank beer all da One at lunch, then a few hours lat another one, and then another ... I don do cocaine or LSD. I do beer," she say laughing. "I love the stuff."

Story: Bunty Avieso

T TO
AGAIN!

*6I go out on a
date with a boy
d he thinks I am
sex expert … it is
nbarrassing. I'm
t a spokesperson
for sex 9*

Fig. 7.1 Sophie Lee in *TV Week*. Photograph by Rob Austen

wherein we've become accustomed to the 'fact' that *characters* (fiction) can have sex but *people* (fact) can only talk about it. Interestingly, however, *Sex* turned out to be generically and ideologically straightforward, not to say suburban, showing and talking about sex across a wide range of people, practices and problems in an informative, matter-of-fact, non-sleazy, non-judgemental, open-minded sort of way. But none of this affected the programme's reputation, which centred almost entirely on its presenter, Sophie Lee, who in turn came to *be* 'sex' for the Australian popular media during 1992 – '*Sex* with Sophie Lee' became the ho-ho headline of the year.[5]

Meanwhile, *Sylvania Waters*'s Noelene Donaher seemed to confirm some people's worst fears about suburban, petit-bourgeois social democracy: she was the Australian Dream incarnate, but was it a nightmare after all? Controversy raged in the media about both shows and both women, and while both received more than their share of criticism, both toughed it out, providing endless extra copy for the popular print media. They finally came together on the same page in the Christmas 1992 edition of *The Australian Women's Weekly*, which allowed them a Christmas wish. One of them – and I won't say which – wanted to shower her loved ones with gifts, the other wanted 'documentary makers to be more honest'.[6]

Although *Sylvania Waters* came as a shock to an unsuspecting Australian public in 1992, Sophie Lee was already a star. She grew up in suburban Newcastle, NSW, but her home would never have been chosen for the archetypal suburbanality of *Sylvania Waters*. The daughter of a professor of philosophy and a schoolteacher, she went without TV throughout her childhood, a curious fact that the weekly magazines never tired of telling us, given that she made her name as presenter of a children's TV show, *Bugs Bunny*. She attracted attention for doing nothing more revolutionary than wearing stylish clothes on the show, and very quickly she became a synonym for sexiness.

Sophie Lee appeared in most of the Australian popular print media within a year and was featured – often as cover girl as well – in *Woman's Day* (twice), *New Idea*, *TV Soap*, *TV Week* (three times), *Cosmopolitan* (Figs 7.1–7.3), *Dolly*, *The Dolly Rock Book*, *Who Weekly*, *Playboy*, *Cleo* and *The Australian Women's Weekly*. She also featured in extensive news copy,[7] in a Samboy Chips TV commercial ('hit me slowly . . .'), and as celebrity gardener on *Burke's Backyard*. She was newsworthy not only as presenter of *Sex* and *Bugs Bunny*, but also in connection with the NSW Family Planning Association's *Fact and Fantasy File* diary ('banned by the PM!'), as saxophonist for The Freaked Out Flower Children (on the cover of *Playboy* as well as *Dolly*), as an actor playing the character of Penny Wellings in *The Flying Doctors* (and its successor *RFDS*), as a fashion model for *Cosmopolitan* and *Cleo*, and she was also frequently reported as being a close friend of Kylie Minogue.

She may be better known to an international audience through her role in the 1994 suburban tragi-comedy film *Muriel's Wedding*,

'They've used me ...it's unfair!'

Sophie hits back at the savaging the press gave her over that teen sex diary

SOPHIE LEE — under attack from critics of the now-banned Fact And Fantasy File diary — is to present a documentary on teenage sex for the Nine Network.

The one-hour special, made in conjunction with A Current Affair, is certain to fuel the fire created by Sophie's association with the diary — a project of the NSW Family Planning Association which was banned by Prime Minister Keating.

Sophie claims certain sections of the press "used her" to sensationalise the aim of the diary, which, she says, was solely to promote safe sex among teenagers and to raise awareness of AIDS.

"I felt the diary idea was fantastic," Sophie says. "I gave a speech at the launch and met the teenagers involved. Then the whole thing blew up. I still can't believe the way it was handled.

"It was really disappointing. Maybe the tabloids didn't have a lead story. It was like 'sexy young starlet in sex diary' on the front page.

"They really used me. It's unfair. This is such a serious issue and these people don't seem to understand that."

For the diary, Sophie, 23, took part in an interview, in which she stated that one-night stands were "okay" — a comment that newspapers highlighted.

"What I'm saying is that if you want to go ahead and have casual sex, that's your business and that's okay, if you practise safe sex," she says.

"That's it. That's all I said.

"I'm not enforcing permissiveness and I'm not even pushing my morals on anyone. I'm merely saying, 'Kids have a right to be educated' . . . otherwise they are going to die if they make the wrong decision."

In her short but successful TV career, Sophie has had to cop a lot of flak — but the latest bout of criticism has obviously had a dramatic effect on her.

"I was appalled at the way the diary was handled by the media," she says angrily. "To dismiss it as smutty, they are missing the whole point.

"This is the biggest issue of the Nineties, indeed the whole century.

"People have a go at me because I'm a young woman, I'm attractive and I'm doing well.

"I find that's another disappointing thing about Australian society. To get a good job and

have credibility, they expect you not to be attractive and to wear a hessian sack.

"The media use me for their own gain. But I don't listen to commercial radio nor do I read second-rate newspapers. So I don't expose myself to it. Obviously, I do hear about it and it's not very nice."

To be screened soon, the A Current Affair documentary's aim is, according to Sophie, to "educate both parents and teenagers about a lot of sexual issues".

"Obviously, I've had to cop flak over launching the diary . . . but if this documentary can save one person's life, then it's worth it to me to cop — from the press," Sophie says.

"I'm really thrilled to be doing the documentary. We are going to cover a really broad range of issues, from homosexuality to safe sex to teenage sex.

"I believe that people — and teenagers are people, too — have a right to know about sex. Teenagers have to make informed choices.

"We are certainly living in dangerous times."

Sophie hopes both parents and their teenage children will watch the documentary.

"It is there to bridge the gap between teenagers and their parents," she says. "I hope they watch it . . . and I hope they have an open mind about sex."

Story: Mark McGowan
Main picture: Rob Austen

> ❝ I'm not even pushing my morals on anyone. I'm merely saying, 'Kids have a right to be educated' . . . otherwise they are going to die if they make the wrong decision ❞

6 TV WEEK, 22/2/92

---

where she plays Tania, a character whose sobbing, mascara-spattered, uncomprehending line, 'But I'm beautiful!' (as if that should have guaranteed her a happy ending in line with Hollywood mythology) when she literally loses the plot to the despised friend, the ugly, fat, uncool Muriel of the title, sums up an Australian, ironic refusal of the standard American teen plot where the good-looking juvenile lead always wins out in the end.[8] That Sophie Lee herself is no fan of some aspects of suburban culture shines through her too-perfect portrayal of the too-awful Tania. As Lee herself commented in a later interview:

> I got her [Tania] from Newcastle [NSW]. It does not have the benefits of a big city where people tend to be more accepting of a wider variety of cultures. In a small town there is more of an accepted norm and

Fig. 7.2 Sophie Lee in *Woman's Day.* Photograph by Barry Sproson

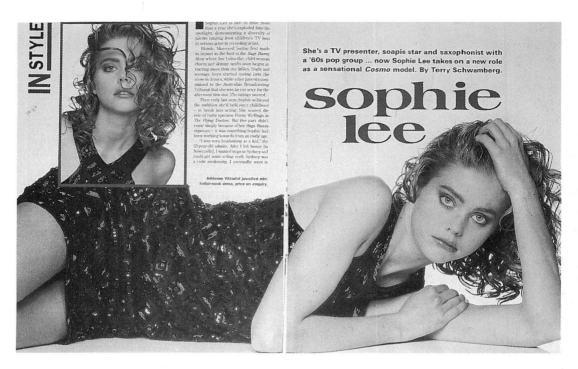

She's a TV presenter, soapie star and saxophonist with a '60s pop group ... now Sophie Lee takes on a new role as a sensational *Cosmo* model. By Terry Schwamberg.

sophie lee

Fig. 7.3 Sophie Lee in *Cosmopolitan*. Photograph by Warwick Orme

people dangerously short of brains run around dictating what the norm is. Tania to me is a real suburban terrorist. Those girls try to be really tough with each other and really ugly and threatening – they have to be really sure no-one steps out of line. It's a power thing.[9]

In other words, within the constraints of possibility offered by her public persona, Sophie Lee is working against the grain of 'suburban terrorism', not uncritically endorsing or exploiting it, but offering glimpses of other possibilities than being 'beautiful' but 'dangerously short of brains'. Indeed, she uses her own beauty, brains and opposition to the 'power thing' to talk *through* the expected stereotypes *to* the suburban Tanias, not to mention the men who were hooked on her *Bugs Bunny* persona: 'As Lee says: "Boys are dumb".' In short, she uses her visibility to *teach* the real Tanias and the boys, who she knows so well, other possibilities than simply to be 'ugly and threatening' to each other.

Although it is quite possible for one person, a Rupert Murdoch or a Kerry Packer, say, to *own* such a multifarious collection of media outlets as Sophie Lee appeared in during her spectacular early career, it is unusual to find one person *appearing* in so many different sectors of the market simultaneously without regard to the usual generic boundaries between fact and fiction, actors and models, presenters and performers, men's and women's magazines, fashion glossies and supermarket weeklies, children's interests and sex. So among other things Sophie Lee functions as a personalized visual marker of this crossover tendency in contemporary popular culture, and the thing that crossed all these boundaries with her was the subject of sex. Naturally, this remained the case whatever she might have thought or said about it, since her critical comments were duly reported in the very organs she was criticizing.[10] In fact the contradiction between her sexiness and her anti-sexism became an accepted part of a developing 'narrative image' in the media, which did however have the positive consequence that her forthright views got prominent billing in outlets not noted for political or social progressiveness.[11]

The Frocks Pop

In Nightmare Abbey, *Peacock makes his reactionary Mr. Flosky lament: 'How can we be cheerful when we are surrounded by a* reading public, *that is growing too wise for its betters?'* ... *In 1828 a barrister told the Westminster magistrates that a forger owed his trip to Botany Bay to 'the march of intellect,' and to this the magistrates (or some of them) responded with 'Hear, Hear.'*

R.K. WEBB[12]

Part of the problem addressed by this chapter is that of repute. As is the case for suburbia itself, and whole media like TV and popular periodicals, it seems that whatever the 'telebrity' person actually does or says has little impact on her reputation, even when it would be seen as progressive or radical in other contexts. And part of the problem of repute is that *popularity* seems to bring with it a poor rather than a high reputation, at least among those in the 'knowledge class' whose cultural function it is to dispense repute (those for whom the phrase 'good television' is an oxymoron). Here the question becomes one of how to account for the power of reputation to determine whole reading practices (it's my view that reputation is a form of class policing: the more popular the medium, whether it be television or Sophie Lee, the more virulent is its dismissal by belittlement and unfair criticism, no matter how good its content or actions; and because this discourse of dismissal emanates from respectable sources like academics, professionals, intellectuals and 'opinion leaders', it makes good copy for the popular media themselves, who thereby teach their own readers and audiences that their most popular symbolic engagements are the most to be despised). The question thus becomes one of how to account for the low repute of people who are, in their own words:

> *a mixture of I look alright, I can sing alright, I can dance reasonably well. People can relate to me because I'm not out of reach or unattainable. It's a kind of ordinariness. That sounds depressing, doesn't it?*[13]

In other words, this investigation is not about looks, singing or dancing as such, but about the politics that makes 'ordinariness' 'sound depressing' – the *reputation* of phenomena that are, in Graeme Turner's words, 'so widely seen as *so* self-evidently bad', serving a 'culturally denigrated audience', via the medium of stars who are held to be '*more* fabricated, *less* talented, *more* "produced" and more of a brainless puppet than any other',[14] that in the end only one name encapsulates both the thing itself and the unanimous contempt in which it is held – and that name belongs to the mixture of 'ordinary alrightness' quoted above – Sophie Lee's friend Kylie Minogue.

Kylie Minogue is held by the best authorities to produce nothing worth disagreeing with,[15] presumably on the principle that bouncing cheerfully up and down to a dance beat is not something with which you *can* disagree.[16] Fair enough, but in the semiosphere it is not only statements which make propositions, but also clothes which make statements. As fashion magazine *Mirabella* put it in relation to Gianni Versace's 1991 collection: '*This* is truly power dressing: not the tired symbolism of the padded shoulder in which women aped the bodies of men', but the power of:

> *confidence, wit and, above all, sexuality. "My ideal woman,"* he [Versace] *says, "can have any type of body and be any age, but she must have the intelligence to adapt her figure and personality to the various proposals of fashion."*[17]

Kylie Minogue is by no means merely a singer, dancer, actor and model. She is also, like her friend Sophie Lee, a *popularizer* of certain 'proposals'. Given their pop-culture careers, popularization is the general cultural function of such entertainers as Kylie Minogue and Sophie Lee, but it does need to be remembered that popularization is always pedagogic, and that Kylie Minogue and Sophie Lee are *teachers*, if their performances are looked at from the point of view of their *readership* rather than from that of their *reputation*. Kylie Minogue's reputation allows critics to have fun at her expense, but her readership – the audience that is as 'culturally denigrated' as she is herself – is the thing that allows certain values, images, energies and changes to be circulated *so* widely that even though she is not a critic she is the *bearer* of meanings which do have a propositional – as well as a spectacular and bodily – component. Kylie Minogue and Sophie Lee are not the *vox populi*, the voice of the people (the thirty-second grab of anonymous opinion that performs the dialogue of a fictionalized democracy), but they are among those celebrities whose showy messages cling to them like a frock – often *as* a frock – in short they're the '*frox populi*': visualizations of certain knowledges, truths and values, and every time they appear, their image, action, 'look' and performance become the idiom of popular pedagogy.

Like any other fashion garment the 'frocks pop' are an expression of their wearer's identity, but simultaneously they are quite obviously 'made up' by someone else. Just as a dress is created by couturiers and their staff, so the public personae of Kylie Minogue and Sophie Lee are created by managers and record companies, by editors, journalists and photographers of the popular media, and – to some extent – by Kylie Minogue and Sophie Lee themselves. Kylie

most shocking, and when prints are bold, his the boldest.

There was a time – in the matt black, androgynous mid-Eighties – when such things were considered outmoded, even tasteless.

Yet there is a discipline in Versace's collection which stops it from ever toppling over into vulgarity. He has always been a designer for whom technology and innovation matter as much – if not more – than craft. He has long experimented with developing new fabrics and methods of production and in this, his best collection to date, he reaps the dividends of that investment.

I F THE EIGHTIES WERE RESPONSIBLE for any one trend, it was that of the body. New developments in fabric technology have brought us clothing that not only moves with the body, but that behaves literally like a second skin. When Versace cuts a short skirt, he twins it with tights in matching tones and of fabrics so durable and covering that they assume a modesty that did not seem possible even five years ago. Sheer tights with short skirts carry quite a different message. The covered, decorated and coloured leg ceases to be erogenous but becomes a part of the whole. These clothes are sexy, certainly, made for women for whom showing off is a matter of course.

In Versace's collections are encapsulated all the concerns of his exclusive clientèle: wealth, power and control. Here is confidence made flesh. Money is stitched into every controlled seam line, it glimmers in the crusted beading and embroidery, it glows from the expensively starved and exercised bodies the clothes are designed to show off. This is truly power dressing; not the tired symbolism of the padded shoulder with which women aped the bodies of men, but power over the flesh, power over the tiresome matter of ageing. These are clothes for spare-fleshed women intent on defying middle age. If strenuous exercise and diet have played their part the covered body looks pretty much the same, whether young or old.

The investment of willpower, money and plain optimism in pursuit of a perfect physique demands a fair return. The body becomes the showcase for the clothes and not, as latterly, the other way around. Versace understands his customer well. He knows how to dress her with confidence, wit and, above all, sexuality. "My ideal woman," he says, "can have any type of body and be any age, but she must have the intelligence to adapt her figure and personality to the various proposals of fashion. That said, my hope is that there are no taboos left." ⬛

Fig. 7.4 Helena Christensen models Versace's 'power over flesh' (*Mirabella* Magazine)

Minogue's image is her own even while it is produced by others (this is a point she was constantly trying to get across in interviews), just as she can choose which outfit to wear without personally creating its fashion style.

From the perspective of the reader, 'frocks pops' are mixed and fragmented images, generating meanings that are well beyond the control of the 'telebrity' whose image they appear to be; Sophie Lee's likeness appears all over the public sphere (which in this case resembles not so much a sphere as a glitter-ball), but no reader (other than the assiduous fan or trudging scholar) is expected to trace each little facet in order to construct a (wholly imaginary) 'real' Sophie Lee out of all the bits. In fact the reputation of popularizers like Kylie Minogue and Sophie Lee is based not so much on who they are or what they do, but on how they're reported and reputed, on how well they fit into the fashions of the season, and on how they look. Their 'speaking position' is determined by their audience (which comprises not only general readers but also journalists who 'read' them for gossip copy and celebrity pix), their value by their consumers. This is a fact of public life that has not been better put than by its first modern philosopher, Thomas Hobbes, writing in 1651:

> *The* Value, *or WORTH of a man, is as of all other things, his Price . . . and therefore is not absolute; but a thing dependent on the need and judgement of another.... And as in other things, so in men, not the seller, but the buyer determines the Price. For let a man (as most men do,) rate themselves as the highest Value they can; yet their true Value is no more than it is esteemed by others.*[18]

It is interesting that Hobbes saw power and value (reputation) as commodities with exchange values, for he included among them natural attributes and abilities, including bodily beauty, which he calls 'Forme' (and, in the custom of the day, associates with men) – 'Forme is Power; because being a promise of Good, it recommendeth men to the favour of women and strangers.'[19] 'Forme' in Hobbes's time was a complex term but, applied to persons, it referred not only to the 'visible aspect of a thing', but also to 'beauty, comeliness', to 'style of dress, costume', and to 'an image, representation, or likeness'. It was 'a body considered in respect to its outward shape and appearance; *esp.* that of a living being, a person' (*OED*). However, as C.B. Macpherson has noted, Hobbes located power not in a person's natural abilities or attributes as such, but in their '*eminence*'; once more it is 'esteem by others' that determines the social value of even such natural gifts as 'Forme'.[20] This Hobbist conceptualization is the political theory of 'frocks pops' too; their contemporary 'power' and 'value' is also the 'eminence' of their 'form'; exactly the situation as described by Hobbes in the mid-seventeenth century. They are significant not so much for their originality as for their destinations; not so much for their own speaking position as for that of their hearers; they are dedicated not to production, origin and identity, but to consumption, destination and exchange. Their meanings are social, communicative, cultural, not authorial or authoritative.

A Sidelong Glance

To argue that women catch psychological disorders from watching television [i.e. eating disorders from seeing images of 'waif' supermodels English Kate Moss and Australian Emma Balfour] is to enter into an undemocratic infantilisation of women's everyday practices. The prevalence and power of this argument needs attention. ABIGAIL BRAY[21]

Perhaps one of the lessons that the 'frocks pop' teach is that identity itself (subjectivity) is mixed, fragmented, dispersed and not entirely in the individual's control. Here they differ radically from the more celebrated Madonna, whose career is dedicated to preserving the fiction of individualism (identity politics), and whose press coverage in this period (1991–92) was generally much more sympathetic than that given to Kylie Minogue and Sophie Lee, perhaps because commentators were lulled by her militant self-invention and her megalomaniacal manipulation of the public sphere into a false sense of ontological security; Madonna seemed to confirm all the old verities of authenticity, originality, creativity and self-identity, not to mention American superiority and the longstanding habit of presuming New York is coterminous with the civilized world. Whether she turned into the things she parodied so well remained an open question, but few critics doubted that Kylie Minogue was copying her, an accusation which dogged her throughout the year.[22]

Certainly, what the 'frocks pop' teach is not confined to what they say, even though they are interminably interviewed, profiled and quoted (and much of the content of such copy is indeed straightforward advice, teaching sensible ideas). But in the main theirs is a performative and dramatic pedagogy, visual and vestimentary, and its message – precisely because it is not spelt out but performed as part of popular entertainment – can be read 'at a glance'. Kylie Minogue finds her possession of an 'ordinary' image that can be apprehended on first glance potentially 'depressing'. But she might take comfort from political and anthropological theory; not only is universal recognition a form of Hobbist 'Value' but – perhaps more surprisingly – the kind of glance on which her value depends has been claimed, by the American anthropologist Marshall Sahlins, as perhaps the very means by which society itself is constituted: 'It is by appearances that civilization turns the basic contradiction of its construction into a miracle of existence: a cohesive society of perfect strangers.'[23]

What Sahlins calls '*la pensée bourgeoise*' is based on a *coherence* of a specific kind; on 'the possibility of apprehending others, their social condition, and thereby their relation to oneself "on first glance"'.

The condition of possibility for this '*pensée*' is the glance, which turns out to be more than merely a 'brief or hurried look' (*OED*). The *OED* offers sufficient historical quotations to show that a glance is indeed a thing of power: it is used to cheat at cards (1591); to convey anger (1592); to fall in love 'with the first glance' (1606); to flirt (1667); to maintain and communicate power – 'in most courts . . . the glance of the monarch is watched, and every smile is waited for with impatience' (1728); to take in information (1828); to apprehend a landscape (1860); and to assess imminent danger (1874). The only entry that suggests that the glance may be flawed as a means of practical reasoning is one from 1799 that opts for the now-familiar privileging of the analytic gaze: 'This arrangement pleases at first glance, but soon fatigues the eye by it's [*sic*] uniformity.'

Sahlins suggests that 'a logic completely foreign to the conventional "rationality" is present in economic and social life', a 'practical reason' that pervades humanity. But far from being a mere epiphenomenon of more basic matters like the economy (material goods) and class (social relations), Sahlins argues that it is the cultural system of meanings based on appearance and the glance which enables the other components of 'civilization' to operate at all – the economy, modern, rational, productive and impersonal, is nevertheless 'totemic' in anthropological terms.[24] The 'miracle of existence' hinted at by Sahlins, a 'cohesive society of perfect strangers', is signified through such bearers of meaning as the clothing and fashion system, which is no less miraculous for being popularized by high-visibility personalities such as Sophie Lee and Kylie Minogue.

Kylie Minogue is the bearer of the logic of the glance; she is a member of what I've called elsewhere the 'smiling professions'.[25] It seems, as true professionals, the smilers can get fed up with their work – and their frocks. As Kylie comments:

> *I'm reacting against the old days, All the suits telling me* 'This *would look nice, Kylie, why don't you put it on?' – all the silly old photographers from weekly magazines, telling me to smile, smile, smile. . .*[26]

Does this 'sound depressing', as Kylie Minogue herself fears? Perhaps so, but only for her, not for the system she personifies. According to the London *Independent on Sunday*, 'It is clear she frets about not being talented or extraordinary enough', and she 'lacks Madonna's burning belief in her own uniqueness'. She is in permanent danger of being superseded, even by her own sister:

> *With a younger sister, Dannii, currently in the process of throwing off Oz naffness (a lead role in* Home and Away*) in favour of Euro-hipness (pop songs and slinky dresses), Kylie has the predictability – and infinite repeatability – of her career placed in unusually harsh light . . . 'Of course I know that there will always be someone younger and more beautiful than me. Sometimes I ask myself, Why am I here? and I really don't know the answer.' Kylie crosses and uncrosses her skinny, black-stockinged legs and tugs at her whouffed-up blonde hair.*

Fig. 7.5 Kylie Minogue in *Free Beat* (Photograph courtesy of Mushroom Records)

> '*There are*,' *she adds wonderingly,* '*probably a million of me out there.*'[27]

A million Minogues – and that's only at the production end; the number of people whose ordinary alrightness resembles hers at the consumption end is indeed a matter of economics (where a million Minogues = a million dollars). But it's a precarious kind of success, almost incomprehensible to current ideologies of artistic authenticity – it's not based on authorship, originality or uniqueness, but precisely on repeatability, on the anthropological glance rather than the analytic gaze, on distribution not copyright. The meanings that circulate around her body – 'dwarfishly ravishing – weirder-looking but also far more beautiful than her glamour shots convey'[28] – are not seen as her private intellectual property but precisely as 'produced', like the smile itself, and produced for suburban, domestic consumption at that.

The Body Politic

I am less interested in music or TV than I am in how these cut across and organize the various time-spaces in which the labor, as well as the pleasure, of everyday living is carried out by Australian women. This is why I do not think of 'tourist sites and sounds' as insignificant. . . . I think of them in the first place as political combat zones.   MEAGHAN MORRIS[29]

During 1991 Kylie Minogue underwent a surprising transformation. Just as Sophie Lee sexualized mainstream children's and lifestyle TV, so Kylie Minogue, icon of pre-teen pop and *Neighbourly* homeliness, sexualized herself. She was literally unfrocked, brought into the realm of the profane, and – to the self-serving astonishment of the magazine media – made synonymous with sex. So surprising was this event, in fact, that it became news in real newspapers, from the highest (the *Independent on Sunday*) to the lowest brow (the *Daily Mirror*),[30] and its meaning was minutely analysed while Minogue's body was photographed from every conceivable angle, in glossy magazines, stylish and otherwise, and in popular media in at least two continents, for several months. Maybe the new image was contrived, maybe Kylie Minogue's 'practical reasoning' was a little too well rehearsed. As the world's most stylish magazine remarked at the time: 'There are, of course, reasons to be suspicious.' But, despite itself, *The Face* devoted nine pages and a cover to the event (Fig. 7.6), and concluded:

> *The strange thing is that it is working. Britain is entranced with Kylie in a way that it rarely gets entranced. . . . It's not just working for the public, but in her life. When most teen stars try to move into more fashionable milieux, they are laughed at. . . . But fashionable London seems to like having Kylie around. She's the girl they talk about.*[31]

Kylie Minogue and Sophie Lee, in Britain and Australia, were media through which the postmodern public domain was sexualized. I don't think that what was happening was merely a matter of sexualizing their bodies – this was the *tabula rasa* upon which social messages could be written. And I don't think they were mere products of commercial manipulation – Kylie Minogue and Sophie Lee were also professionals; troupers. Their 'moral competence' for their job was precisely that which Ian Hunter wants for arts-academics: 'self-abnegation, strict adherence to procedure, and dedication to professional expertise'[32] – in short they were 'produced' to the extent that they were good at their job. They were sexualized and produced, certainly, but beyond that, and more importantly, was their cultural function as popularizers of meanings. In this sense their bodies and frocks *were* the public sphere, they were *spatial practices* in the semiosphere, a place that is as small as a photo and as large as suburbia. This is not space as classically conceived, but after Morris's *Great Moments in Social Climbing*, it's hard to decide what constitutes space *as such*, never mind public space, but as she says, the real concern is 'with the problems of historicising particular spatial practices', not with space in general.[33] The particular spatial practice I am seeking to explain is the 'virtualization' of the public sphere, its relocation into the 'frocks pop'.

Once again in this context, it's worth noting that, as Elizabeth Wilson has reminded us, fashion has developed hand in glove with the public sphere of democratization and urban life ever since the nineteenth century:

> *Fashion in the city served to signal to the other strangers in the crowded streets and public places the class and status of the individual, thus countering to some extent the social disorientation threatened by urban life.*[34]

And so, it could be argued, as post-Frankfurt School cultural theorists trace the history of what Richard Sennett entitles *The Fall of Public Man*,[35] it becomes ever more clear that 'man' is precisely the subject of the discourse of the public sphere from Hobbes onwards, and that, meanwhile, the shift from public to private domains, from political power to spending power, marks a contrary kind of history for women, one which can be read optimistically, as Wilson suggests.

> *So far as women are concerned – and fashion is still primarily associated with women – contemporary fashions arguably have liberatory potential (whether or not this is realized). . . . As fashion increasingly extends its ambiguous sway over both sexes, . . . it creates a space in which the normative nature of social practices, always so intensely encoded in dress, may be questioned. Fashion, as the most popular aesthetic practice of all, extends art into life and offers a medium across the social spectrum with which to experiment.*[36]

The 'space' created by fashion not only draws our attention to the politics of the body, but also introduces a new space for the body politic, and perhaps, thence, 'a site from which to speak' for women and others, 'as opposed to the Western modernist male intellectual who believed he stood at the cutting edge of history'.[37] The popular aesthetic spatial practice of wearing clothes in public is also political, whether self-consciously, like the demotic avant-garde punk (called by Wilson 'a walking art object and performance', designed to collapse the boundaries between art and life),[38] or the more diffused emancipation of social-democratic mass clothing, which

THE FACE

No 37/OCTOBER 1991 £1.50 • US $4.95
ITALY L6000 GERMANY 8.90DM SPAIN 435PTAS BELG. 138BFR

TALKIN LOUD

LOUIS FARRAKHAN
AND MUSLIM RAP

MEN IN FROCKS:
NEW YORK DRAG

YOUNG DISCIPLES,
INCOGNITO, OMAR

too sexy!

KYLIE
REMADE

KYLIE MINOGUE
photographed by
Andrew Macpherson

9 770263 121002

10

Army Of Lovers / Adeva / Spike Lee on Malcolm X / fat rap /
future cities / Brandon Lee: son of the dragon / bootleg wars

Fig. 7.6 Kylie Minogue in *The Face* (Photograph by Andrew Macpherson)

Sophie wears make-up by Guerlain. On face: Elysemat Liquid Foundation No.3, and Loose Powder in Perlee. On cheeks: Pomponnette Powder Blusher in Peche. On eyes: Powder Shadow Duo in Casablanca, Black Eye Pencil and Black Treatment Mascara. On lips: Corail Treatment Lipstick. Net bodysuit by Seafolly.

Close friend Kylie

Fig. 7.7 Sophie Lee in *Cleo*. Photograph by Daniela Federici (courtesy of ACP Publishing)

functions not only to expand individual *difference* but also to make it impossible, for the first time in history, to 'know a woman by her dress' – an anonymity which is one of the historic attractions of popular culture, as Leslie A. Fiedler tried to get the critics of 'mass culture' to see as long ago as the 50s.[39]

In my view (I don't think Wilson, as an avowed urbanist, would be a party to this extension of her argument), a further diffusion of the 'logic of equivalence' of democracy has extended the politics of fashion from urban to suburban locations, from boulevard and high street to shopping mall and home entertainment. If the tendency to feminize and sexualize the public domain continues, and if it is to be taken seriously by cultural analysts, then it follows that the prejudicial reputation of suburbia will also have to be rethought. The popular media, as is their wont, have begun to think through certain long-term, historical transformations *via* the 'calculating machine' of Kylie Minogue's and Sophie Lee's visual attractiveness (i.e. the hold of the 'telebrity frocks pop' at the point of contact between media and the public exemplifies, and is the focus of, larger trends towards the privatization, feminization and more recently the sexualization of the public sphere) – but the same cannot yet be said for the suburbs. Sexy they *ain't* (yet), despite the fact that this is where homes are traditionally set up by couples at the start of their sexually active careers, where children are begotten and where teenagers first learn about sex, in short where sex actually happens in Australian and other societies. So little are the suburbs associated with sex that noticing it has the force of a literary innovation: Robin Gerster notes, for instance:

> *Alan Wearne's verse-novel set in post-sixties Melbourne,* The Nightmarkets *(1985), is a contemporary text that explodes the myth of suburban deadness. In one scene, Sue Dobson, cynical veteran of the urban counter-culture, takes a friend to the family home deep in the suburbs as part of a tour of the city. 'Take any normal street of average length and just consider all that fucking!' she advises her companion.*[40]

Considering all that fucking may, however, produce other than pleasant visions of passion and fecundity. The quintessentially Australian 'class' which lives in 'the' suburbs is the petit bourgeoisie, now for ever identified with *Sylvania Waters* and in particular with Noelene and Laurie. Sex, in this context, is challenging to the onlooker to say the least, surfacing startlingly on occasion to produce what for Graeme Turner 'gets my vote as one of the most embarrassing moments in Australian television', namely 'Noelene's expression of pride in her lust for a black stripper, a lust that is actually fuelled rather than undercut by her racism'.[41] In short, sexualizing suburbia may only increase the problem of its reputation.

In fact the unsexiness of suburbia in so many discourses of loathing suggests that in the semiosphere suburbs generally occupy the position of ugly sister; their negativity is required, as is that of personalizations like Noelene Donaher, as a rhetorical foil for whichever desirable *urbs* they *sub*tend.[42] However, as I've tried to show, the 'frocks pop' indicate that the story of Cinderella applies to the suburbs in another way: it's the 'ugly sisters' of urban decline who have tried to clothe themselves in the desirable garb properly belonging to the despised but beautiful 'other' sister working in the scullery. Perhaps her time has come for an 'outing'?[43]

I've argued that the classical public domain is fully fictionalized and rhetoricized in contemporary representative politics, and that the 'smiling professions' exist within the great institutions of government, education and the media to produce and circularize the Sahlinesque symbols that allow society to cohere at all (to the extent that it *does* cohere at all). Suburbia is just as fictional as the classical public domain. It too is rhetoricized. This can occur positively, for instance in the form of 'the' suburban family on the cover of *TV Extra* (Fig. 7.8), where the 'family' turns out to be two local newsreaders and three not very feral kids (not their own) posing for a fake picnic outside the Telethon Home (publicizing a charity auction).[44]

Home is where the heart is: Susannah Carr and Rick Ardon, with some young friends, at the Telethon Home in Phillips-Fox Terrace, Woodvale. It will be auctioned on site at 11am today.   **SUNDAY, Seven and GWN, until 8.30pm.**

Fig. 7.8 Newsreaders as family. Photograph courtesy of Channel Seven Perth and the Perth *Sunday Times*

Or, negatively, suburbia can be made to symbolize the destruction of the classical body politic, as it was most tellingly in *Time* after the 1992 LA riots, putting to shame the democratic sentiments of the Woody Guthrie song: 'this land' (downtown) 'is your land' (black, poor, male); 'this land' (suburbia) 'is my land' (white, affluent, female) ... the democratic vistas of America are divided, a social fact symbolized in *Time* by putting the images of downtown and suburbia on succeeding pages, requiring the reader to *enact* the 'two Americas'.[45]

Meanwhile, in what used to be the real public domain – the city centre – the only time crowds turn out in this forum nowadays is to come in from the suburbs to catch a glimpse of supermodel Elle Macpherson, whose tour of Australia to promote her 'own' brand of lingerie turned into the contemporary equivalent of a royal progress, lovingly recorded in the weeklies, and in Perth at least rating two consecutive front-page colour lead stories in the *West Australian*, the newspaper of record for that State (Figs 7.9 and 7.10). Rob Sitch, comedian and 'host' of the ABC's parody current affairs show *Frontline*, has been quoted in *Australian Fashion Quarterly* as saying: 'Women are attracted by power and success, and men are attracted by lingerie ... You have to worry about our priorities.'[46]

He's right, especially as these two sets of priorities are now merged. Elle Macpherson, admired by women and men alike,

Fig. 7.9 Elle Macpherson in *The West Australian* . . . 'power and success'

pictured signing lifesized photographs of herself in lingerie, performs exactly the same function as Queen Victoria once did, the body politic now literally revealed *as* 'The Body', successfully symbolizing the 'dignified part' of the constitution even in her underwear, effortlessly uniting 'the people' around a figure which is clearly understood by the crowds (who fight each other for the right to get a glimpse of her) as the smiling professional *par excellence*, a representative of Australianness in a way that the actual Queen's actual representative at the time, Governor General Bill Hayden, could never hope to match.

Fig. 7.10 Elle Macpherson in *The West Australian . . .* 'lingerie'

Notes

1. Rita Felski (1995) *The Gender of Modernity*. Cambridge, Mass.: Harvard University Press, 34.
2. Vanessa Paradis, 'France's leading cover girl', quoted in: Paris passion – the new French starlets, by Amy Raphael, *The Face* 40, January 1992, 32–9.
3. See Cherise Saywell (1994/5) Post-sacred sex: melodramatic discourse and the erect penis in *Sophie Lee's Sex*. Paper presented to *Intellectuals and Communities*, conference of the Australian Cultural Studies Association. Saywell argues that this documentary series' over-coding of

emotion, visualization, feminization and the moral order places it in the tradition of melodrama, rather than current affairs.

4. Sex on TV comes in three forms of absence:
   metonym – bits of bodies and movements associated with sex;
   metaphor – flowers/ocean waves/ceiling fans (etc.) plus music and a quick cut to the morning/cigarette after;
   modification – the evil MAO or 'Modified Adults Only' classification, which deletes even fully fictionalized sex from Australian commercial TV screens for fear of offending someone, or more exactly some*thing*, namely the Australian Broadcasting Authority.

5. E.g. a full-page ad for Channel 9 in the *West Australian* (13 August 1992) showing photos of Sophie Lee and Elle Macpherson, captioned SEX WITH SOPHIE LEE 8-30 TONIGHT', and 'ELLE McPHERSON [*sic*] CALENDAR GIRL 9-30 TONIGHT'.

6. All I Want for Christmas. . . *The Australian Women's Weekly*, December 1992, 4–5. The spread featured a kind of 'Australian community' of different people, ranging from some worthy unknowns to Prime Minister Paul Keating, Olympic swimmer Kieren Perkins, author Elizabeth Jolley, Professor Fred Hollows and *Strictly Ballroom*'s star Tara Morice.

7. The most interesting story was about some advertisers' responses to *Sex*, though it was misleadingly headlined 'Some *viewers* don't like "Sex"'. Despite high ratings, viewer approval, and a primary audience of the desirable 'females aged 16 to 39' demographic, some advertisers were unmoved: 'General Motors-Holden's advertising manager David Venticich said: "We choose to advertise on programs which are wholesome and *Sex* simply doesn't fit our bill in terms of being a wholesome program".' Luckily, Channel 9 had the good sense to stick with the show (and, with the increasing tendency for women to decide motor car purchases, GMH might have to reconsider their amazingly outdated notion of wholesomeness). See 'Some viewers don't like "Sex"', Perth *Sunday Times*, 14 June 1992, 4.

8. See Tom O'Regan (1996) *Australian National Cinema*. London: Routledge, Chapter 10, where he quotes the film's director to show how this decentring of expectations is explicitly anti-Hollywood. O'Regan argues that it is by no means confined to *Muriel's Wedding*, however, being a characteristic gesture of Australian national cinema.

9. Sophie Lee (1995) interviewed by Catharin Lambert in *Australian Style* 12, 1995, 62–3.

10. For instance her cover-girl picture in *TV Week* (16 November 1991) is superimposed, in big red letters, with the headline: 'IT HURTS. . .'. On reading the story inside, it transpires that what has hurt her is sexism and gossip, the very things that *TV Week* displays and celebrates *via* Sophie Lee, and so the readers, if not Sophie Lee herself, can have their sex-and-gossip cake and critically eat it too. See also Fig. 7.2.

11. As always, the uneditorialized voice of the readership is hard to trace, but one fan letter did show up – in *Playboy*. After asking 'What does Soph wear under her miniskirt?', a reader's letter (from one C. Marks, Sydney South, NSW) concludes: 'What better subject for some good old-fashioned cheesecake photography – subtle, tasteful, but all the more naughty – than the lady who has become the leading spokesperson for the safe sex campaign of Australia?' To which 'Ed.' appends a reply: 'Wow, that's one weird question! We also would have thought

that the answer to what she wears under her miniskirt is pretty obvious: panties. Still, you're obviously after more detail. As far as a more revealing look at Sophie goes, you can rest assured that we are on the case – *Ed'. Australian Playboy*, November 1992, 5. (Needless to say, Sophie Lee never appeared as a pin-up.)

12. Opening lines of R.K. Webb (1955) *The British Working Class Reader 1790–1848: Literacy and Social Tension*. London: George Allen & Unwin, 13.

13. Kylie comes clean: Minogue on sex, drugs, and naked ambition, by Adrian Deevoy, *Cleo*, January 1993, 112–15, 153.

14. Graeme Turner (1991) Return to Oz: populism, the academy and the future of Australian studies. *Meanjin* 50(2), 19–31.

15. Meaghan Morris (1991) Responses to Graeme Turner. *Meanjin* 50(2), 32–4. Turner and Morris were engaged in a dialogue in *Meanjin* as to whether or not John Fiske was the Kylie Minogue of cultural studies. Morris thought not, because unlike Fiske, Kylie did not produce work with which she could *disagree*.

16. Even Kylie Minogue's lyrics can be controversial, and have been subjected to close textual analysis, as in the case of her 1991 hit song 'Shocked'. According to an analysis in the opening paragraph of her *Cleo* profile, the lyrics go like this: 'I was shocked by the power, Shocked by the power of love, Yes, I was shocked, Fucked to my very foundations'. To which the typical bad-faith question immediately asked by *Cleo* (which either does, or does not, reckon 'pop kids' among its own readership), is this: 'Must we fling this filth at our pop kids?' *Cleo*, January 1993, 112.

17. Power over flesh, by Sally Brampton, *Mirabella* UK, February 1991, 110–13.

18. Thomas Hobbes (1968, first published 1651) *Leviathan*. Ed. C.B. Macpherson. Harmondsworth: Penguin, 151–2.

19. Hobbes, 150–1.

20. Hobbes writes: '*Naturall Power*, is the eminence of the Faculties of Body, or Mind: as extraordinary Strength, Forme, Prudence, Arts, Eloquence, Liberality, Nobility' (150). See also C.B. Macpherson (1962) *The Political Theory of Possessive Individualism: Hobbes to Locke*. Oxford: Oxford University Press, 35–7.

21. Abigail Bray (1994) 'The edible woman': reading/eating disorders and femininity. *Media Information Australia* 72, 4–10, this quotation 7.

22. For example, on a planned Minogue book with nude poses, see *TV Week*, 21 November 1992, 22: A leaf from Madonna's book.

23. Marshall Sahlins (1976) *Culture and Practical Reason*. Chicago: University of Chicago Press, 203–4.

24. Sahlins argues for an anthropology of meaning in which culture is understood both as a unified symbolic structure, and as a form of practical reasoning with material effects. He writes: 'Much of anthropology can be considered a sustained effort at synthesizing the original segmentation of its object, an analytical distinction of cultural domains it had made without due reflection, if clearly on the model presented by our own society. But the project was doomed from the beginning, because the very first act had consisted in ignoring the unity and distinctiveness of culture as a symbolic structure, hence the reason imposed from within on the relations to an external nature. . . But it follows that a retotalization is not effected merely by considering material goods, for

example, in the context of social relations. The unity of the cultural order is constituted by a third and common term, meaning'. Sahlins, 205–6.

25. John Hartley (1992) *The Politics of Pictures: The Creation of the Public in the Age of Popular Media.* London and New York: Routledge, Chapter 5.

26. Kylie evolved, by Zoe Heller, *The Independent on Sunday*, 27 October 1991. This interview was a promo for an upcoming concert at Wembley Arena, but it was headlined FASHION and accompanied photographs by Mark Lebon of Kylie Minogue dressed by John Galliano.

27. Heller.

28. Heller.

29. Morris, *Ecstasy and Economics.* Sydney: EMPress, 122. Along with three other interestingly titled books – *Fraud, Sin,* and *The Pleasure of Reading* – Morris's stylish book rated a review in *Vogue*, headlined 'The fantastical reality of others' lucid dreams', which brought cultural studies (or at least Morris's) into direct dialogue with the feminized public domain I've tried to describe herein (*Vogue Australia* XXXVI (11), November 1992, 66). But of course Morris was happily ensconced in the virtual public sphere long before I stumbled upon it: the author's photo on the back cover of *Ecstasy and Economics* shows her, a true professor of smiling, sitting outside a motel called, appropriately, 'The Forum'.

30. 27 October 1991 and 1 September 1991 respectively.

31. In bed with Kylie . . . , by Chris Heath, *The Face* 37, October 1991, cover, 3, 46–53, 128.

32. Ian Hunter (1992) The humanities without humanism. *Meanjin* 51 (3), 479–90, this quotation 488.

33. Meaghan Morris (1992) *Great Moments in Social Climbing: King Kong and the Human Fly.* Sydney: Local Consumption Publications, 4–5. For Morris, such problems are associated with places well to the side of the traditional public domain (she lists Sydney Tower, three suburban shopping malls, a motel and a memorial park); apart from the beach, they are at least *buildings.*

34. Elizabeth Wilson (1990) These new components of the spectacle: fashion and postmodernism. In Roy Boyne and Ali Rattansi (eds.) *Postmodernism and Society*, London: Macmillan, 209–36, this quotation 211.

35. Richard Sennett (1974) *The Fall of Public Man.* Cambridge: Cambridge University Press.

36. Wilson, 233. See also her essay All the rage. In Jane Gaines and Charlotte Herzog (eds.) (1990) *Fabrications: Costume and the Female Body.* New York and London: Routledge, 28–38, where she hints that the British radical (Fabian) dislike for fashion may have the same roots as suburbia itself, namely late Victorian lower-middle-class respectability (29). If so, then the hip dislike of suburbia is understandable, but it is as outmoded as the radical dislike of fashion.

37. Wilson, These new components . . ., 232–3.

38. Wilson, New components, 216.

39. See Leslie Fiedler's essay in B. Rosenberg and David Manning White (eds.) (1957) *Mass Culture: The Popular Arts in America.* Glencoe, Ill.: Free Press.

40. Robin Gerster (1990) Gerrymander: the place of suburbia in Australian fiction. *Meanjin* 49(3), 565–75.

41. Graeme Turner, Suburbia verité, 39.

42. See Kathleen Mee (1994) Dressing up the suburbs: representations of western Sydney. In Katherine Gibson and Sophie Watson (eds.) *Metropolis Now: Planning and the Urban in Contemporary Australia*. Sydney: Pluto Press, 60–77.

43. While it may be time for suburbia to 'come out', both Kylie Minogue and Sophie Lee signed off 1992 in the popular picture papers by saying that they would (or would like to) disappear, by turning to study; in Sophie Lee's case this was enough to make front page news: 'It's back to school: Sophie swaps Sex for study!' squealed the cover of *TV Week*. The first benefit of study, we learn inside, is to avoid the *glance*: 'at the Actors' Centre in Surry Hills, Sydney, no-one gives Sophie a second glance'. (A class act! by Di Stanley, *TV Week*, 12 September 1992, cover and 6–7.) Meanwhile, 'Kylie has also recently admitted that she hopes one day to go back to her first love – acting – and that "there are times when I hate what I do. I often consider giving it all up," she confesses. "I'd like to study at university or maybe backpack across Thailand." (Nice Men Aren't Interested in Me, by Vici McCarthy, *Woman's Day*, 5 October 1992, 10–11.) It seems that for both Sophie Lee and Kylie Minogue study represents a return to the private, anonymous personal life they do not enjoy as 'frocks pop'.

44. Home is where the heart is, Perth *Sunday Times*, *TV Extra Magazine*, 18–24 October 1992, cover picture and caption.

45. The two Americas: e pluribus unum?, *Time Australia*, 18 May 1992, cover story, 28–33.

46. *Australian Fashion Quarterly* 8 (Summer 1994) 176.

CHAPTER

8 *The Triumph of the Still*

(Gunners and Gallantry)

Now though we know of old that looks deceive
And always have done, somehow these good looks
Make more impression than the best of books.
                                        LORD BYRON[1]

This chapter considers the use of pictorial, commercial, popular journalism in nation-building. Photography is of course the most spectacular new development in journalism of the twentieth century; it dominates TV journalism, and in print journalism the rule is clear – the more popular the outlet, the more driven by pictures it must be. But along with this development has continued an anxious chorus of critical denunciation that says pictorial, commercial journalism is not an extension of the democratic energies of the French Revolution, but an invasion. In come aesthetics, out goes politics; in come media tycoons, out goes democracy; in come pictures, out goes reality. This Habermasian fantasy of the imminent defeat of actuality by semiosis, of the public by publicity, of the real by the sign, has retained its hold throughout the twentieth century, despite (perhaps because of) the fact that one of journalism's main jobs during that whole period has been to visualize actuality by means of semiosis, the public by means of publicity, and the real by means of the sign. Far from destroying the public with too much visual stimulation, pictorial news creates the public sphere *within* the semiosphere, and has been doing so for over a hundred years.[2]

Although this chapter is about photojournalism, I want to begin with something that is neither journalism nor a photo; it's an advertisement, and unlike most ads these days it comprises four columns of copy, with no photographs at all (Fig. 8.1). What's really unusual about it is that it advertises both newspapers (as opposed to television) and advertising; it's a 1987 newspaper ad for the Newspaper Advertising Bureau of Australia.[3] Despite being an ad, this is a useful,

Have you ever wondered why one newspaper advertisement works better than another?

Why, for instance, has *this* particular advertisement attracted your attention?

Is it because the headline offers you an intriguing benefit?

And speaks to you in a personal way?

Or could it be the typestyle that is deliberately inviting and easy to read?

In truth, every single element in this advertisement is carefully calculated to attract your interest and keep it.

It is, in effect, an ideal ad, created entirely to demonstrate some proven principles of newspaper advertising.

Many more are contained within the copy below.

All you have to do is read on.

We'll simply swap a few minutes of your time for 80 solid years of well-researched wisdom.

Higher potential readers.

To start with, the very fact this advertisement is even *in* a newspaper gives it a head start.

Almost 90% of readers see every page of their newspaper, excluding the classified sections. And spend, on average, some 40 minutes with their favourite daily paper.

In addition, newspaper readers are more receptive to advertising.

According to Starch readership surveys, they actually give *equal value* to the information received via ads as they do editorial.

The same can't be said of television, where advertising content is viewed as an intrusion. (A phenomenon known in the trade as the "flush factor".)

Nor does it apply to radio, often referred to unkindly, but perhaps accurately, as "wallpaper sound".

Listeners aren't standing with one ear cocked for the commercials.

Given the unique advantage of the newspaper medium, it's really up to you to capitalise on this natural curiosity.

And there are proven ways to do this.

Strong headlines lead to strong bottom lines.

The key to being noticed is to target the message by means of the headline.

A good headline should say "this message is for you, read on".

Such an effect is most often achieved when a headline promises or infers a benefit.

You see an example above.

A headline should also involve the prospect emotionally. It doesn't have to use the word "you" or "your" but it's amazing how often these words can help.

David Ogilvy maintains the reader must be "flagged down" in the headline.

Bill Bernbach urged that headlines "go to the essence of the product".

Headlines then, are crucial to capturing prospects.

Lose them there and the rest of the advertisement is academic.

The laws of gravity.

Once having gained a reader's attention, layout and typography take over to help guide it through safely.

Some age-old maxims are borne out in recent research conducted by Colin Wheildon, Publications Editor for the NRMA.

In the Western World, reading is done from top left of the page to bottom right.

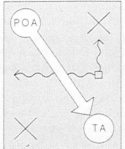

Figure 1. Gutenberg diagram charts basic reading eye movement. Picture-captions like this, by the way, also help make your advertisement more information-rich.

The same applies to eye travel through an advertisement (See Fig. 1).

The eye falls initially on the top left, the Primary Optical Area (POA) and leaves the page at the bottom right, the Terminal Area (TA).

Crosses indicate dead corners, and wavy lines track "backward" movement which the reading eye resists.

(You may have noticed this advertisement adheres closely to these dynamics.)

This is known as reading gravity, the laws of which are broken with grave results.

For example, test layouts complying with the principles of reading gravity (Fig. 2) score 73% good comprehension.

This is the ideal position for a headline.

Figure 2. An example of a layout which complies with the principles of reading gravity.

But turn the page - and the diagram - upside down, and you see an example of a layout which completely opposes these principles.

And causes the comprehension scores to become totally reversed; 37% as against 73%.

How long is a piece of copy?

If good layout guides readers through an advertisement, it is body copy which holds them.

The extent to which body copy is read has always been a vital question, even a hotly contested issue, for advertisers.

But the amount of copy which prospects are willing to read is often completely underestimated.

Ogilvy's own research shows that "although readership falls off rapidly up to 50 words, it drops off little between 50 and 500 words".

(As a matter of interest, this ad contains over 1000 words.)

Long copy can often convey the impression that you have something important to say, whether it is read or not.

Copy length ultimately depends on the fascination of the subject matter.

If you were to be handed six tightly spaced pages someone had written about you, you'd probably read every word.

	%
1. Roman old style lower case	92
2. Sans serif lower case	90
3. Roman modern lower case	89
4. *Roman old style italic lower case*	86
5. *Roman modern italic lower case*	86
6. *Sans serif italic lower case*	86
7. Optima lower case	85
8. *Optima italic lower case*	86
9. ROMAN MODERN CAPS	71
10. ROMAN OLD STYLE CAPITALS	69
11. Square serif lower case	64
12. *ROMAN MODERN ITALIC CAPITALS*	63
13. *ROMAN OLD STYLE ITALIC CAPITALS*	62
14. *SANS SERIF ITALIC CAPITALS*	59
15. *OPTIMA ITALIC CAPITALS*	57
16. SANS SERIF CAPITALS	56
17. OPTIMA CAPITALS	51
18. SQUARE SERIF CAPITALS	44
19. *script lower case*	37
20. ornamented lower case	32
21. *script caps*	26
22. ORNAMENTED CAPITALS	19
23. text letter lower case	10
24. TEXT LETTER CAPITALS	3

Figure 3. Legibility of headline styles comprehension scores.

It takes all types to make a world. But not an ad.

The most common and legible newspaper typefaces are serif styles, such as we've employed on this page.

(Serifs are the little "feet" on the extremities of the characters.)

Sans serif type - such as you see in this example paragraph - is demonstrably less readable, especially when the copy runs to any sort of length.

One school of thought argues that capital letters in headlines achieve more impact. But the eye is presented with A SERIES OF SOLID RECTANGLES AND RECOGNISING WORDS BECOMES A TASK INSTEAD OF A NATURAL PROCESS.

The argument for lower case headlines has human physiology on its side.

When a person reads a line of type the eye recognises the letters by the shape of their upper half.

In fact, a line of lower case type with the bottom half completely missing is still quite legible, as you can see.

This is because the top half of lower case letters are quite distinctive, and, when framed by the white space around them, permit easy recognition.

Again, various other tests have shown conclusive - even brutal results - in favour of lower case letters.

With headlines set in Roman Old Style lower case scoring highest with 92% legibility, and black letter capitals coming a bad 24th, with 3%. (See Fig. 3.)

The same principles apply to text.

Tests have shown serif type leads to 67% good comprehension and sans serif a mere 12%.

There are other, but equally important, principles worthy of note.

Justified body copy, such as you see here, where the text is lined up on the left and right-hand margins, tends to rate more highly in comprehension tests, scoring 62%.

Set it ragged, however, the way you see it in this example paragraph, and suddenly the comprehension level drops down to an alarming 10%.

Columns too, should be no wider than 40 characters or one-and-a-half alphabets. (The column width you are reading now averages 40 characters.)

But once a column width drops below a 20 character measure, so does the score.

Even the tightness of letterspacing, or kerning as it's called, can influence legibility.

Set it too tight, like this (where characters are kerned 4 units) and you get an almost total loss of comprehension.

The ideal is to kern around one unit, as demonstrated in this line.

Words of Caution.

Of course, you can't simply do great ads "by the numbers" in this fashion.

Otherwise every ad in this newspaper would look exactly the same.

Thus defying the very first principle of advertising - to stand out.

The skill comes in knowing the rules so you are able to break them creatively.

There are thousands of permutations of these guidelines and just as many success stories behind them.

So finally, let us give you one more guideline of good newspaper advertising.

Close the sale.

Further information can be obtained from The Newspaper Advertising Bureau of Australia, 77 Berry Street, North Sydney 2060. (02) 92 1044.

The Newspaper Advertising Bureau is a marketing organisation established by Australia's major metropolitan and regional newspaper publishers as a service to industry.

As such, the NABA is a non-profit organisation.

Which it can afford to be, given that so many of its advertisers aren't.

Newspapers work.

Incidentally, it has frequently been shown that the best place for your company logo or brand is down here. In the bottom right-hand corner. After all, where do you place the signature on a personal letter?

The creative partnership of Jack Vaughan and Rob Tennant at the Campaign Palace, Sydney, has resulted in some of the most effective and memorable Australian advertising produced in the past few years. They created this ad for the Newspaper Advertising Bureau of Australia.

Fig. 8.1 An ad for ads – and newspapers – courtesy of The Campaign Palace, Sydney

informative, interesting and well-designed piece of analysis (it repays detailed attention if you're interested in the tricks of the trade), and what's more it gives away the greatest trade secret of advertising; namely that advertising 'works' by very detailed and sophisticated techniques which are used not to make people *buy* but to make them *read*. Advertising, like news, is a textual system, and the 'influence' it has over people is to train them in a certain kind of literacy. If advertising did indeed 'make' people buy there'd be nothing left in the shops; if it 'worked', we wouldn't need it. This ad, pursuing advertisers, gives the game away:

> *In truth, every single element in this advertisement is carefully calcu-*
> *lated to attract your interest and keep it.*
>
> *It is, in effect, an ideal ad, created entirely to demonstrate some*
> *proven principles of newspaper advertising.*
>
> *All you have to do is read on.*

Like journalism, advertising has a vested interest in constructing and instructing a readership, and like advertising, journalism has to work on the basis of Lotmanesque mutual attraction to get its readers to look at its copy; to 'read on' (it's all they *can* do in practice). Advertising and journalism have lived together since the outset of both, and have come up with the same techniques for attracting readers, techniques which of course include the use of pictures. But because advertising has if anything an even worse reputation among social critics than does popular journalism, the fact that advertising was first to capitalize the semiotic potential of pictures has only served to deepen the puritan suspicion of visual excess ('we know of old that looks deceive' as Lord Byron put it in *Don Juan*), a sixteenth-century prejudice against both (Catholic) icons and women that has persisted throughout modernity in the form of educated prejudice against the visuality of popular media.[4] This chapter seeks to work against that prejudicial grain by showing how news and advertising share the same semiotic space, and are in constant dialogue with each other – at least from the point of view of the reader. And as the ad for ads says of newspaper readers: 'According to Starch readership surveys, they actually give *equal value* to the information received via ads as they do editorial'.

A Rupert

Journalism's poisonous, contaminated reputation among artists, writers and intellectuals is best summed up by a sick joke of British TV playwright Dennis Potter, who publicly named his own pancreatic cancer 'Rupert' (after Rupert Murdoch, controlling shareholder of News Ltd.), just before it killed him in May 1994 – although of course Potter couldn't avoid using journalism, in the form of international television news, to broadcast his gallows humour to the public.[5] Since the media are the world's most fully capitalized mode of discourse, where economic power is connected not with production (Potter) but with success in distribution, circulation, marketing, publicity and social pervasion (Murdoch), it is not surprising that traditional producers of discourse and knowledge (intellectuals and artists) are dubious about the most popular media forms, which are driven by sales rather than being disciplined by truth.

But is journalism – even at its most popular, tabloid and highly capitalized – a terminal disease inside the very body of contemporary writing? Or is it simply postmodern, an 'impure' and supplementary form without essence, totality or malignancy, that happens to be supplanting the regime of knowledge it supposedly contaminates? I argue in this chapter that in the twentieth century, journalism 'as a whole' has become the practice of rendering visible the continuous (and necessary) dialogue between truth and communication, between a rational public sphere and the fantasy layers of the semiosphere. The process of rendering visible, which is in principle a *discursive* matter, since visualization can be done in any medium (print and oral as well as visual), has in the twentieth century become more and more literally a visualization, and so this chapter will concentrate on the photographic media, showing that the habit of thought which separates news from more frankly 'visualizing' communication like advertising is at variance with the facts, for while news and advertising are fairly strictly kept apart at the production end, the same is not true at the so-called consumption end of the communication process – readers see news and ads on the same pages and screens, and read them with the same literacy, the same cultural and public knowledges, within the same symbolic and imaginary semiotic landscape; both news and advertising have the same origin in *publicity*, creating a public for a campaign (civic and commercial respectively).

It is the 'contamination' of the body politic by the 'cancer' of commerce that perturbs many who are of the same mind as Dennis Potter, but their concern arises not so much from the malignancy of commercial involvement in media (which has been there throughout modernity), but from the insecure position of journalism itself *as a realism*: a vulnerability to 'self-contamination' which is structured into the 'heart' of journalism not as some external infection but as a founding property that makes journalism what it is, namely *communication*. Journalism is a realism, committed to having its account of the socio-political world agree with referential reality. But simultaneously, like advertising, it is a textualization of the world into a form which is nonetheless constructed and imaginary for being matter-of-fact and familiar. Also like advertising, news has not only to textualize its subject-matter but also to attract and sustain a readership. And like advertising, news is a textual system which has its own history, conventions, innovations, genres, personalities and features, i.e. it is a cultural form which is also the literacy of its readers, who do not come to the news each day fresh as a daisy and with the same amount of knowledge of the mediasphere, but as fully formed readers. As a result of being inserted in this diachronic, collective stream of consciousness, journalism is (and always has been), like any textual system, a developing, self-referential mode of discourse which refreshes itself and its readership with liberal doses of image innovation, including the devices of fiction, faking and fabrication, to reproduce and circulate 'new' narratives and images for its global semio-consumers. The interesting paradox is that the more journalism has turned to the supposedly realistic imperatives of photographic modes of representation, the more it has become self-consciously emancipated from mere referentiality.

Journalism has exceeded the *political* terms of its modernist manifesto, and can no longer be seen purely as a virtuous, revolutionary rhetoricization of the energies created by the inauguration of the sovereignty of the people. Alongside that history has developed another, namely *commercial* journalism; a very different kettle of fish, apparently, since it provokes the routine response of horror in observers from the modernizing, public sphere of writing, who are all too prone to pathologize it as a 'Rupert'. But in fact modernity always was associated with comfort as well as sovereignty; 'freedom' meant freedom from want and freedom to choose diapers as well as deputies. Whether the bourgeois freedoms (of labour, contract, exchange and accumulation) have ever co-existed peacefully with popular freedom is of course a matter of long debate, a debate which has tended to obscure the *promise* of popular sovereignty, from 1789 onwards, a promise of freedom from dearth, fear and coercion, and a promise of comfort, progress and reason for all. It is this aspect of modernity – the pursuit of comfort – that has been most completely colonized by commerce, and commercial journalism was both an early manifestation of this modernizing tendency and simultaneously a major mechanism for promoting it. Journalism is, by its existence, an 'advertisement' for modernity, a visualization of the promise of comfort, progress and freedom. The construction of reading publics around promises of comfort has of course leaked over from the commercial sphere of dubious sales techniques into the public sphere, and is everywhere the small change of political campaigning.

Meanwhile journalism, which as I've been arguing *constituted* the public sphere from the start, has shown a tendency throughout the twentieth century to take over and textualize the democratic function of nations. It is now the place, means and agent of political participation for populations which are otherwise showing a marked and increasing disinclination to vote, to join political parties, or otherwise do their civic, constitutional or political duties as citizens of nation states. Governments of the oldest democracies are driven to recruiting representatives from their supposed binary opposite, i.e. entertainers from the furthest reaches of popular entertainment, to seduce their own citizens – as for example the US government's TV commercial starring Madonna, a US flag and some male African-American dancers, which was designed to persuade ethnic minorities to register and to vote in the 1992 (Clinton/Bush) presidential election. This too is a 'contamination' of the body politic by commerce, sex, fantasy and a well-delivered joke, but it is done precisely to keep that body healthy and operational in a nation where fewer than 50 per cent of eligible adults exercise their democratic right to vote for the presidential candidate of their choice. As a realism, journalism like government seeks in principle to conform to the facts, to agree with reality, not to be based in fantasy, fiction and fabrication; this is what its readers are encouraged to believe above all else as the guarantor of truth. The semiotic enunciation of this guarantee is, nevertheless, and ruinously for the purity of the guarantee, a discursive style – a set of complex textual tricks designed to prove that the facts are talking by themselves. In communicating public truths (and virtue) to a post-revolutionary public, contemporary commercial journalism mixes seduction with reason, pop with politics, commerce with communication, as it has done since 1789, in the very service of public-sphere virtues. To make my argument clear here, I am not berating journalism for these properties; I am merely reporting them, and pointing out that journalism is therefore not exempt from textual construction just because it refers to something outside of itself (the so-called real), or just because its practitioners' motives are pure (even when they are). In short, I'm drawing attention to the inevitability of textuality even in the most magisterially truth-laden realisms: journalism, democracy, politics, government, as well as being what common sense says they are, *are all also fantasies.*

The Real = Photography + Readers

But of course, twentieth-century journalism has done the critics' job for them, by showing a tendency to test modernist realism to destruction. Clearly quite a bit of journalism is post-truth; many stories are lies, and we have 'tabloid' and 'trash' news media that glory in them. Sometimes these media, which specialize in sex stories and sightings of Elvis, Hitler and flying saucers, cross over into the traditional public domain, without bringing truth with them, of course, as for example the unsubstantiated allegations about Bill Clinton's sex-life during his presidential campaign, which were initiated in the *National Enquirer*. This was topped by a story which had ALIEN BACKS CLINTON, complete with photograph, in the US weekly *National News*, a mad joke that then became a useful photo-opportunity for the governor of Arkansas, and was republished around the world, not least in the *Australian* (see Introduction). More important, perhaps, is journalism's post-truth tendency, in quite a lot of the most successful contemporary outlets, i.e. the texts with the largest readerships, to make no propositions for which there is a possible 'true/false' response. This type of journalism doesn't rely on aliens, but equally it doesn't refer to an external world beyond the intertextual semiosphere of contemporary symbolic culture, nor does it invoke a reality which takes precedence over its narrative renditions.

Among the major examples of post-truth journalism is the one thing that makes it a commercial product, whether in print or screen form – its pictorial content. Where would Rupert (not the tumour) be without Page Three – pictures of women with girl-next-door looks, in their late teens and early twenties, photographed without their tops on, looking direct to camera and smiling – for instance? Page Three is legendary for being the mechanism that converted a whole population into the *Sun*'s readership. Larry Lamb was the *Sun*'s first editor under Murdoch's ownership, and the man who, according to his own account, 'helped to make Page Three a part of the language'. He is coy about the effect of topless women models on circulation, although it is clear they were used to attract a readership: 'Important though they were to the paper's development – mainly because they got us talked about – the girls were not nearly as significant as was generally supposed' (this is in a chapter called 'Page Three or Bust'). Lamb, who was knighted by Margaret Thatcher, also reproduces a picture of the model Vivien Neves which was the original topless pose in a British daily; but although Neves became a favourite 'Page Three Girl', this celebrated shot was actually published in *The Times*, in an advertisement for fertilizer (Fig. 8.2).[6]

But the pictures on Page Three do not make propositions, neither about truth nor about relationships. Although they rescued an ailing newspaper they're not even journalism. They are community-building mechanisms and marketing devices. They are designed to attract and hold readers, not establish truths. They are a visualization of Lotman's 'language of smiles', the pre-semiotic mutual attraction of reader and text in the semiosphere which enables dialogue to start and meaning to be created (see page 114–15). But of course it would be wrong to consider the sexualization of journalism as anything new; on the contrary, it is precisely the journalism of tits, bums, scandals, pornography and celebrity gossip that pre-dates the liberatory 'big bang' of the French Revolution, being, as we've seen in Chapter 4, one of the major sources of political journalism.

Ironically, it is the pictorial content of journalism, in both print and screen media, that is said to be the most imperative guarantor of its truth, of its realism, or at the least of its reference to something outside of itself. But the idea that pictures can't lie and must refer to something real is patently absurd, so the ideology of the photographic imperative is in practice a kind of shared tact or trust, a treaty perhaps between publisher and reader, proposing that readers can rely upon what they see. However, that trust does not extend to boring readers to death, and so reality has to be selected, framed, composed, processed, edited, cropped, airbrushed, captioned, and where possible coloured, to make it look as much as possible like advertising. The commitment to readerships over reality is endemic in all textual systems, as it must be, but in journalism, especially

Fig. 8.2 The *Sun* borrows an idea – and Vivien Neves – from *The Times*. Photograph by Michael Boys, from Larry Lamb's *Sunrise*

TOP PEOPLE'S PIN-UP: Long before *The Sun* made the phrase 'Page Three girl' part of the English language, readers of the Top People's Paper, *The Times*, had been treated to – or infuriated by – this sensational picture of Vivien Neves. It wasn't in the editorial columns, however. It was in a full-page advertisement. For fertilisers!

pictorial journalism, this is counted in the most widely available and respectable frameworks of critical explanation as a crime against truth.

In fact the matter is policed vigorously precisely because there is no truth component in pictures (they make no propositions); in photography truth is in the eye of the beholder. A faked, staged, touched-up or altered photograph cannot easily be distinguished from a straight one by the viewer, and so the guarantee of its authenticity comes in the end from the viewer's belief in it, a belief sustained not as an individual opinion but via literacy in the social ideology of realism. Realism, then, is not so much a textual property as a cultural propaganda campaign designed to persuade readerships (no matter what the evidence) that what they see is so. Hence the more familiar the subject the better for realism, because it's easier for the viewer to verify from previous knowledge that the picture shows what it purports to show. Thus it's easier to fake a photograph of a nuclear installation than a celebrity face, for actors and models may be more familiar faces around the house than many of our own family members, but few of us know what a nuclear dump in Cuba or Iraq or Muroroa *ought* to look like, especially one photographed from miles up by a U2 spy-plane. But the familiar is nevertheless routinely given a helping hand to enhance its realism, for instance where fashion photos are airbrushed into perfection. Eyes are clarified, skin smoothed, colours toned in, blemishes removed – even 'blemishes' that take the form of (women's) nipples, as was discussed in relation to Kate Moss's *American Photo* cover in the Introduction to this book. So naturalized do these artfully faked images look that anything less 'produced' begins to look fake. In short, realism is a *code of reading*, a regime of truth, not a technical rendition of reality.

Meanwhile, we sometimes marvel at gloriously blatant fakes that come from other regimes, such as the disappearance of the Gang of Four from the official photo of Mao Zedong's funeral in 1976 (Fig. 8.3). The picture was published in the *People's Daily* the day after Mao's funeral *with* the Gang of Four; a month later it was published again *without* them. But whatever the status of its *photographic* realism, there's no doubt that the airbrushed Gang of Four photograph expresses Chinese political realities very accurately, and it is for this purpose that Chinese official photographs are published. But the strangeness of Chinese political iconography to those trained in the habits of Western realism shouldn't be taken as evidence that the West's familiar icons are any more real than this, or this more faked than Kate Moss's nipples.

Accepting that realism is a product of the relation between texts and readers, rather than being a property of the world, is made more difficult because realism's basic tenet is precisely that it *does* refer to a reality outside of itself. It effaces its own textuality, its own status as discourse. In these circumstances it seems to require even journalism's critics to accept that basic tenet, otherwise surely there would be no basis upon which to criticize it. In other words, accusations of media bias, inaccuracy, distortion, misrepresentation, lies, mistakes, fabrication, faking, propaganda (etc.), are hard even to imagine, let alone 'prove', if there is no 'real' outside of journalism to act as an objective yardstick against which its performance can be

measured. This difficulty is why criticism of popular journalism so often forgets journalism's *discursive reality* and denounces it from a position which apparently 'knows' reality personally, as it were, from *outside* of discourse. Unfortunately for such criticism, in the human semiosphere there is no such place – realism itself is a 'place' in the semiosphere, as is criticism. But still, given the propensity of certain media to commit atrocities against truth on a regular basis, and thence apparently to misinform and mislead their readership the public, it seems that it is a brave (or reckless) critic who gives away the main weapon in the critical armoury ('Bias!' 'Distortion!' 'Lies!') before entering the fray. And so most public discussions of journalism, especially those which circulate within the media themselves, accept its claims to realistic transparency. Meanwhile there's silence about the *reality* of the very stuff that journalism is made of: words, images, sequence, visualization. I think this amounts to bad faith, and would suggest that while journalism, like the public sphere, criticism, realism and even truth itself, is made of discourse, it is nevertheless possible to analyse commercial, pictorial journalism without seeing it as a cancer or as a distortion of pure, pre-semiotic reality. Truth has power to command, but only if it is known and communicated; communication in its industrial forms, i.e. drama and journalism, is achieved by rhetorical, narrative and visual means, and

Fig. 8.3 Mao's funeral: the day after, and one month later the 'Gang of Four' has disappeared

made into 'well-known facts' by marketing and promotional activities, which have no necessary connection with truth.

But just in case you, like Dennis Potter, are still afraid of big bad media wolves (foxes?) like Rupert Murdoch, it might be worth pointing out that no one today gives two hoots for Charles-Joseph Panckoucke, though there are some (like me) who admire Marat, Desmoulins, Etta Palm, Hébert. But in the period leading up to and into the French Revolution, C.-J. Panckoucke was a 'publishing tycoon',[7] the 'most substantial newspaper owner of the time, employing over 800 workers'.[8] Panckoucke was a 'pragmatist' who rose to prominence in the 1760s and 1770s 'through an adroit mixture of political deference and commercial acumen'.[9] He bought up rival papers and amalgamated them with his own, producing large (but fluctuating) readerships, and he attracted government support for his monopolies, during both the *ancien régime* and the Revolution. The 'Rupert' of his day, he combined an acceptance of the restraints of censorship and market regulation by the state with 'astute commercial acumen and genuine commitment to the progress of the Enlightenment'. He was 'also a business man, providing his newspapers with a sound financial base through careful promotion, the buying up of rivals, skilful marketing and the recruitment of first-rate editorial staff'.[10]

Similarly, few today will have heard of Joseph Duplain, who was responsible for the most advanced distribution technology of revolutionary France; his *Courier extraordinaire ou le premier arrivé* was printed in Paris and distributed by private coach to Lyons, Calais, Rouen, Dunkirk and Orléans. By taking copies from the front end of the print run and dispatching them at 3 a.m. by light coach, Duplain could get his paper to Lyons within 56 hours – 40 hours ahead of his competitors; he was also 24 hours ahead of the pack in the politically important north-east departments and the low countries.[11] By such means Duplain capitalized on the 'newness' of news rather than its content, which like everyone else he sometimes copied from other sources (a fatal misjudgement, as he was guillotined for counter-revolutionary content in 1794). In other words, like Panckoucke and Murdoch, he epitomizes the business side of journalism; this hasn't left too many traces in the annals, but it has left annals themselves. Business, routine, large-scale management, technical innovation, distribution, and promotion of the ideology of modernizing progress towards comfort – this is the legacy of the French Revolution's right-wing media moguls.

What the likes of Panckoucke, Duplain (or Murdoch) *believed* is not recorded by history; but eventually, in 1941, to be exact (as we shall see later in this chapter), the 'comfort' and the 'sovereignty' (right wing/left wing) aspects of revolutionary modernization were to come together in *Picture Post*, with the use of popular, commercial, consumer journalism to promote a version of popular sovereignty which was designed to emancipate the free but poor sections of society into welfare, if not wealth. And all this was done under the aegis of an owner, Edward Hulton, who was 'a staunch Conservative'. Tom Hopkinson relates how he and editor Stefan Lorant resolved the question of *Picture Post*'s politics in classic journalistic style:

> For Lorant and myself the main interest was that it should be strongly political, 'anti-Fascist' in the language of the time; we also believed that the magazine's success depended on its taking such a line. But being 'anti-Fascist' meant being 'left-wing' – and our proprietor, Edward Hulton, was a staunch Conservative. . . . Mr Hulton told us that the cover for the first number had got to show a battleship. When I said privately to Lorant that there could only be one thing on the cover of the first number, and that was a girl, he replied, 'Tom, there will be two girls!'[12]

The Formula of (British) Conquest

It is one of those commonsensical 'well-known facts' that among the opposites of truth is advertising. As a form of commercial propaganda, advertising deals in information rather than knowledge, and while it is designed to communicate facts – the product name for instance, or its bigness, newness, and price – advertising is also well known to work on the emotional and symbolic resources of its readers, rather than on their critical reason. Advertising is therefore not regarded as an archivable source of information in most libraries, nor is it often cited for scholarly purposes – it is undisciplined, iconic, emotional non-knowledge. News, conversely, is obsessively archived, and news reports are frequently quoted as history, both for the stories they contain and for the way they tell them. While news functions *as truth itself*, being a major documentary database for historians, advertising does not even count as archival raw material. Here we glimpse an archival binarism, which continues to separate the semiosphere from 'the real' in critical discourses. An absurd image of the past has arisen wherein it is reduced to economic forces and political actions, but it is shorn of *signification*. People and communities of the past are allowed to have material but not semiotic needs, semiosis has no history, and we're left with a fantasy of past time as semiotically purer, more innocent, when commodities were not suffused with signification. Part of the genesis of this historical fantasy is of course the fact that the evidence was suppressed, by not keeping and counting the communicational publicity of the past, and refusing to see such material *as* documentary evidence with the same status as 'historical' (i.e. journalistic) facts. Our pasts are therefore like our cathedrals: big, empty, stone places, run by a mostly male clerisy in splendid monastic isolation, bereft of what made them meaningful to their pre-modern users – stories, sights, sounds and symbols, in paint, colour, voice, glass, fabric, monument and narrative, all carried and communicated in

PEARS' SOAP IN THE SOUDAN.

"Even if our invasion of the Soudan has done nothing else it has at any rate left the Arab something to puzzle his fuzzy head over, for the legend
PEARS' SOAP IS THE BEST,
inscribed in huge white characters on the rock which marks the farthest point of our advance towards Berber,
will tax all the wits of the Dervishes of the Desert to translate."—Phil-Robinson, *War Correspondent
(in the Soudan) of the Daily Telegraph in London*, 1884.

Fig. 8.4 The formula of British conquest

the memories and rituals of the 'readers' of these complex and colourful 'texts'.

Like a cathedral today, which is relatively meaningless to its visitors but nevertheless treated reverentially (perhaps for that very reason), truth is kept reverentially separate from the contaminations of commerce. News is supposed to be sacrosanct too, and in fact the boundary between news and advertising is one of the most heavily policed in contemporary society, not only in the sense that 'advertorial' copy is frowned on within media, but in the more general sense that readerships – whole populations – have learnt to treat advertising as one thing, news as another; to keep them categorically separated in their minds, classified into different taxonomies. So it might come as a surprise to find that what has been claimed by Thomas Richards, in his book *The Commodity Culture of Victorian England*, as 'perhaps the largest promise made by an advertisement in the nineteenth century', is an incredible mixture of news, advertising, imperialism, visualization, and soap.[13]

The advertisement is from *The Illustrated London News* of 27 August 1887, and illustrates the following news report from 'Phil Robinson, War Correspondent (in the Soudan) of the *Daily Telegraph* in London, 1884':

> *"Even if our invasion of the Soudan has done nothing else it has at any rate left the Arab something to puzzle his fuzzy head over, for the legend*
>
> > *PEARS' SOAP IS THE BEST,*
> *inscribed in huge white characters on the rock which marks the farthest point of our advance towards Berber, will tax the wits of the Dervishes of the Desert to translate."*

That quotation is headlined: 'PEARS' SOAP IN THE SOUDAN', but the advertisement as a whole is headlined: 'THE FORMULA OF BRITISH CONQUEST', this being the claim that Richards suggests may have been the whopper of the century. The engraved illustration shows puzzled Dervishes gazing on the huge white caption, the fuzziest one on his knees in what looks like an obeisance.

This is a complex text. It is a visualization of an actual event – a proto-news-photo, in which the elements of war and commodity culture, exoticism and homeliness, the creation of 'they' and 'we' communities, are mutually defining, just as they are in any contemporary prime-time bulletin. It illustrates a piece of imperial vandalism, graffiti on what may well be a sacred site, a Kilroy-Was-Here message using a commercial catchphrase of the day – the very kind of youthful excess that nowadays earns young offenders a short sharp shock in the boot camp (where they are subjected to the very military discipline and comradeship that might find expression in a prank by gallant young army officers far from home). As an example of imperial cockiness it is hard to beat; as an ad for Pears' Soap it is hard to read, for its actuality and fantasy components, its visualization of the Sudan and its glorification of British imperialism, are not easy to reconcile with the actual function of soap.

Clearly we have already moved well beyond the realm of the referential, into another place where a slogan is a popular joke, and soap is a marker of the high tide of conquest. The cotermination of empire and commodity is true enough, and not only in this instance; it's telling the blatant truth about imperial capitalism, done from

THE BIRTH OF CIVILIZATION — A MESSAGE FROM THE SEA ☀

PEARS' SOAP.

"THE CONSUMPTION OF SOAP IS A MEASURE OF THE WEALTH, CIVILISATION, HEALTH, AND PURITY OF THE PEOPLE." *LIEBIG.*
Specially drawn by H.S.MARKS,R.A.for the Proprietors of PEARS' SOAP.

Fig. 8.5 The birth of civilization – a message from Pears' soap

the point of view of the domestic consumer, for whom the Sudan, the Arabs, Dervishes and Berber are all less real as physical objects than either Pears' Soap itself or Pears' ads, for this is only one of a long series of such punning, peculiar advertisements, and in any case many imperial schoolchildren would have learnt all they wanted to know about the world from *Pears' Cyclopaedia*, a popularization of the imperial archive which survived well past the use-by date of the Empire itself.[14]

For the readers of the *Illustrated London News*, of course, all this was banal – just another ad, literally familiar, in which the whirling Dervishes, fuzzy-wuzzies, Arabs of the Desert and 'our boys' in the Sudan are familiar denizens of the symbolic world of story, narration, symbol and stereotype, where the boundaries between news, fiction, empire and commodity are erased.[15] The most telling emblem of this *in*distinction is the figure of Rudyard Kipling – a journalist from the *Allahabad Pioneer* whose fictional writing did more than any other single thing, including conquest, to make the British Empire real for its subjects. It was his *Stalky & Co.* stories that promoted a patriotic larrikinism among the imperial servitors, of exactly the kind illustrated in the Pears' Soap ad.[16]

Nation-building

What men call gallantry, and gods adultery,
Is much more common where the climate's sultry.
LORD BYRON[17]

News is a visualization of society, an actuality-discourse that calls into being as its readership a public for modern political communities, a semiotic guarantor of the existence, identity and actions of the nation for which it is news. But news narration, visualization, and mode of address are the semiotic tail that wags the dog of truth – these are the supplementary formal elements to which journalism is wilfully blind, mere techniques for audience-building and maximization, devices to keep viewers and readers happy and tuned in, necessary fictions to convey unarguable truths. However, news in the British press at least has always been found in the company of its discursive opposite, advertising (this was not true in France till the mid-nineteenth century).[18] And while news has retained its commitment to referential realism, advertising has naturally maintained a commitment to the reader. What I am attempting to show throughout this chapter, in relation to pictures from both political and commercial campaigns, is that the two systems are not *opposed* at all; the techniques of news are 'silent' versions of the techniques of advertising, while the referent of advertising is not laundry but life. Ads and news from the very beginning of modernity are in unstoppable dialogue with each other's designated part of the semiosphere. Readers have always faced two kinds of reality: the sort made familiar in news, and another sort over in adland, the equally real but entirely imaginary world of symbol, intertextuality, narrative, character, plot and story which is already familiar to any viewer literate enough to look at the news.

In this world, the nation is a resource, a deposit in the public image-bank, ready to be drawn on in whatever denominations a particular product or campaign requires, and where national emblems like Shakespeare, Empire and the white cliffs of Dover are part of a running gag in the service of soap. In adland there's more to national identity than mere territoriality. This is the independent world of the semiosphere – it does not have its referent in the geography and institutions of nation states, but only in other parts of the semiosphere. Looking at the signs of national identity in the Pears' Soap ads with the benefit of hindsight, however, it's clear that what's on offer is not clean laundry but a national fiction, addressed to the 'what we already know' image of the nation-empire (i.e. the literacy) that may have been taken for granted among users of soap who are also citizens of empire and of popular media.[19] The Pears' ads may be centenarian, but clearly they rely on a readership used to their over-coded jokiness, and they ambiguate history (news) with propaganda (ad) in time-honoured fashion. Their existence suggests that the sophisticated reader of commercial media is not a new phenomenon, but a stable expectation of popular journalism from the earliest days of brand-name advertising.[20]

Certainly the sophisticated reader is a stable expectation in soap advertising, as shown in some turn-of-the-century advertisements for the (still-familiar) products of Lever Bros.; Sunlight laundry soap, Lux flakes (Figs 8.6 and 8.7).

These full-colour ads were distributed as inserts in popular magazines, in a convenient form for decorative display in the home. They work largely by dressing adult themes in children's garb – by infantilization. In 'So Clean and White' the joke is on race – black child dresses as imperial baby in celebration of whiteness, a cheerful racism and reminder of the multiracial Commonwealth all in one. In 'Lux won't shrink woollens' infantilization co-exists happily with what on an older body would pass for soft porn, or at least fetish-wear.

In the 'Gallantry' ad (Fig. 8.8), the word – translated from military dash into its original sense of (upper class) sexual conquest[21] – is also rendered apparently harmless by infantilization. The

Fig. 8.6 So clean and white

Fig. 8.7 Why don't they use Lux?

'Gallantry' of 'boy meets girl' is universalized and abstracted, the 'otherness' of the top hat (people in top hats didn't wash clothes) depoliticized by its literal ludicrousness, and the whole image is detached from the product, except that the boy carries a box of Sunlight soap as if it were a love-token – 'love me, love doing my washing'?

These banal curiosities *domesticate* gender, race, class and the body, not to mention drudgery, since the only truth-claims, spelt out on the back of each card, are that 'A CHILD can use SUNLIGHT SOAP in the "Sunlight Way"'; 'This simple way Makes washing play'; 'SUNLIGHT SOAP Lessens the Worries of Life'; 'SUNLIGHT SOAP Adds to the Pleasures of Home' (and so on). The pictures are not referential in any easily explainable sense, but they require a certain generic and referential literacy: the black baby in the 'So Clean and White' upper-class European clothes signifies not herself, not racial equality (nor even assimilationism) but 'whiteness' and cuteness defamiliarized by an unexpectedly 'black' visualization; the picture's

Fig. 8.8 Gallantry

racial offensiveness (the 'charm' is in the otherness of a black person, 'Theydom' in 'Wedom's' clothes) almost completely masked by showing an attractively smiling child. These defamiliarizations of homely truths (children, affection, play) are naturalizations of class, empire and race. They seem at once to require and to deny the existence of a real world of hierarchy and conflict, and their tendency towards de-referentialization prefigures postmodernity by about eighty years.

Fig. 8.9 Hot work for Australian gunners

While Lever Bros. were pouring sunlight, whiteness, gallantry (and postmodernity) out of the magazines and into the homes of the imperial public, sterner events were of course afoot, culminating in the war that put an end to toy-soldier notions of gallantry, and put the machinery of industrial destruction in place of the gleam in the officer-class's eye. But like soap, world war needs careful semioticization, translation from the grim brutality of big-gun battle into an idiom already familiar to the folks at home. For instance, the image of Australian gunners (Fig. 8.9), unites news with propaganda (Fig. 8.9), manly (white) bodies (mildly eroticized) with imperial effort, the war front with the home front. It is both a postcard for domestic correspondence and a *Daily Mail* 'OFFICIAL WAR PICTURE' (series 15, No. 113), 'PASSED BY CENSOR', Crown copyright.

The postcard is captioned 'Hot Work by Australian Gunners' on the image itself, and on the back: 'These Australian gunners stripped to the waist, are enduring the double heat of a summer's day and the working of their big gun.' Child's play really, in the heat of a summer's day, stripped down and 'working' the washing machine of history for the benefit of a nation to which these gallant soldiers don't actually belong but which is visible in the combined efforts of the six men, united in their common purpose, partially obscuring each other and individually unidentifiable, in a landscape at once benign (green, cultivated) and nondescript, certainly not Australia, who for some reason not apparent in the homely image itself are 'working' on the other side of the planet killing Germans.[22]

The Photograph that Won the War

But there it is. Sitting here, one is glad to be alive – a bit ashamed, maybe, but glad.   JAMES CAMERON[23]

'Hot Work by Australian Gunners', a strange little flake of imperial war, is of course almost forgotten, a bizarre private memento for those like me who live in Australia, or whose fathers, like mine, served in that war, as did my only uncle, a gunner who was killed in action in 1917 at the age of 19, in a setting just like this, more than thirty years before I was born. But there is a much more public and celebrated icon which does remarkably similar 'work'; it is also a photograph of six masculine soldiers, facing right, united in effort, obscuring each other, individually unidentifiable, facing an enemy on the other side of the planet from their own country, in a nondescript landscape, signifying national unity and victory (Fig. 8.10). This too began life as journalism (it was taken by Joe Rosenthal for Associated Press), but graduated immediately to the status of national and then global emblem. It is perhaps the limit case of what a photograph can mean, and how the furious, turbulent energy of the global semiosphere can transform one four-hundredth of a second into an infinity of signification.

It is a photograph that 'will live for ever', according to Harold Evans, formerly editor of the (London) *Sunday Times*, who discusses it in his manual for professional photojournalists and picture editors, *Pictures on a Page*.[24] He may be right; certainly the image of US marines planting the US flag on the summit of Mount Suribachi on the little Japanese island of Iwo Jima in February 1945, is well known to non-specialists, and has had a remarkable military and

Fig. 8.10 The photograph that won the war. Photograph by Joe Rosenthal, Associated Press, and the *Los Angeles Times*

professional career over the past fifty years. Its most famous reproduction is in the form of a huge bronze statue in the Arlington
National Cemetery in Washington DC, a three-dimensional realiza-
tion of the picture that 'nationalizes' it, recoding it ready for retrans-
mission around the semiosphere in the form of postcards,
bumper-stickers, calendars, subsequent news events held in that
space, and US postage stamps.

The photograph is interesting in itself. Its largest feature is in fact
nothing at all – much more blank sky than you'd normally see in a
newsphoto (though it is frequently cropped); a sky whose very
featurelessness might be said to bespeak transcendental values
rather than being tied to the historical here and now; 'the
empyrean' is an important element in Western art, from the conventional use of sky and clouds to represent the sublime in paintings,
to Leni Riefenstahl's use of them at the beginning of *Triumph of the
Will* to visualize Adolf Hitler's arrival (in a plane) as national destiny.
The overcast sky gives the Iwo Jima picture plenty of abstract potential, its calm emptiness being enhanced by its opposite at the bottom
of the frame: the detritus and mess of war underfoot in the
foreground. These 'natural' features are of course separated and
joined by the main event; the marines raising the Stars and Stripes.
By everyday news or photojournalism values, this is a 'bad' picture:
there are too many men, too crowded, their faces are obscured, the
flag is half-furled, there's too much sky. The 'right' thing to do in
such cases is to line up your marines under an unequivocally flying
flag and take their names for the caption. This is in fact what
Rosenthal did: 'I got them together to wave and cheer under the
flag.'[25] But the photograph that resulted from this exercise has been
forgotten, while the Iwo Jima image for which he is famous is a
success for other reasons than news values. The fact that the marines
cannot be identified individually, and are so crowded that they
become one body, gives the image a sculptural quality. This is
enhanced by the overcast sky which gives depth to their bodies and
fabric-folds, and also by the repetition of the shape of their legs and
their upstretched arms – a 'redundancy' which means we see the
effort not the men. This effort is itself enhanced by the energy of
the diagonal (and heavy) flag pole, and by the shape of the just-
unfurling flag that both opposes the men's bodies around the diagonal of the pole and reaches for the empty sky-space that the framing
of the picture reserves for it. Out of the detritus of war, into the
empyrean of destiny: the marines' effort enacts American
supremacy. To test this, try to imagine this picture as a shot of
American marines not raising but lowering the flag (there's nothing
in the frame to say which way the pole is travelling); try to make this
a picture of withdrawal and defeat.

It is clear that there are elements in the picture itself which determine what it can mean, not only referentially but also symbolically.
But historically its meaning is determined not by the war in which
it was taken but by the political realities of the postwar period; it is

a reminder that to the victor go the spoils, one of which is the semiosphere, which proceeded to be colonized . . . coca-colonized . . . by Americana, pax and otherwise. This is why the Iwo Jima picture has become what Harold Evans claims as the 'most reproduced photograph of all time'.[26] It is so perfect an emblem of American supremacy that it has been called a 'fake', in the sense that the marines were doing what they were doing for the benefit of the reporters and photographers who accompanied them; it was part of a staged sequence in which the soldiers posed for the cameras. But of course, while the scene was a set-up, the shot could never have been staged in its significant details; the 'decisive moment' quality of the picture results from a split-second coalescence of ground, bodies, pole, flag and sky which could not have been staged, not least because the shot breaks all the rules. Rosenthal may have been well-enough tuned to the potential of the scene to press the shutter at the right split second, but his visualization of 'American destiny' works because the marines were not interested in the camera at this precise moment.

However, the status of the image itself, and its career as the world's most reproduced photograph, was only a beginning. Once 'nationalized', the Iwo Jima image was quickly converted into a kind of permanent deposit in the international image-bank, eventually being available to signify anything at all. It has featured (and still does, fifty years on) in political cartoons, ads, birthday cards, computer clip-art, cover graphics, children's comics, teen movies. Even Japanese companies use it as a neutral icon, its former status as an image signifying American victory over the Japanese quite forgotten. It has been made into an icon of peace, of youth, of Croatia, football fans, business, Central Lancashire . . . you name it. It has demonstrably lost all referential status: no longer a photo of these men in this place on this occasion, it is also no longer a mythologized image of abstract values like 'America', 'victory', 'war'. It is just an image of itself, and refers only to our familiarity with it. It makes no truth claims, no propositional statements. It's not even propaganda, being well past the stage where it could be claimed as the exclusive semiotic property of any 'we' community. At what point do such images cross over from news to some other domain in the semiosphere, and when do they then cease to be journalism? At what point does this quintessential image of American national supremacy cease to be American? When is 'Iwo Jima' *not* Iwo Jima? The answer to all of these questions must be the same – it is the point of *readership*, where public sphere intersects with semiosphere, and people who were not alive when this picture was taken, have no personal connection with the USA, and are interested neither in marines nor in war, nevertheless instantly recognize the image and have sufficient generic knowledge of it to sustain a whole industry of homage, pastiche, rip-off and inversion, and to service a popular memory which is not false but has no recollection of the facts.

(11)

"We were just about ready to admit defeat. And then we discovered Central Lancashire."

STM 13-12-31
by Alan Thorpe, Managing Director, Holbro Steel Tubes Ltd.

"In late 1979, two friends and I decided to set up our own steel stockholding business.

Had we known what awaited us, I think the three of us would have been tempted to stay in our nice, comfortable, salaried positions.

We gave up our jobs early in 1980. And spent six months in a frustrating, fruitless search for premises.

We saw old properties, often with poor access. New properties, which were frequently too expensive.

We saw people who wanted us to give financial guarantees to the year 2005. People who didn't want us because we weren't a manufacturing business.

Finally, late in June 1980, I saw an advert for the Central Lancashire Development Corporation.

Expecting miles of red tape and months of delay, we went to see them one Friday morning.

Three working days later, we moved into our new 3,000 sq. ft. CLDC factory at Roman Way, Preston.

Today, our factory is double that size. We're now planning a move to a 20,000 sq. ft. unit.

And we employ seven people, all of whom were redundant or unemployed before we came along.

It's my belief that without the practical help and positive encouragement of the Development Corporation, our business would never have got off the ground at all."

Thanks Central Lancs.

Central Lancashire
BRITAIN'S BIGGEST NEW TOWN

CENTRAL LANCASHIRE HAVE WORKSHOPS, NURSERY AND STANDARD FACTORIES READY FOR IMMEDIATE OCCUPATION. PHONE BILL OGDEN, OUR COMMERCIAL DIRECTOR, IF YOU'D LIKE TO KNOW MORE.

(12)

SPRING BREAK

(15)

Like it's really, totally, the most fun a couple of bodies can have.

You know?

UMBRA PICTURES Presents a SEAN S. CUNNINGHAM Film "SPRING BREAK" DAVID KNELL · PERRY LANG · PAUL LAND · STEVE BASSETT · JAYNE MODEAN · CORINNE ALPHEN · DANIEL FARALDO · DONALD SYMINGTON · JESSICA JAMES and RICHARD B. SHULL · HARRY MANFREDINI · STEVEN POSTER · MITCH LEIGH and MILTON HERSON · FOGBOUND INC. · DAVID SMILOW · SEAN S. CUNNINGHAM · Released by COLUMBIA-EMI-WARNER Distributors

(14)

(13)

(15)

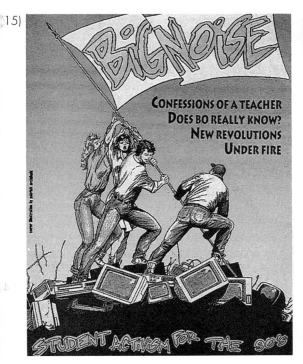

(16)

(17)

(18)

Fig. 8.11–18 (11) Iwo Jima as regional development. (12) Iwo Jima as holiday romance. (13) Iwo Jima as postcard from Arlington National Cemetery (from Terence Hawkes). (14) Iwo Jima as postage-stamp nationalism. (15) Iwo Jima as media pathology. (16) Iwo Jima as peace. (17) Iwo Jima as Japanese computerware. (18) Iwo Jima as Croatian nationalism

The Iwo Jima photograph – the photograph that won the war – demonstrates that the reality which is the bedrock of news is only 'universal' when it is completely detached from its referential specificity. The Iwo Jima photograph won the war, not least because it was conscripted into service to fight the *next* one: the propaganda war with the Soviet Union, whose Marshall Zhukhov and Red Army had done militarily what six US marines did semiotically. Iwo Jima fought in the cold war as an icon of American supremacy, effort, potential, energy, victory, confidence. While few in the West today have heard of Zhukhov and fewer still could recognize a picture of him, the marines are willed to 'live for ever' in the visual semiosphere, as we've seen. Theirs is of course an unrelentingly masculine and military image of victory, and while it obviously does signify American success in the Pacific war it does not in fact signify the actual victory over either Germany (Zhukhov) or Japan ('Little Boy' and 'Fat Man').[27] Iwo Jima itself is a little island, long since returned to the Japanese, whose capture did not win the war for the Allies and which was in any case not captured until some two weeks after this shot was taken (the military function of the flag was to signal US presence on Mt. Suribachi to troops further north on the island and to ships offshore). Finally, the Iwo Jima picture does not signify a victory *for* anything or anyone. It is the *photograph* – no more, no less – that won the war.

A Plan for Readerships

The people of the new age, the technicians, mechanics and skilled workers in light industries, were exactly the people who . . . seemed to worry George Orwell: they led a 'restless, cultureless life', he said, centred around tinned food, Picture Post, *the radio and the internal combustion engine.*

JOHN TAYLOR[28]

I turn now to another kind of picture journalism which was also part of the war effort, this time in Britain. I have to admit that I admire *Picture Post* and its most celebrated editor, Tom Hopkinson, as the most successful British exponent of a popular journalism that was equally committed to the communicative impact of pictures (under the inspiration of its first editor, Stefan Lorant) and to the sovereignty and welfare of its readers. It may be that during the Second World War 'Britain became more genuinely egalitarian than ever before or perhaps since',[29] so perhaps the sense of popular sovereignty and social democracy that shines though the big, stylish pages is a mere reflection of social realities. Certainly *Picture Post* was not alone – the amazing propaganda films of Humphrey Jennings of the same period give exactly the same attention to pictures and to politics; films like his *Listen To Britain* (1941), *The Silent Village* (1943), *Fires Were Started* (1943) and *Diary for Timothy* (1944) never show an enemy but concentrate on what the people of Britain were

Fig. 8.19 'The office girls go ashore' in *Picture Post* (© Hulton Picture Library)

fighting *for*, and as a socialist Jennings didn't include the government that funded his productions in that number, but created a photopoetic vision of Britain as a community of different but purposeful people, fighting for what was already theirs – freedom, culture, tradition, socialism, work, countryside, schools, music, each other. So perhaps something was in the air; the British had been taken to war by their imperial governments once too often, and this time wanted something out of it for themselves.

In *Picture Post* that something could be a better Home Guard, or air-raid shelters, or critical free press; or it could be the new wonder-fabric nylon to replace aristocratic silk and frumpy cotton with egalitarian and easy-care transatlantic style (NY-Lon = New York- London);

or it could be pictures not of Australian gunners but of Australian office workers leaping off the Sydney Harbour ferry (Fig. 8.19) in a long-legged hymn to verve (1 March 1941); pictures and stories that still impress with their mixture of war-wariness (not a misprint) and optimism, struggle and possibility, democratic determination and desirable starlets.

But the most talked-about issue that *Picture Post* ever did, which mobilized its own readership and may indeed have had a hand in winning the war (for the Labour party, despite the fact that *Picture Post*'s owner, Edward Hulton, was a conservative), was Volume 10, No. 1, the first issue of 1941. Its cover-picture (Fig. 8.20), like the Iwo Jima photograph and that forgotten group of hot Aussies from the First World War, shows a tightly bunched group of six bodies. But unlike those other war pictures, this one, taken when Britain was at its lowest ebb militarily – 'a time when it seemed doubtful whether any independent Britain would survive',[30] as Tom Hopkinson himself has put it – is different. It shows six toddlers, boys and girls, naked except for their shoes and socks, not all smiling, on a slide (slippery-dip) – facing left. It is captioned: A PLAN FOR BRITAIN. Tom Hopkinson has written of the motivation for this issue, for which he enlisted the help of the scientist Julian Huxley:

> *Churchill as war leader was against talk about 'War Aims', fearing the argument might breach national unity. But papers such as* Picture Post, *which was receiving hundreds of letters from men and women in the armed forces, knew what they were thinking. They were ready to fight, but wanted to know what they were fighting for. One of the things they were* not *fighting for was two million unemployed living on £2 a week or less. For 4 January we decided to prepare a special issue summing up what we believed our country's 'War Aims' should be. We called it 'A Plan for Britain'. The plan – for its day – was revolutionary.*[31]

The issue opens with a scene-setting feature by unemployed Welsh miner B.L. Coombes, 'This is the problem', and then goes on to propose a series of solutions: work (by Thomas Balogh), social security (by A.D.K. Owen), town planning (by Maxwell Fry), home planning (by Elizabeth Denby), land reform (by L.F. Easterbrook), education (by A.D. Lindsay, Master of Balliol), health reform (by Julian Huxley), a medical service (by Maurice Newfield), leisure policy (by J.B. Priestley). Later issues proposed reform of local government and of democracy, floating the idea of the abolition of the House of Lords.[32] The articles proposed 'a job for every able-bodied man'; minimum wages; a building programme for 'everybody to live in cheerful, healthy conditions'; planned kitchens at home and 'new municipal services everywhere; municipal hot water, scientific refuse disposal, a municipal laundry service'; a 'rural civilisation', 'a career for farm workers' and education for every farmer to ensure 'he is fit to control his part of our common inheritance';

Fig. 8.20 A plan for Britain – *Picture Post*'s finest hour (© Hulton Picture Library)

common education for all until age thirteen, then 'Youth Service for everybody' and reform of the university curriculum; healthy diet, public health policies, child welfare; a state medical service; holidays for all, facilities for the arts, 'civic centres of music, drama, films and talk'. In other words, A Plan for Britain was the blueprint for the welfare state, for the planned economy and for a transformation of government priorities from state security to social security. As Tom Hopkinson himself points out, these proposals went on to become the common-sense, consensual bedrock of postwar reconstruction. They lasted for nearly forty years until Thatcherism, when the next-but-one generation of Welsh miners followed B.L. Coombes into idleness and frustration.

'Two Nations' – Still

A flight sergeant, who had been decorated, said, 'After we've finished with Hitler we can start on them [the rich].' JOHN TAYLOR[33]

Perhaps just as remarkable as the Plan itself, with all its (occasionally fussy) detail and its (naive) faith in science and planning, was the response to it. The letters poured in by the sackful, and *Picture Post* printed pages of them in issue after issue; from MPs and lords (including Lord Leverhulme of Sunlight Soap), writers like Sean O'Casey, and trades unionists, ordinary people and experts (not all complimentary), including this from No. 1597548 Gunner G.N.H. Gardner: 'At last, in all our rather hazy war aims, here is one outstanding and beautiful ideal. You have the humble but sincere support of a gunner.'[34] Eventually the 'virtual community' of readers proved too active to stay on the page, and the magazine organized a conference of readers and experts to discuss and refine the plan. The conference was reported back to the people through the pages of *Picture Post* in a feature called 'Readers Work on the Plan for Britain' (8 March 1941). Editor Tom Hopkinson describes the hesitations and difficulty involved in preparing the Plan issue (lack of staff, pictures, paper, space and confidence that readers would like it), and his doubt that it would 'make a very wide appeal'.[35] However, he writes, the '"Plan for Britain" was the most successful issue we have ever had. Our readers made it so.' Hopkinson goes on to editorialize about his own feelings at the conference:

> *What an immense fund of intelligence, common sense, courage and humour there is in the ordinary people of this country. . . . The first business of democracy – in war or in peace – is to find means to draw on this store, to release these energies. What is the good of the common sense of our housewives – if it is never to have the slightest say in the sort of houses we put up? What is the good of the courage and adventurous spirit of our young people – if after the war we are going to set them to selling one another vacuum cleaners? What is the good of the*

A day in the life of 'PICTURE POST'

Here comes "Picture Post" through the letter-box. It's a funny thing but young Tony is generally down early on a Wednesday and he's on to it like a flash.

Tony can't read all "Picture Post" before breakfast. But this morning he's lucky — Dad has a letter from the Income Tax which demands his undivided attention. For once, he goes off to town without his copy of "Picture Post."

Mother finds the "Picture Post" when she's dusting. Over her eleven o'clock cup of tea, she has a good dip into it — almost forgets the time.

After lunch, Dora the maid finds it. She dreams over it, while the washing-up water gets cold.

Daphne gets home from her A.R.P. duty and she's in a hot bath, reading "Picture Post," as fast as she can make it.

Daphne leaves "Picture Post" in the bathroom. The plumber who's come in to put new washers on the taps reads it during his tea break.

Dad arrives home and after dinner he makes himself thoroughly comfortable for an hour with "Picture Post."

Dad's gone to the Home Guard — and taken "Picture Post" with him. His corporal is very glad he did. He says when you're on all night, you want something to read.

And there in the guardroom we leave "Picture Post." It's going to start a new cycle of life tomorrow. It will be going on for months to come — you never see "Picture Post" thrown away.

Read POST in comfort — order it at home

PICTURE POST

Fig. 8.21 A day in the life of *Picture Post* – an ad for popular reality. Note that this is a visualization of readers responding to the Plan for Britain. Compare with Figs 2 and 3 (pp 14–15), for changes in the image of popular readership. *Picture Post*, 22 February, 1941.

spirit of self-sacrifice so easily aroused in all of us – if we live in a society that pays respect above all things to successful greed? . . . I say that we cannot possibly afford this waste. Some millions of readers of PICTURE POST, through their representatives at these meetings, seemed to say that we cannot either.

Hopkinson signs off by hoping, on behalf of the Plan for Britain: 'May it play even a small part in producing a new kind of Britain.' What ordinary people expected that new kind of Britain to be was not entirely a matter of guesswork, thanks to the efforts of the social research organization Mass Observation. Its co-founder, Tom Harrisson, wrote to *Picture Post* with some statistics from recent investigations. The item which the largest percentage of people, especially women, expected, was 'less class distinction'.[36] Harrisson comments: 'On the whole, social changes expected are largely those making for less social discrimination, less private ownership of essential services, better mutual understanding and more equality of opportunity.' The *reason* such an expectation is so high is not given in Harrisson's letter, but is certainly hinted at in one that *Picture Post* chose to print right next to it. It is from two gunners and two army drivers:

We were extremely interested in your plans for a new Britain. But a trifle dubious as to whether we shall ever improve this democracy of ours. . . . Four of us entered a café [in Watford] and asked for tea. The manager asked us to leave, saying that he only served officers. We were soaked to the skin and freezing cold. Can you wonder that we read your articles rather cynically; and that Mr. Bevin's and Mr. Churchill's speeches fail to have the effect they should.[37]

The 'two nations' described by Disraeli in 1845 were still alive and kicking a century later; and this of course was the problem *Picture Post*'s Plan for Britain addressed. But in proposing solutions it had also to visualize the problem, and in this case it chose what has become in its own way just as celebrated a picture as the Iwo Jima photograph (Fig. 8.22). It was published in the Plan for Britain with the caption:

THE TWO SYSTEMS OF EDUCATION: A Picture That Sums Up Our Main Problem. *Two boys stand top-hatted outside Lord's cricket ground. Three boys stand bare-headed and stare at them. Between the two groups there is a barrier – deliberately created by our system of education. Our task is to remove the barriers – to bring the public schools into the general scheme.[38]*

The same picture is reproduced in Tom Hopkinson's 1970 compilation of *Picture Post* with a shorter but equally descriptive caption; he calls the picture '"Two Nations"'.[39]

Harold Evans reproduces this picture in his manual for photojournalists as the 'symbol for an era'.[40] Is this in fact the picture that won the war in Britain? From the evidence I've presented of journalism's

Picture Post, January 1.

THE TWO SYSTEMS OF EDUCATION: *A Picture That Sums Up Our Main Problem*

Two boys stand top-hatted outside Lord's cricket ground. Three boys stand bare-headed and stare at them. Between the two groups is a barrier—deliberately created by our system of education. Our task is to remove the barrier—to bring the public schools into the general scheme.

A PLAN FOR EDUCATION

by A. D. Lindsay

Author is Master of Balliol College, Oxford. He has been there since 1924. University men look up to him as an outstanding teacher and administrator. One of the leaders of progress in educational ideas.

THE things most obviously wrong with English education to-day in my opinion are :—

(1) There is still, on the whole, one system of education for the poor and another for the rich.

(2) For the poor, education ends at too early an age.

(3) The conditions under which boys from the primary school can climb the educational ladder to the Universities are such that we are paying for a great blessing—democracy in the universities—with a new curse—the production of an intelligentsia in the worst sense of that term.

(4) The excessive specialisation of our higher secondary and university education is producing the same effect.

I should like, as a corrective background of these criticisms, to say that the great advantage of the English educational system is its variety and

WHAT WE WANT

● *The same kind of education for all up to the age of 13.*
● *"Educative control" for all up to the age of 18.*
● *The child's future education to be decided at 13.*
● *The public schools brought into the general system.*
● *Some Youth Service for everybody.*
● *A break between secondary school and University.*
● *An overhaul of the curriculum in Universities.*

PICTURE POST

adaptability—if you like, its unsystematic character, its happy mingling of statutory and voluntary organisation. I hope we shall resist all attempts to make our education over-tidy.

This is important to bear in mind when we consider the first of the evils I have mentioned—the fact that there is in this country one system of education for the poor and another for the rich. For we might try to cure that evil by saying that there should only be one system of education for everybody. But the great variety of types of secondary schools in this country—from the public schools at the one end to technical schools at the other—is not an evil. The variety is a different one. The decision as to which boys should go to which schools, or be trained in which system, depends not on ability or fitness, but on wealth and class. The social division thus created is the outstanding evil.

visualization of popular demand for an end to class division (and people's disgruntled irritation with its petty manifestations), it is safe to say that the 'plan' of the picture itself, as published in *Picture Post*, is to realize – make real – the demand for social equality. It demands dialogue between these two nations, and a coalition between the modernizations associated with capital (top hats) and popular sovereignty (smirking boys) respectively, i.e. material comfort, equal opportunity, scientific progress and political democracy. Certainly picture journalism was here in the vanguard of propaganda for the 'logic of democratic equivalence' (see Chapter 4), in a form which is not only suited to the mass markets and pictorial conventions of the day, but also well ahead of politicians themselves in pushing for social justice. That *Picture Post* knew what it was doing is indicated by Tom Hopkinson's own insistence on the primacy of pictures in the article he wrote about the readers' conference on the Plan, where he devotes four paragraphs to describing the process of picture selection, including this:

> *Whereas a daily paper, and most weekly papers, start with the written word – with news, articles, editorials – and find what pictures they can for illustration, we begin with photographs. No matter how fascinating, or how important, an idea may be, if it will not go into pictures it is not, as a rule, an idea for us.*[41]

Having by some inspired research found this (prewar) photograph, he gives it half a right-hand page, to make sure readers get the message. Again, this decision needs to be seen as a deliberate political provocation, because he was so pressed for space (a planned 100-page issue was squeezed into 44). Hopkinson goes on to berate the government for not allowing *Picture Post* extra paper for the Plan issue:

> *We had imagined that a Plan for a juster, healthier, happier Britain, produced in the middle of war, might be considered by the Ministry of Information a worthy subject. Apart from its importance to us all, it would obviously be of the greatest propaganda value abroad. The Ministry were sorry. They could not help. . . . Engaged in a life-and-death struggle with Dr. Goebbels, they had just cut off one of their own fingers as a method of increasing their own strength.*[42]

There was no doubt in Hopkinson's mind that *Picture Post* was part of the war effort, and that the justice, health and happiness of the people was the aim of his own picture-war, *despite* the government. His judgement, his picture, eventually won; as soon as they were given a chance in 1945, the gunners and their families voted decisively for the welfare state.[43] Top-hat gallantry was – wasn't it? – a thing of the past.

Notes

1.   Lord Byron (1977, first published 1816–24) *Don Juan*. Ed. T.G. Steffan, E. Steffan, W.W. Pratt. Harmondsworth: Penguin, 518 (Canto XV. 84).

2. For a useful introduction to the unhappy relations between political and media theory/teaching in the twentieth century, see Ian Ward (1995) *Politics of the Media*. Melbourne: Macmillan Education Australia, Chapter 1: The press, television and the public sphere.

3. Created by Jack Vaughan and Rob Tomnay of the Creative Palace, Sydney, for the Newspaper Advertising Bureau of Australia; published in *Marketing World* (journal of the Australian Marketing Institute), 7(8), August 1987, 27.

4. See Rita Felski (1995) *The Gender of Modernity*. Cambridge, Mass.: Harvard University Press.

5. Dennis Potter's last interview, with Melvin Bragg for the *South Bank Show* in the UK, April 1994; shown in full on Australian TV on the ABC *Sunday Arts with Peter Ross* programme in June 1994, although the 'Rupert' extract had been shown earlier on ABC-TV news on the occasion of his death.

6. Larry Lamb (1989) *Sunrise: The Remarkable Rise and Rise of the Best-selling Soaraway Sun*. London: Macmillan, 110–17.

7. Robert Darnton (1982) *The Literary Underground of the Old Regime*. Cambridge, Mass.: Harvard University Press, 76.

8. John Gilchrist and W.J. Murray (1971) *The Press in the French Revolution: A Selection of Documents Taken from the Press of the Revolution for the years 1789–1794*. Melbourne: Cheshire, London: Ginn, 30. See also Suzanne Tucoo Chala (1977) *Charles-Joseph Panckoucke & la librairie française*. Pau and Paris.

9. Hugh Gough (1988) *The Newspaper Press in the French Revolution*. London: Routledge, 8–11.

10. Gough, 9.

11. Gough, 207.

12. Tom Hopkinson (ed.) (1970) *Picture Post 1938–1950*. Harmondsworth: Penguin, 9–10. Lorant won, of course, and the 'two-girls' cover became even more celebrated when *Picture Post* used it again for its last cover (1 June 1957). Lorant was *Picture Post*'s inspiration and first editor (1938–40); Hopkinson was its most celebrated editor (1940–50).

13. Thomas Richards (1991) *The Commodity Culture of Victorian England: Advertising and Spectacle, 1851–1914*. London: Verso, 121. The illustration of the advertisement is reproduced in Richards's book (122). See also Tony Bennett and James Donald, advised by Francis Frascina and Gill Perry (1982) The image and mass reproduction. In *Popular Culture*, Open University Course U203. Milton Keynes: Open University Press, Unit 25, where this and other Pears' advertisements from the nineteenth century are reproduced (in the Illustration Book) and discussed in the booklet *Science, Technology and Popular Culture (1)*.

14. My friend Roland Denning, a London film-maker, tells me he consulted *Pears' Cyclopaedia* (with its reassuringly red world map) throughout his childhood for such things as advice on mice-rearing, the flags of foreign nations and the rules of whist, wondering at the time what all this had to do with that little brown bar of translucent, floating soap in the bathroom.

15. That nineteenth-century publics were fully literate in catchphrases and crazes associated with popular commercial culture is amply evidenced in Charles Mackay (1841, 1852) *Memoirs of Extraordinary Popular Delusions and the Madness of Crowds*. London. Republished (1932) New York: Farrar, Straus & Giroux. See especially 619–31, Popular follies of great cities.

16. Angus Wilson (1977) *The Strange Ride of Rudyard Kipling: His Life and Works.* London, Toronto, Sydney, New York: Granada Publishing, 75–81.
17. Lord Byron, 61 (Canto I. 63).
18. See Gough, 219.
19. See Graeme Turner's very thoughtful analysis of national emblems in the Australian semiosphere in his (1994) *Making It National: Nationalism and Australian Popular Culture.* Sydney: Allen & Unwin.
20. Kathy Myers (1986) *Understains: The Sense and Seduction of Advertising.* London: Comedia, traces the history of advertising from the early days of branding (products) which gave way in the twentieth century to targeting (consumers).
21. 'Gallantry' as aristocratic sex, usually illicit, is at least as old as the Renaissance; see for instance the sixteenth-century classic by Pierre de Bourdeille, Seigneur and Abbot of Brantôme (1943, first published c. 1600) *The Lives of Gallant Ladies.* London: Pushkin Press.
22. The landscape is obscured by the gun, but its features are generic, recalling 'peasants working in the fields' paintings, such as the aptly named, in the light of the Australians 'working' their gun, *Laborare est Orare* ('Work is prayer') by John Rogers Herbert (1862), in the Tate Gallery.
23. James Cameron, reporting on the US Marines' landing at Inchon in September 1950, during the Korean War: INCHON *Picture Post* 49(1), 7 October 1950.
24. Harold Evans (1978) *Pictures on a Page: Photo-journalism, Graphics and Picture Editing.* London: Heinemann, 145–8.
25. Evans, 145. *See also* William J. Mitchell (1994) *The Reconfigured Eye: Visual Truth in the Post-photographic Era.* Cambridge, Mass.: MIT Press, 42–3.
26. Evans, 147 (caption). *See also* Karal Ann Marling and John Wetenhall (1991) *Iwo Jima: Monuments, Memories and the American Hero.* Cambridge, Mass.: Harvard University Press.
27. These were the names given to the atomic bombs dropped on Hiroshima and Nagasaki in August 1945. See Brian Easlea (1983) *Fathering the Unthinkable: Masculinity, Scientists and the Nuclear Arms Race.* London: Pluto Press, 111–12.
28. Quoted in John Taylor (1991) *War Photography: Realism in the British Press.* London: Comedia/Routledge, 75, from George Orwell (1941) *The Lion and the Unicorn: Socialism and the English Genius.* London: Secker & Warburg, 15. It should be noted that Orwell himself wrote for *Picture Post*, e.g. a very early version of *Boys from the Blackstuff* – a feature called 'The roadman's day' – in *Picture Post* 10(11), 15 March 1941. As Taylor comments, 'the photographs that were offered to [these people] in *Picture Post* should have allayed Orwell's fears': in other words Orwell is voicing educated prejudice against popular culture, not describing the facts of his own experience, much less theirs.
29. Laurence Thompson (1970) 1941. In Hopkinson (ed.), 88.
30. Hopkinson (ed.), 15.
31. Hopkinson (ed.), 90.
32. Reform democracy by W. Ivor Jennings, *Picture Post* 10(4), 25 January 1941; Reform our local government by W.A. Robson, 10(7), 15 February 1941.
33. Taylor, 65.
34. *Picture Post* 10(5), 1 February 1941, 32. O'Casey's long letter is in 10(5),

18 January, and Lord Leverhulme's in 10(6), 8 February. An article called 'What happens to your letters' says that *Picture Post* received over 3000 letters since 1 January 1941, nearly 2000 on the 'Plan'. *Picture Post* 10(11), 15 March 1941, 17.

35. Tom Hopkinson, Readers work on the Plan for Britain. *Picture Post* 10(10), 8 March 1941, 14–18.

36. Tom Harrisson, What you think. Letter to *Picture Post* 10(13), 29 March 1941, 3. See also Tom Harrisson (1978) *Living Through the Blitz.* Harmondsworth: Penguin.

37. James Reedy, C. Bevan, L.E. Jones, J. Sharkey, That snobbery curse again. Letter to *Picture Post* 10(13), 29 March 1941, 3.

38. *Picture Post* 10(1), 4 January 1941, 27.

39. Hopkinson (ed.), 90.

40. Evans, 9. Evans dates it to 1937 and credits it to James Jimmy Sime and Central Press.

41. Hopkinson, Readers work on the Plan for Britain, *Picture Post* 10(10), 14.

42. Hopkinson, Readers, 14.

43. The plan for Britain that eventually went to Parliament was the Beveridge Report, which *Picture Post* strongly supported (see *Picture Post* 18(10), 6 March 1943), and see also Chapter 9 below. *Picture Post* was blamed by Tory grandees for the victory of the Labour party by a large majority in the 1945 election, but Hopkinson himself thought the *Daily Mirror* 'deserved the lion's share of the credit'. See Hopkinson (ed.), 15. It's also worth recording that the Beveridge Report was stoutly defended in the pages of *Picture Post* 18(10) by Quentin Hogg, later Lord Hailsham, explicitly as the fulfilment of Disraeli's 'one nation' Toryism (see Introduction and Chapter 3).

9 *Journalism Matters*

(Radical Ratbags)

Theory must take account of the impermanence, fluidity and compromised nature of commercial cultural products, not by memorialising them but by engaging with them on an equally shifting, though by no means insubstantial, level. Once the mutuality of the battlegrounds of cultural studies and cultural products is established, exchanges productive of cultural transformation become all the more possible.
PAULA AMAD[1]

Radical Ratbags are the Essence of Good Journalism

The best work on journalism tends to be written by people who are thinking about something else. This chapter discusses two paradigmatic studies of news from the research field, and then some approaches to journalism and the media from a number of what I take to be *readership* perspectives, as a way of raising issues about the study of journalism. They demonstrate as ever that scholarly research tends to find what it is looking for; the most important part of any research project is the perspective it adopts, its theoretical orientations and its methodological predilections. Hence I have chosen to begin with two studies which may help to isolate some of the most important currents in the research field. Although the two approaches contrast with each other they should not be regarded as opposites in any adversarial sense; both are incisive and revealing, and when read in Lotmanesque dialogue with each other are especially productive of understanding. I'm calling the two approaches 'Hallism' and 'Ericsonism', after their principal investigators. This is how their perspectives may be seen to differ from one another:

Hallism	*Ericsonism*
British	North American
Marxist	criminologist
1970s	1980s
organic intellectual	social science methodology
theoretical	empirical
critique	ethnography
intervention	documentation
power	control
class conflict	bureaucratic procedure
hegemony	administration
ideological	useful

Ericsonism has a pervasive, diffusionist view of journalism, which from its perspective can be seen as a social talcum powder: very small, slithery and amorphous, being applied several times a day, most vigorously to organs and areas on the body politic that are perceived to be embarrassing or bothersome, but spreading to nooks and crannies everywhere, absorbing some of the dribbly irritations from the armpit of public life; a minor but useful product for making what Thorstein Veblen once called 'modern associated life' run more comfortably. Hallism on the other hand sees journalism as an enclosing straitjacket, slipped over the heads of the 'subordinate classes', constraining every move they make, blinkering their view, rendering them incapable of autonomous movements and susceptible to being pushed around by a journalism which from this perspective is just another one of those imperial, institutional, coercive, 'caring' forces whose corrective, protective, educational, propagandistic and ideological efforts are apt to drive the poor workers crazy even if they weren't before. Ericsonism is interested in how bureaucratic life is administered in a 'knowledge society', Hallism wants knowledge as a weapon to wrest hegemonic authority from the administrators, to pull off that straitjacket so the workers can be taught to dance to a different tune.

Now journalism can indeed be understood from both of these perspectives, which despite what I've just written are not mutually incompatible, because there's no doubt that both Hallite and Ericsonian journalisms exist from time to time, or even alongside each other as tendencies in a larger social field. And it is interesting that there's no contest between Hallite and Ericsonian conceptualizations of that larger field; for both, journalism is a discursive agency of social control. It is also interesting that neither approach takes much notice of readerships, either by theorizing the textual system under analysis from *their* point of view, or even by empirical/demographic study of their discursive practices.

The reader may have noticed that I neither do nor care for empirical studies of populations; I think they are control mechanisms themselves (see Chapter 2), and they tend to sample the efficacy of (political or commercial) campaigns that have already been carried out *upon* audiences (I exempt Mass Observation from this criticism – and recommend it as a good example of democratic statistical work). Another way of studying readerships is by conceptualizing 'them' as 'us'; this entails abandoning altogether the idea that there's some natural, impervious barrier between producers and consumers, writers and readers, leaders and led. It's one of the great injustices of social theory, to set up endless research projects which look at *production* from an institutional, corporate, socialized point of view, analysing news*makers* in their full panoply of power, but then looking at *consumption* as an individual 'behaviour', buttonholing unrehearsed, dis- or uninterested, non-professional individuals, in a context where neither benefit nor blame attaches to their answers, and using their responses to make claims not about them as individuals, but about something which is in fact bigger than the mighty institutions of production themselves, i.e. the reader*ship*, the public. If you look at a very complex piece of communicational machinery – a truck, say – whose intricacies you admire but whose power you fear, and then you look at a laboratory mouse, and you ask: if I put this mouse on this road in the way of this juggernaut, how is the mouse going to interact with it? – the answer is going to be obvious but not worth listening to. Wrong comparison; silly question.

I think a methodology which pays due respect to the social, institutional, historical and productive context of journalism production should do no less to the context of its consumption. This means abandoning the habit of taking media producers to be monsters and consumers to be mice; media moguls are paper tigers, in the long run, they're all dead. Readerships, on the other hand, are *part* of the intricate communicational machinery of modern journalism, produced by it and actively driving it, all at once. One simple way of resisting the 'mogul–mouse' syndrome is to look for evidence of reading practices which are not individual, not consumerist, and not confined to reception. This 'method' is to look for what has been written about journalism from the point of view of more or less organized, identifiable reader*ships*, especially those who've got some 'outside' perspective which can be used to give a bit of proportion to the distorted image of the journalistic juggernaut familiar from social science. Such readerships include radicals, women, ethnic and 'racial' groups, youth, environmentalists, and peace-seeking groups. All of these are historically outside of the traditional public domain; all are traditionally in journalism's 'Theydom', all of them are subject to the most offensive misrepresentation in journalism itself. They are the best people to speak about journalism from the perspective of the reader, because they have something to say, something to lose, something to win. They can and do answer back. All the student of journalism has to do is listen. They prove the only 'law' I've been able to discover while writing this book, which is this: radical ratbags make the best journalists, and radical ratbags make the best guides and critics to journalism. This is hardly surprising, since they started the whole thing rolling in the first place.

Hallism

The formal study of news, from a perspective compatible with the one adopted in this book, requires an interdisciplinary approach. History, semiotics and literary theory, cultural studies, social and political theory, feminism, Marxism, media and communication studies, technology, even anthropology – all have something to offer the student of popular reality. But at the same time there are books and approaches which have concentrated on the study of news, and among these are some which have had a decisive, shaping effect on what comes afterwards. Among the most substantial contributions yet made to the critical understanding of journalism are studies led by Stuart Hall in the UK and Richard Ericson in North America. It is interesting to note that neither study is simply 'about' news or journalism, but is concerned with questions of social order and control, and of how the discursive field of representation intersects with the traditional political institutions of power during the contemporary period.

Stuart Hall is well known as one of the driving forces behind the establishment of British cultural studies during his time as Director of the Birmingham Centre for Contemporary Cultural Studies in the 1970s. Working to an explicitly Marxist theorization of both social relations (conflict) and intellectual work (collective), the Centre sought not to study popular culture for its own sake, but as part of a strategy which sought to reinvigorate intellectual work in the context of British Left politics. The Centre's ambition was not to produce research reports but *organic intellectuals,* in the Gramscian sense: people who (and publications which) would be able to assist in the class, gender, ethnic and other political struggles of the day *as* intellectuals, providing a theorized base to political action and pointing to areas of conflict and control which the Left had traditionally neglected, to its political cost. It is in this context that *Policing the Crisis* needs to be understood.[2]

The book is an extraordinary *tour de force,* as important for the way it was written, its ambitious theorizations, authorial asides, passionate engagement in work that clearly *matters* both intellectually and politically, as for its analytical mapping of 1970s journalism. *Policing the Crisis* does something that had never been attempted before, by putting journalism centre-stage in a project which is actually designed to understand what the authors saw as a deep and general crisis in the 'British way of life'. It takes the textuality and discursive materiality of journalism just as seriously as it takes such sociological staples as deviancy, crime and control, and by holding very firmly to this general perspective it inaugurates the first truly *cultural* study of news, showing how the social production of meaning works textually, culturally and politically. It avoids both the formalism and the judgementalism of the then dominant forms of textual and popular-culture analysis, and equally it resists the pseudo-explanations of empirical sociology, which at least in their officially funded, populist forms tend to isolate a symptom of social conflict and present it as a cause (i.e. they accept moral panics at face value and use scientific language to blame the poor for not being rich). Against such consultancy-driven work, *Policing the Crisis* takes the textual and sociological commonplace as its own raw material, seeking to understand: 'why and how the themes of *race*, *crime* and *youth* – condensed into the image of "mugging" – come to serve as the articulator of the crisis, as its ideological conductor'.[3]

In other words, it is not race, crime, or youth that explain 'mugging', but the *articulation* of such themes to a more general social 'crisis of hegemony' that explains 'the Britain of the 1970s'. Notice too from the quotation above how for the first time three different fields of knowledge are put together: common-sense knowledge as circulated in the public/media domain ('mugging'); the sociological categories of *race, crime* and *youth*; and the discursive field of 'image . . . articulator . . . ideological'.

Like other passionately imagined historically based studies of British class conflict (from Disraeli to E.P. Thompson), *Policing the Crisis* is narratively interesting in its own right. The book takes a little, local event – a 'mugging' (and its equally savage judicial aftermath) – and pursues this tiny flake of history relentlessly, back to Victorian ideologies of crime, to Marxist theorizations of ideology and the state, to the crucial Gramscian concept of hegemony, and, in the other direction as it were, into the detail of headlines in the local press, statements by judges, politicians, parents, lobbyists and journalists, so that what starts as a journalistic anecdote ends as an exploration of nothing less than the social structure, the intellectual context, state agencies and cultural history of Britain as it slid out of consensualism (from 'Butskellism' to Thatcherism) and revealed how *behind* the stark photoflash contrast of the emblematic event just how divided the 'two nations' still were. *Policing the Crisis* is a vision of the whole semiosphere, as it enabled, determined, and reacted to the signification of this grubby event in a grotty suburb, and the grotesque over-reaction of those who spoke and acted as if they were one nation at war with the other.

The study shows how the 'mugging' was taken up by various agencies (the police, the judiciary, Parliament, local councils, as well as by oppositional and reform groups, from social workers to anti-racists); how it was constructed ideologically in the national and local press and articulated to political and control issues; and how this ideological closure might be explained via an innovative cultural-Marxist theorization of social conflict and crisis. The book starts with the theft of thirty pence by three 'coloured' youths, and the subsequent handing down of twenty-year and ten-year sentences, and it ends with an account of British cultural conflict in a period of decolonization and deconsensualization, where the state and the media together seek to regain lost control by ever-tougher 'law and order' policies against their own citizens, policies which are themselves justified as being demanded by 'public opinion'. In this vision, journalism is both a 'relatively autonomous' institution with its own imperatives and priorities, and at the same time a major player in the conduct of relations between conflicting classes, groups, ideologies and politics.

How is journalism a major player? According to Hall *et al.*, it is in the business of 'mapping problematic reality'.[4] In traditional socio-logical vein, they distinguish between 'primary definers', agencies whose views are given privileged access to news coverage (the police, judiciary, etc.), and 'secondary definers' who are the news media and the discursive agencies which 'orchestrate' (manufacture) 'public opinion'. This residual sociologism on their part is unsatis-factory, because it puts into a subordinate position the very textual system and discursive process which actively 'maps reality' for a 'society' in modernity. Of course it is important to avoid anachro-nism here; it was only after the extraordinarily influential work undertaken by the Birmingham Centre had gained some currency in the intellectual domain that the very idea took hold that media might themselves be *primary* agencies of social control, and that their words were also deeds, not 'definers' of popular reality but *the thing itself*. But *Policing the Crisis* was published before fully fledged theories of discourse and knowledge had been articulated to theories of power and control (i.e. before Foucauldianism was thoroughly elaborated in the English-speaking world), and it retains a Marxist tendency to downplay the cultural field (and with it the media) into a secondary role, seeking to explain sense-making from the perspec-tive of class struggle and state crises. The idea that culture – the discursive, media, knowledge-producing and sense-making sphere of life – might itself determine such matters as class, conflict, and the state, had not yet found a way of being proposed, never mind argued. In the 1970s when this book was being written the unset-tling provocations of deconstruction, postmodernism and the infor-mation age were still somewhat inchoate; the idea that 'reality' – problematic or otherwise – is not a self-evident thing out there, but something which is discursive, and created in the act of being mapped, was still unthinkable in this period. However, the perma-nent value of *Policing the Crisis* is not in its particular concepts but in its *scope*, its ambition and seriousness, and in its attempt to inter-vene in social power conflicts from a theorized and unapologetically intellectual position. It makes journalism matter, not just as a self-contained professional or institutional practice, but more impor-tantly in the context of a century and more of social conflict (and social analysis).

Hall *et al.* move confidently between the tiny details of different newspaper headlines and what was known then as 'grand theory', making them mutually illuminating, and showing how it is in fact possible to 'read' topical meanings in the light of formal structures of knowledge. The very narrative of the book is an enactment of the idea that discourse and social structure are connected, mutually determining and illuminating, inexplicable without each other.

Policing the Crisis is therefore not the kind of book you can race through to raid for applicable concepts and essay 'quotes'; it is self-consciously anti-pragmatic in this sense (it avoids 'solutions' to the 'social problems' it addresses, and it is certainly not written as a student textbook). However, it does try to understand how professional media ideologies and practices are produced, how they fit with other agencies and institutions of power, and how the public domain of press, opinion, and common sense is manufactured by definite practices which can be analysed.

In the light of its crash-through-or-crash explanatory style, it hardly seems to matter that all this energy is spent in pursuit of an explanation of something which the book never establishes in the first place; its thesis about a crisis in hegemony brought on by class and cultural conflict actually requires that there was at one time, say in the 1950s, an *achieved* hegemonic equilibrium in Britain which could then be put into crisis. The book makes this presumption because its theory generates the need for it to be so, but doesn't argue it through on the ground, because its Marxist agenda requires it to dismiss as *a priori* a sham any actual 'period of social unity and cohesion' that it finds.[5] Consensus is state policy, not a state in which people find themselves naturally, as it were. Listen:

> *When a ruling-class alliance has achieved an undisputed authority and sway over all these levels of its organization – when it masters the political struggle, protects and extends the needs of capital, leads authoritatively in the civil and ideological spheres, and commands the restraining forces of the coercive apparatuses of the state in its defence – when it achieves all this on the basis of consent, i.e. with the support of 'the consensus', we can speak of the establishment of a period of hegemony and hegemonic domination.*[6]

Their certainty about all of this is complete; there's no room even to ask 'What if it *doesn't* achieve "all this"?' 'All this' is not hegemony, it's domination, and there are no counter-forces, no exemptions, nothing going on *outside* the 'undisputed authority and sway' of the 'ruling-class alliance'. Consensus is domination of the whole *universe*, literally:

> *What the consensus really means is that a particular ruling-class alliance has managed to secure through the state such a total social authority, such decisive cultural and ideological leadership, over the subordinate classes that it shapes the whole direction of social life in its image, and is able to raise the level of civilisation to that which the renewed impetus of capital requires; it encloses the material, mental, and social universe of the subordinated classes, for a time, within its horizon. It naturalises itself, so that everything appears 'naturally' to favour its continuing domination.*[7]

This claim, that the 'ruling-class alliance' (which here is strictly economic) actually 'encloses' the whole semiosphere, and therefore that any improvements in civilization can be dismissed as a capitalist plot, is Pythonesque.[8] While the concern for ideology, authority, image, civilization, and the 'mental universe' (Lotman's 'universe of the mind'), is laudable in the context of a theorization of power in a period of unequal social relations, this clearly overstates the completeness of such a 'consensus', giving it the delicious paranoiac twist that makes it read like a synopsis for a futurefright TV series like *House of Cards, A Very British Coup, GBH,* or *To Play the King.*

Perhaps it's not surprising to see such universal power being imputed to a phenomenon – 'consensus' – which would have been encountered by the activists at the CCCS not only in the form of theory but also out on the door-knock when getting people to vote Labour was an uphill struggle, never mind getting them to think about an economic liberationism (Marxist class-struggle) to match the political modernization of popular sovereignty (which *Policing the Crisis* dismisses anyway as 'the pluralist theories of political democracy'). Indeed, Hall *et al.* follow their theoretical fantasy to its logical conclusion, namely paranoiac fictionalization. After the passage quoted above they go on to end the same paragraph with a claim that this universal 'naturalization' of domination in the form of consensus had in fact occurred, in 1959, with the third election victory of the Tory Prime Minister Harold Macmillan: 'No wonder he announced (no doubt hoping it would become a self-fulfilling prophecy) that "The class struggle is over". Perhaps he added, sotto voce, "and we have won it".'[9]

And – 'no doubt', 'no wonder', 'perhaps' – he didn't. Perhaps we should add, quite loudly, that the 'self-fulfilling prophecy' is on the other foot, and this reduction of the semio-cultural and 'mental' universe of 'everything' to the status of a mere by-product of the machinations of the Carlton Club is not only wrong in fact but an impediment to understanding.

CCCS could observe but not account for the workings of language itself, since they'd 'enclosed' it and put it into the hand of the godlike 'ruling-class alliance'. They themselves were struggling in the arena of knowledge, media, information, imagery, symbol and culture, and were contesting the build-up of anti-democratic tendencies in the 'knowledge class'. But they could not see such tendencies among popular media readerships – they never mention readerships in *Policing the Crisis*, leaving an unstated but pervasive impression that 'the people' are passively manipulated, since they seem to be constantly pushed around, dominated, hegemonized, by the ideological closures of the capitalist press. Hall *et al.* never consider that readers may be just like them – 'relatively autonomous' from what they read. They may read the *Sun* and not give two hoots for Rupert Murdoch. Equally, the CCCS position does not account for its own practice as a player in the internal struggles of the knowledge class; *Policing the Crisis* is a contestant in a struggle *among* members of the 'knowledge class' for the right to speak on behalf of 'the people' – in short they need to theorize a *hegemonic* ideology which has the population at its mercy because they want to ride into town as organic intellectuals and impose a *counter-hegemonic* consciousness on those same people, in order to mobilize resistance to the 'ruling-class alliance'. They don't *really* give two hoots for what 'the people' might be thinking, saying, knowing and imagining for themselves.

Ericsonism

From a more traditional sociological and political perspective, but still an innovative work which was the most comprehensive organizational analysis of both press and TV news of the 1980s, is Richard Ericson, Patricia Baranek and Janet Chan's trilogy: *Visualizing Deviance, Negotiating Control* and *Representing Order*, on the production, sources and content (respectively) of press, radio and TV journalism.[10] Combining a comprehensive literature survey of current scholarly approaches to journalism with a large-scale ethnographic study, including participant observation of the industrial process, study of the relations between news organizations and their sources, and textual (content) analysis of the institutional output of newsmakers, the Ericson *et al.* trilogy is an exemplary analysis from the North American, empirical school. Interestingly, this work too is motivated by a desire to understand *society*, rather than journalism *per se*; Ericson and his colleagues are criminologists and experts in the field of justice, not in the first place in media or news analysis.

It is this outsider perspective which gives them a position from which to look at journalism as an active agent in culture, control, and politics,[11] of 'all of organized life, all of society'.[12] They are well aware of the discursive nature of news, saying that 'visualization – making something visible to the mind even if it is not visible to the eye – is the essence of journalism as a method'.[13] They are therefore alert to the practices by means of which journalism works as a form of knowledge, as a creator of common sense, and as an active textual system which makes (and fakes) the impression of truth in the service of a social order to the maintenance of which the entire textual system of journalism is dedicated:

> *Journalists are central agents in the social construction of reality about deviance and control. . . . They are control agents themselves, using their power of imprinting the reality in the public culture to police what is being done in the microcultures of bureaucratic life, including especially the activities of other control agencies.*[14]

According to Ericson *et al.*, the old oxymoron that 'bad news is good news' can be explained literally; social order is represented and circulated to the public via a Saussurian discourse which continuously maps out *what it is not*:

> *Our cultural identity, our sense of what we are, derives from pointing to what we are not: that which is bad, wrong, faulty, in error, straying,*

etc. Bad news provides a barometer of how good our life is. It is at once an abstract vision and practical template for constructing order and managing change. News is the most common stock of knowledge generated to meet the desire to control and command the environment. Its focus on information about deviance and control, disorder and order, stability and change, is part of the insatiable quest to reduce equivocality in the environment and attain a workable level of certainty. . . . Talk about wrongs, errors, faults and cracks in every nook and cranny of organized life gives a sense of how organization can be improved to make things better, to progress.[15]

This nook-and-crannyism is the high-water mark of modernity, with news at the service of progress by seeking out deviant procedural and behavioural practices and generalizing knowledge of them across the public sphere of mediated visualization. Ericson *et al.* make news equivalent to science and policing in its social reach – like them it takes the whole world as its imperium. They also equate news with the law in its need to seem impartial – like justice, journalism must be seen to speak on behalf of the general public, translating sectional interests and specialist knowledges into the public domain. Small wonder, then, that journalism constantly uses the rhetorics, personalities, methods and press releases of science, police and the law to legitimate itself:

> *By giving such predominant attention to the law and legal authorities, the news media can go a long way towards making convincing the image that they are an objective, impartial, universal and general voice of the people.*[16]

In what Ericson *et al.* call a 'knowledge society' there are few professions apart from the police, social scientists and journalists who have free range across the whole of organized life; each adds lustre to the other by mutual association. But in modern organized life, which in its public and control functions is increasingly institutionalized and bureaucratic, knowledge is also power, and here I think the *Visualizing Deviance* conceptualization of news in functional, societal terms shows its limits. They conclude:

> *As we have argued, politics in the knowledge society seeks perfection in administration (the perpetual cleaning up and repairing of flawed procedures) and reflection in entertainment (the perpetual propping up and staging of prefabricated spectacles).*[17]

In other words they retain at the end a distinction between internal control discourse for the knowledge class (journalism as administrative modernism), and external entertainment for the ignorant masses (journalism as circus). But in the contemporary American empire of information, it is clearly wrong to think in terms of a generalized, neutral, self-adjusting 'knowledge society'. On the contrary, it is clear that journalists are part of a 'knowledge *class*', which takes or retains power by controlling knowledge. To the extent that there is a distinction between administration and entertainment, 'perfection' and 'reflection', procedures and spectacles, it is a distinction between power and powerlessness in the knowledge economy, not a functional division of labour to which everyone naturally assents. But my analysis of journalism in modernity suggests that this binary vision of functional journalism in an information society is historically back to front. The politics of *journalism* (rather than of imperial administration and control of deterritorialized but colonized satellites by means of knowledge) has its origins in what is here dismissed as 'reflection', 'entertainment', 'prefabricated spectacle'. Ericson and his colleagues certainly describe something real in everyday journalism, but they make the essence of *journalism* that which is the essence of modern *imperialism*, i.e. bureaucratic control of populations and institutions by means of knowledge. It may even be that the knowledge class has progressively *colonized* journalism and appropriated its historic power to create readerships and a 'mediasphere', and it may be that everyday journalism, with its nook-and-cranny deviance detector, has taken over the logic of democratic equivalence from revolutionary journalism. But this is not to describe the essence, nor even the function, of journalism; rather it is to describe a phase in a continuing power-play over what counts as true in the information age, and who gets to do the counting. Ericson, Baranek and Chan's trilogy is an astute, detailed and to date unsurpassed account of what routine journalism is and how it is done; it's currently the 'industry standard' of institutional or organizational research into journalism. But like others before it, its modernist, progressive, functionalist methodology eventually forgets the greatest creation of modern journalism; the readership which is also the public, and the sovereignty which is also popular reality.

Langtonism

Hall and his colleagues, Ericson and his colleagues: between them they provide a insight into two schools of explanation for contemporary news practice, from a critical (theoretical) and an organizational (empirical) perspective respectively. Of course there are many other books on news, but few which seek to *account* for journalism, and fewer still which are interested in how it all works out from the point of view of the reader/audience/public, or in what it all means in relation to liberty, comfort and democratic equivalence. I turn now to what I take to be some readership perspectives.

As always in this context, feminism is instructive, since its enabling question is precisely that of the 'logic of democratic equivalence', interrogating a discourse which in both its institutional and its textual form has constructed women as outside the productive apparatus, as consumers, subjects and readers. All too often women are pathologized, and their longstanding habit of reading popular media texts is turned into an illness. Abigail Bray has shown how women are seen to read in the same way that they are seen to eat; they catch 'reading disorders' from too much fictional romance, too many weekly magazines, too much long-form TV drama, just as they are supposed to catch 'eating disorders' like anorexia and bulimia from being put in the context of readily available food. Their reading practices are pathologized in the same way as the discourses of 'eating disorders' pathologize their everyday lives.[18] Indeed, the two 'disorders' are often explicitly linked: women catch 'eating disorders' from reading fashion magazines and seeing pictures of Kate Moss or Emma Balfour. One feminist response to this anti-democratic policing of women's reading practices is to point out something that I too would wish to argue: that readerships are not mere bodily functions at the mercy of capitalist rhetoric, but precisely readers, whose practices are so little understood in the public/intellectual sphere that they are more often colonized by silly psychology than recognized as liberated and autonomous activities within a mediasphere of democratic equivalence. It is interesting to note too that the pathologization of women as victims of what they read, invaded by semiosis, infected by images, corrupted by culture, is that in this very respect they stand as a metaphor for readerships in general – 'the people' – who have frequently been represented as a helpless, disordered, pathologized body, who must of course be given counselling, therapy or a good telling off (for their own good of course) by the caring professions of social and political science, the social equivalent of the house-parent with the keys to the fridge (and the back door). However, things can be done better than this, and it is often the analyses from the perspective of some supposedly helpless and victimized outsider-group that turns out to have the most explanatory power when it comes to representing readerships' perspectives on journalism. From feminism, for instance, Liesbet Van Zoonen's book *Feminist Media Studies*, and Catharine Lumby's *Bad Girls: The Media, Sex and Feminism in the 90s*,[19] differing from each other in purpose and allegiances as they do, would make a useful starting point for further consideration of journalism from a critical readership perspective.

In another social domain, but one with some of the same topographical features, for instance the habit of infantilizing its subjects, is the area of ethnicity and journalism. Here I am interested not so much in the racism *of* the media, which is a control-culture problem, but the perspective of those from whatever ethnic or racial community is excluded from a given discursive 'Wedom'. Such perspectives are often surprisingly tolerant, given what they have to put up with; see for instance Marcia Langton's '*Well I heard it on the radio and I saw it on the television*'.[20] Langton is not all that tolerant of those who are less interested in dialogue between different but equal semiospheres than they are in colonizing the Aboriginal semiosphere, a point she tellingly makes by directing it not against the media, popular or otherwise, but against the very highest strata of intellectual culture:

The complaint, 'This is all so tiresome and infantile; why do we have to listen to this chorus of "I want", "I demand"?' is part of an intellectual malaise. Some intellectuals even demand that the Native answer back in a refereed journal, say something about the French intellectuals Jacques Derrida or Jean Baudrillard, and speak from the hyperluxury of the first world with the reflective thoughts of a well-paid, well-fed, detached scholar. The notion of social justice appears to have become boring and has disappeared from the rhetoric. But this . . . is a symptom of postmodernism and economic rationalism.[21]

Point taken, but I can't help noticing that Langton's position, which is founded on the struggle for social justice in the political and cultural spheres, is worthy of anything you'd find in the most advanced refereed journals; it is in fact a 'Native answer back' in the language of liberation, which however *starts* by recognizing the existence of difference between Aboriginal and non-Aboriginal subjectivities and representations: like Lotman, Langton argues for intersubjectivity and dialogue between the Aboriginal and non-Aboriginal semiospheres, through the media.

'Aboriginality' is remade over and over again in a process of dialogue, imagination, representation, and interpretation. Both Aboriginal and non-Aboriginal people create 'Aboriginalities'.[22]

She identifies three main 'categories of intersubjectivity': Aboriginal people in dialogue with each other inside Aboriginal culture; 'stereotyping, iconising and mythologising' by people with no substantial contact with Aboriginal people; and 'the construction generated when Aboriginal and non-Aboriginal people engage in actual dialogue, where the individuals test and adapt imagined models of each other to find satisfactory forms of mutual comprehension'. She goes on:

It is in these dialogues that working models of 'Aboriginality' are constructed as ways of seeing Aboriginal people. Both the Aboriginal subjects and the non-Aboriginal subjects are participating. The results of this self-conscious dialogue are meanings and analyses which, ideally, do not mystify 'race' and other ideological concepts.[23]

Langton is clear that this dialogue is both public, i.e. set *within the mediasphere*, and 'equivalent', i.e. on terms set by Aboriginal people, not a communication across demographic lines where all the power is assumed to reside with those who live in the lap of hyperluxury:

Aboriginal people have invented a theatre of politics in which self-representation has become a sophisticated device, creating their own theories or models of intercultural discourse such as land rights, self-determination, 'White Australia has a black history' and so on.[24]

In short, the readership can and will 'answer back', in ways that 'refereed journals' have trouble noticing, because of Western intellectual culture's longstanding habit of infantilizing readerships. Instead, as I've argued in Chapter 2, and following Rita Felski's work, it is clear that communally identifiable readerships form their own public spheres – there are or have been feminist, Aboriginal, environmental, working class, and even 'style' public spheres within, alongside, and in dialogue with each other and with 'the' public sphere.[25] Like everyone else, Aboriginal people are 'citizens of media', and are doing something about it.

There are of course plenty of specialist approaches to news: press history, TV news, studies by country or topic (from racism to the economy). Such specialist studies are best used as archive, not explanation. For an overall perspective on journalism, news and popular media, it is often best to contextualize these specialist subjects within an even broader framework. Modernity, culture, politics, racism, feminism, Marxism; these are the larger epistemological discourses which will make sense of news as a cultural form. Unfortunately, in academic work, news has been 'disciplined' as a sub-set of empirical social science in the American tradition, or of government in the Anglo-Australian tradition. Neither of these disciplinary traditions has much to say about meaning, and both are notable for an interest in managerial interventions into professional and governmental strategies, rather than seeking to understand how the human species makes sense. They have no theory of discourse, textuality or culture, which is a pity, since this is in fact what journalism is made of. They are more likely to show you *how* professional, bureaucratic, top-down journalism attempts to pull the wool over the eyes of the public it creates than to contest that particular brand of corporate journalism. It follows that for the most interesting and thought-provoking insights into the role of journalism in society it is probably best to consult books which are not about journalism itself; to feel the pull of the currents of the intellectual tradition from which cultural studies draws its sustenance – Marxism, feminism, structuralism, semiotics, postmodernism, Foucauldianism, even the works of Derrida and Baudrillard (alongside those of Langton and Lotman); it's here that journalism has an outside from which it can be observed, interrogated and listened to. It's also instructive to put journalism into a context where its history and development can be mapped on to other developments in the history of ideas, of politics and of the public. Since contemporary bureaucratic journalism of the American type – Ericsonian journalism – can be seen as a continuation and diffusion of the American empire of information and control by colonizing knowledge, it might be wise to think about journalism as you read Thomas Richards's book *The Imperial Archive*, which is not about journalism at all, but is very thought-provoking and radical (beyond its own purposes, I think) on the politics of information in late imperial history.[26]

Painism

Personally I think books on journalism by journalists are only interesting once everyone involved is dead, unless they are offering craft skills. But even these need to be treated with caution. For instance, the craft skill that the most authoritative books actually offer the unsuspecting cadet may turn out to be *counter-revolution*. I have argued in this book that modernity, popular sovereignty and journalism – the public sphere of democratic equivalence and citizenship of media – are all products of the revolutionary energies of the French Revolution in particular, together with its cognate developments in America and elsewhere in the European semiosphere. One of the champions of this liberatory energy was Thomas Paine, a journalist-politician whose work played no small part in three revolutions (two successful, in the USA and France, and one not, in his and my country of birth). By 1792 he was a citizen of France, a deputy of the French National Assembly, a former citizen of the USA (a country he had helped to invent) and secretary for foreign affairs to the American Congress.

At this point Tom Paine had published *Rights of Man*, to bring to Britain what he thought was imminent and inevitable across Europe – in his hope and optimism he predicted that monarchy and aristocracy would be a thing of the past in seven years – i.e. by the dawn of the nineteenth century.[27] He argued for reform of government, lowering of taxes, popular representative democracy, alliance instead of war between Britain, France and the USA, and something like a welfare state. His belief in popular sovereignty was based on 'reason and discussion':

> *If it [the nation] prefer a bad or defective government to a reform, or chuse to pay ten times more taxes than there is occasion for, it has a right so to do: and as long as the majority do not impose conditions on the minority, different from what they impose on themselves, though there may be much error, there is no injustice. Neither will the error continue long. Reason and discussion will soon bring things right, however wrong they may begin.*[28]

Paine's proposals are also based on mutual self-interest and commerce, which he saw as the antidote to war: 'It is a pacific system, operating to cordialize mankind, by rendering nations, as well as individuals, useful to each other.'[29] He advocated tax reform, to lower taxes overall by cutting defence spending, and redistributing revenues from war to welfare:

> *By the operation of this plan, the poor laws, those instruments of civil torture, will be superseded . . . . The hearts of the humane will not be shocked by ragged and hungry children, and persons of seventy and eighty years of age, begging for bread. The dying poor will not be dragged from place to place to breathe their last, as a reprisal of parish upon parish. Widows will have a maintenance for their children, and not be carted away, on the death of their husbands, like culprits and criminals; and children will no longer be considered as encreasing the distresses of their parents. The haunts of the wretched will be known, because it will be to their advantage, and the number of petty crimes,*

*the offspring of distress and poverty, will be lessened. The poor, as well
as the rich, will then be interested in the support of government, and
the case and apprehension of riots and tumults will cease.*[30]

I quote from Paine's modest proposals, not all of which have been
taken up yet in his country of birth, and for which he was indicted
for treason, because I am interested in what newspaper proprietors
think their journalists ought to know. To explain, I must turn to the
Kemsley Manual of Journalism, which was published in 1950 by
Kemsley Newspapers (*The Sunday Times, Sunday Chronicle, Daily
Graphic (Daily Sketch), Daily Dispatch* and a swag of provincial papers).
Viscount Kemsley, one of the Berry brothers (the other was Lord
Camrose, also a press baron, owner of the *Daily Telegraph*) writes in
a foreword to this manual that 'there is no more important respon-
sibility to the community than that of journalists; and if the public
is to be fully and accurately informed of the world's news, their
educational standards must be high and their training thorough'.[31]
Turning to the section on training, we find this syllabus for a
'DIPLOMA COURSE IN JOURNALISM (*as established at the Technical
College, Cardiff*)':

SUBJECTS OF THE COURSE
Section A
   Practical Journalism
Section B
   Current Affairs for Journalists
   English Literature (Drama and Novel)
   English Literature (Poetry)
   English Literature (Shakespeare)
Section C
   English Composition (Advanced)
   Elements of Economics
   Public Administration
   Economic and Social History
   Psychology
Section D
   Shorthand (Speed)[32]

The Cardiff course was the only one in Britain at that time, and was
part of the 'Kemsley Editorial Plan' – a national training scheme for
journalists which survived long enough (under another name) to be
joined by Britain's only university diploma in journalism, founded
by Tom Hopkinson at University College Cardiff in 1970. In case
you should be surprised at the dominant hegemony of English literature on this syllabus, it has to be said that the emphasis was deliberate. The most substantial chapter in the training section of the
Kemsley *Manual* is on what journalists should *read*. Beginning with
the Bible, Shakespeare and Macaulay's *Essays*, the list takes in a
couple of historians (Gibbon) and biographers (Boswell), and then
turns to politics:

Coming to politics, I scarcely think one can expect the journalist, even the political journalist, to have read much that is earlier than Burke. But Burke is essential; no author on our list more so. Read the two great speeches on America. . . ; read the Address to the King*; and read the* Reflections on the French Revolution, *so often now misrepresented and decried, yet full of treasure from end to end.*[33]

There's the rub. Edmund Burke was 'so often misrepresented and decried' in the egalitarian 1940s because he was an anti-democratic defender of heredity, monarchy, aristocracy and the unwritten 'constitution' of a Britain which resisted to the death of its own subjects the revolutionary energies of France and America. It was in answer to Burke's *Reflections on the French Revolution* that Paine wrote *Rights of Man*, which includes long passages of detailed critique of that 'treasure'. But *Paine* – journalist, modernist, democrat – is not mentioned in the Kemsley manual as being worth reading, even by a political journalist. Similarly, the young journalist is enjoined to read Milton; but it's *Lycidas, L'Allegro* and *Il Penseroso, not* the *Aeropagitica* of 1644, which is Milton's stirring pamphlet to Parliament arguing for the freedom of the press. The reduction of politics to style – Burke's flowery prose preferred over Paine's simple sentences; Milton's 'perfection' over his passion for reason and free speech – only serves to hide the politics: counter-revolution.

For the owner of Kemsley Newspapers was the same ennobled Viscount Berry-brother (Viscount Kemsley, the brother of Lord Camrose) who benefited from the hereditary system, who used his own 'press freedom' to harry the British reading public with his own ghastly political views, and who had been denounced by Tom Hopkinson a few years earlier as the 'chief opponent' of the 1943 Beveridge Report – the very document which sought at last to unite the 'two nations' of rich and poor, by creating a system of social rather than state security; putting put a stop to the conditions which had persisted from the time Paine himself describes in the passage quoted above, by the very means Paine had advocated. As Hopkinson points out in *Picture Post*, where he prints unflattering mugshots of the two anti-poor aristocrats, the newspapers of lords Kemsley and Camrose (the *Daily Sketch* and *Daily Telegraph*) were the 'most persistent of all critics of the Beveridge Report', running 'leading articles, feature articles, and letters attacking the scheme day after day'.[34] In a long article criticizing the parliamentary (Tory) 'filleting' of the Beveridge proposals, Hopkinson recommends something that doesn't quite come to the storming of the Bastille, but certainly suggests that a sovereign people (citizen-readership) should take direct action *against* their parliament, even in time of total war, and he causes this incendiary paragraph to sit next to the mugshots of the two heartless class-supremacists:

How can we once more make our voice heard in high places? Only by speaking. The nation has other voices than the voice of parliament. Separately those voices may be only squeaks, but enough squeaks make a roar. Every factory, workshop and office has a voice. Clubs have voices. So have trade union branches. Political societies and groups have voices. Universities, colleges and schools have voices. Every kind of woman's organization has the power of speech. Now, if they are interested, let them speak.[35]

Of course, the mouse that roars won't be heard by Kemsley, Camrose or any other baronial journalists, because these well-trained newshounds will be busy reading Burke and writing feature articles. Well, what's sauce for the goose is sauce for the gander: *I say* read Paine and Hopkinson, not Lord this and Viscount that, men whose only real interest in Burke is *Burke's Peerage*. As Tom Paine says (and he should have the last word on this):

As the republic of letters brings forward the best literary productions, by giving to genius a fair and universal chance; so the representative system of government is calculated to produce the wisest laws, by collecting wisdom from where it can be found. I smile to myself when I contemplate the ridiculous insignificance into which literature and all the sciences would sink, were they made hereditary; and I carry the same idea into governments. An hereditary governor is as inconsistent as an hereditary author.[36]

Transcendental Journalism

Wisdom can usually be found well to the side of what press barons think. One of the *least* ideologically corrupted manuals for journalists that I've come across, and one of the most useful, is a book published by the United Nations, in co-operation with a group called the Asian Forum of Environmental Journalists.[37] A preface by Aditya Man Shrestha indicates why this is such a good book: it is motivated not by interest in journalism as such, but by a wish to contribute 'as best we can to protecting the environment in Asia by generating environmental consciousness at both the people and government levels through the media'.[38] Its real quarry, then, is to avoid another Bhopal, to raise awareness of the dangers of pesticides, fertilizers, deforestation, atmospheric pollution, desertification, overfishing, waterlogging, salinization, and to raise public and governmental awareness of the 'key global interrelated environmental issues of sustainable development, over-population and poverty'.[39] Its chosen method is to produce *good journalists*:

You have your professional duty to consider all the different strands of a story and to bring them together in a coherent manner. You also have a professional ethic of objectivity and fairness which does not allow you to favour one particular view over another. In such circumstances, you cannot, almost by definition, be specialists; and yet as generalists you must still strive to know enough about all of the various specializations so that an informed balance is maintained. The successful accomplishment of such a difficult and complex balancing act is worthy of anyone's admiration and respect.[40]

And what follows is indeed an admirable balancing act, providing practical guidance on issues, education, the specifics of environmental reporting, research, interviewing, story-writing, journalistic constraints (and how to cope creatively with them), a checklist for reporters, and various informative appendices. Because it is interested in something else, something that matters, the handbook is deft, useful and trustworthy in its advice. As it says:

Being an educator and a watchdog requires a great deal from a reporter, but one who wants to do an effective job in covering the environment can do no less. . . . Since environmental events transcend administrations, reigns and lifetimes, you can help to keep public attention focused on an issue until something gets done. There is no question that the role of the environmental journalist is an important one.[41]

The handbook is innovative in what it counts as media:

Another effective form of creating public awareness is the use of alternative media in the form of dramatic plays, songs, puppet shows and advertisements. Because this is a volume primarily for journalists, this subject is not addressed. However, again some of the basic guidelines, particularly those on how to translate technical information for laypersons, should prove helpful for those working in the alternative media.[42]

The whole semiosphere is put at the service of the whole biosphere. But as ever, the trouble is government. Within a year of the publication of the Asian Forum of Environmental Journalists' *Handbook*, things were going badly for them in Indonesia. As David T. Hill reports: 'Opposition groups suffer particularly. The environmental activist group SKEPHI had its *Berita Hutan* [*News of the Forest*] closed in March 1989, while the *Indonesian Human Rights Monitor* was banned in February 1990, both ostensibly for failure to obtain the required permits.'[43] The government wants 'national security', environmental journalism wants to save the planet. Who wins in the short term is not an issue; governments, barons and moguls trundle blindly on, over readers', journalists' and the environment's dead bodies, figuratively or literally. But such aggressive tactics are only necessary because in the end the forces of state reaction are actually weak. Even in Indonesia, as Hill points out, pressure to change comes from the readership, and from journalism which seeks to serve that readership. His analysis of journalism in one of the most tightly controlled regimes on the planet shows the state to be a leaky vessel:

Firstly, the analysis highlights the sharpening contradiction between the interests of business in maximising the profit-making potential of the print-media industry and the desire of the State to control the flows of information in order to maintain the 'security' of the State. . . . In the early 1990's atmosphere of greater political 'openness' . . . cautious publications risk losing readers to newer, bolder, rival papers unless the traditionally prudent papers follow suit. . . . Secondly, also challenging State constraints is the burgeoning middle-class with its growing desire for open access to information and greater plurality of voices in the press.[44]

In other words, *readers* (construed here as a market and a class) are leading the charge for 'bolder' political openness and plurality. Add to this the fact that even in Indonesia readers already have access to alternative media, via the availability of uncensored international satellite television, photocopiers, faxes and the internet, not to mention the traditional forms of 'dramatic plays, songs, puppet shows and advertisements', and you have all the ingredients for a journalism/readership push *against* government 'security' – not 1789, necessarily, but a Painite move to turn this particular 'New Order' into an '*ancien régime*'. Who wins in the long term – the time that 'transcends administrations, reigns and lifetimes' – is still an open question, just as it was in 1789, and it still matters; but now the outcome is up to you.

Notes

1. Paula Amad (1994) *Radical Inauthenticity and Cultural Anxiety: The Benetton Advertising Phenomenon*. MA thesis, Department of English, University of Melbourne, 128.
2. Stuart Hall, Chas Critcher, Tony Jefferson, John Clarke and Brian Roberts (1978) *Policing the Crisis: Mugging, the State, and Law and Order*. London: Macmillan.
3. Hall *et al.*, viii.
4. Hall *et al.*, 66.
5. See Hall *et al.*, 215.
6. Hall *et al.*, 215–16.
7. Hall *et al.*, 216.
8. *Monty Python's Life of Brian*: the scene where zealot John Cleese (modelling his truculence on 1970s ultra-leftism) wants to know 'What have the Romans ever done for us?' (apart from raising the level of civilization. . .).
9. Hall *et al.*, 216.
10. Richard V. Ericson, Patricia M. Baranek and Janet B.L. Chan (1987) *Visualizing Deviance: A Study of News Organization*; (1989) *Negotiating Control: A Study of News Sources*; (1991) *Representing Order: Crime, Law, and Justice in the News Media*. All Milton Keynes: Open University Press.
11. Ericson *et al.*, *Visualizing Deviance*, 345.
12. Ericson *et al.*, *Visualizing Deviance*, 15.
13. Ericson *et al.*, *Visualizing Deviance*, 4.
14. Ericson *et al.*, *Visualizing Deviance*, 356.
15. Ericson *et al.*, *Visualizing Deviance*, 356.
16. Ericson *et al.*, *Visualizing Deviance*, 53. see also 15, for comments on science.

17. Ericson *et al., Visualizing Deviance*, 363–4.
18. Abigail Bray (1994) The 'edible woman': reading/eating disorders and femininity. *Media Information Australia* 72, 4–10.
19. Liesbet Van Zoonen (1994) *Feminist Media Studies*. London: Sage; Catharine Lumby (1996) *Bad Girls: The Media, Sex and Feminism in the 90s*. Sydney: Allen & Unwin.
20. Marcia Langton (1993) '*Well I heard it on the radio and I saw it on the television*'. Sydney: Australian Film Commission. Her title is from the Yothu Yindi song 'Treaty now'.
21. Langton, 84.
22. Langton, 81.
23. Langton, 81–3.
24. Langton, 84.
25. See also Ross Poole (1989) Public spheres. In Helen Wilson (ed.) *Australian Communications and the Public Sphere: Essays in Memory of Bill Bonney*. Melbourne: Macmillan, 6–26, especially 22.
26. Thomas Richards (1993) *The Imperial Archive: Knowledge and the Fantasy of Empire*. London and New York: Verso.
27. Thomas Paine (1937, first published 1792) *Rights of Man: Being an Answer to Mr. Burke's Attack on the French Revolution*. Ed. Hypatia Bradlaugh Bonner. London: Watts, 127.
28. Paine, 246.
29. Paine, 189.
30. Paine, 228.
31. Viscount Kemsley (1950) *The Kemsley Manual of Journalism*. London, Toronto, Melbourne, Sydney, Wellington: Cassell, v. My copy of this book is stamped as belonging to Australian Consolidated Press's London office; it was the then publisher of the *Sydney Daily Telegraph, Sydney Sunday Telegraph* and *Australian Women's Weekly*. It is now the (renamed) core of the Kerry Packer empire; this is how baronial ideology stretches all the way from postwar Fleet Street to postmodern Channel Nine.
32. Lionel Berry, Recruitment and training for journalism, in *Kemsley*, 396.
33. R.C.K. Ensor, Books for journalists, in *Kemsley*, 401.
34. *Picture Post* 18(10), 6 March 1943.
35. *Picture Post* 18(10), 6 March 1943.
36. Paine, 148.
37. Asian Forum of Environmental Journalists (AFEJ/UN) (1988) *Reporting on the Environment: A Handbook for Journalists*. Bangkok, Thailand: AFEJ and ESCAP (the UN Economic and Social Commission for Asia and the Pacific). For a copy write to United Nations/ESCAP, UN Building, Rajadamnern Avenue, Bangkok 10200, Thailand.
38. AFEJ/UN, iii.
39. AFEJ/UN, 27.
40. S.A.M.S. Kibria, Executive Secretary of ESCAP, in AFEJ/UN, vi.
41. AFEJ/UN, 25.
42. Kibria, in AFEJ/UN, vii.
43. David T. Hill (1994) *The Press in New Order Indonesia*. Perth: University of Western Australia Press/Asia Research Centre, 113–14.
44. Hill, 21–2.

Bibliography

AIJAZ AHMAD (1992) *In Theory: Classes, Nations, Literatures.* London: Verso.

RICHARD ALTICK (1957) *The English Common Reader: A Social History of the Mass Reading Public 1800–1900.* Chicago: Chicago University Press.

PAULA AMAD (1994) *Radical Inauthenticity and Cultural Anxiety: The Benetton Advertising Phenomenon.* MA thesis, Department of English, University of Melbourne.

ASIAN FORUM OF ENVIRONMENTAL JOURNALISTS (AFEJ/UN) (1988) *Reporting on the Environment: A Handbook for Journalists.* Bangkok, Thailand: AFEJ and ESCAP (the UN Economic and Social Commission for Asia and the Pacific).

ANTOINE DE BAECQUE (1989) Pamphlets: libel and political mythology. In Darnton and Roche (eds.), 165–76.

WALTER BENJAMIN (1973) The work of art in the age of mechanical reproduction. In *Illuminations.* Ed. Hannah Arendt, trans. H. Zohn. London: Fontana, 219–53.

TONY BENNETT AND JAMES DONALD, ADVISED BY FRANCIS FRASCINA AND GILL PERRY (1982) The image and mass reproduction. In *Science, Technology and Popular Culture (1),* Unit 25 of *Popular Culture,* Open University Course U203. Milton Keynes: Open University Press.

PIERRE DE BOURDEILLE, SEIGNEUR AND ABBOT OF BRANTÔME (1943, first published 1600) *The Lives of Gallant Ladies.* London: Pushkin Press.

ABIGAIL BRAY (1994) The 'edible woman': reading/eating disorders and femininity. *Media Information Australia* 72, 4–10.

BERTHOLD BRECHT (1977) Against Georg Lukacs. In E. Bloch *et al.,* *Aesthetics and Politics.* Trans. and ed. R. Taylor. London: New Left Books, 68–85.

JOHN BUNYAN (1928, first published 1666) *Grace Abounding to the Chief of Sinners.* London: Dent; New York: Dutton.

[LORD] BYRON (1977, first published 1816–24) *Don Juan.* Ed. T.G. Steffan, E. Steffan, W.W. Pratt. Harmondsworth: Penguin.

JAMES CAMERON (1950) INCHON. *Picture Post* 49(1), 7 October.

WILLIAM CANE (1991) *The Art of Kissing.* Sydney: Harper Collins.

JAMES W. CAREY (1977) Mass communication research and cultural studies: an American view. In James Curran, Michael Gurevitch and Janet Woollacott (eds.) *Mass Communication and Society.* London: Edward Arnold, 409–25.

PETER CAREY (1991) *The Tax Inspector*. Brisbane: University of Queensland Press.

JACK RICHARD CENSER (1976) *Prelude to Power: The Parisian Radical Press 1789–1791*. Baltimore and London: Johns Hopkins University Press.

MIGUEL DE CERVANTES SAAVEDRA (1902, first published 1605) *The Life and Exploits of the Ingenious Gentleman Don Quixote De La Mancha*. Trans. Charles Jarvis. London: Sands.

SUZANNE TUCOO CHALA (1977) *Charles-Joseph Panckoucke & la librairie française*. Pau and Paris.

DEBORAH CHAMBERS (1992) Women and suburban culture: investigating women's experiences of the transition from rural to suburban living. In Brian Musgrove and Rebecca Snow-McLean (eds.) *Signifying Others: Selected Papers from the Second Cultural Studies Association of Australia Conference*. Toowoomba: USQ Press, 121–9.

JOHN CLARKE AND JANET NEWMAN (1993) The right to manage: a second managerial revolution? *Cultural Studies* 7(3), 427–41.

JAMES CLIFFORD (1983) On ethnographic authority. *Representations* 1(2), 118–46.

COUNCIL FOR ABORIGINAL RECONCILIATION (1995) *Together We Can't Lose: A Report to the Nation*. Canberra: Council for Aboriginal Reconciliation.

T.W.H. CROSLAND (1905) *The Suburbans*. London: John Long.

GEOFFREY CROSSICK (ED.) (1977) *The Lower Middle Class in Britain*. London: Croom Helm.

ROBERT DARNTON (1982) *The Literary Underground of the Old Regime*. Cambridge, Mass.: Harvard University Press.

ROBERT DARNTON (1989) Philosophy under the cloak. In Darnton and Roche (eds.), 27–49.

ROBERT DARNTON (1990) *The Kiss of Lamourette: Reflections in Cultural History*. New York: W.W. Norton.

ROBERT DARNTON AND DANIEL ROCHE (EDS.) (1989) *Revolution in Print: The Press in France 1775–1800*. Berkeley and LA: University of California Press.

JACQUES DERRIDA (1976) *Of Grammatology*. Baltimore and London: Johns Hopkins University Press.

JEAN DHOMBRES (1989) Books: reshaping science. In Darnton and Roche (eds.), 177–202.

BENJAMIN DISRAELI (1980, first published 1845) *Sybil: Or The Two Nations*. Ed. Thom Braun. Harmondsworth: Penguin.

GEORGES DUBY (ED.) (1988) *A History of Private Life. Vol. II: Revelations of the Medieval World*. Trans. Arthur Goldhammer. Cambridge, Mass.: Harvard University Press.

BRIAN EASLEA (1983) *Fathering the Unthinkable: Masculinity, Scientists and the Nuclear Arms Race*. London: Pluto Press.

UMBERTO ECO (1987) *Travels in Hyperreality*. Trans. William Weaver. London, Picador.

UMBERTO ECO (1990) Introduction to Lotman, vii–xiii.

FREDERICK ENGELS (1971) *The Condition of the Working Class in England*. (2nd edn., trans. W.O. Henderson and W.H. Chaloner) Oxford: Basil Blackwell.

HANS MAGNUS ENZENSBERGER (1976) Constituents of a theory of the media. In *Raids and Reconstructions: Essays on Politics, Crime, and Culture*. London: Pluto Press.

RICHARD V. ERICSON, PATRICIA M. BARANEK AND JANET B.L. CHAN (1987) *Visualizing Deviance: A Study of News Organization*. Milton Keynes: Open

University Press.

RICHARD V. ERICSON, PATRICIA M. BARANEK AND JANET B.L. CHAN (1989) *Negotiating Control: A Study of News Sources.* Milton Keynes: Open University Press.

RICHARD V. ERICSON, PATRICIA M. BARANEK AND JANET B.L. CHAN (1991) *Representing Order: Crime, Law, and Justice in the News Media.* Milton Keynes: Open University Press.

HAROLD EVANS (1978) *Pictures on a Page: Photo-journalism, Graphics and Picture Editing.* London: Heinemann.

RITA FELSKI (1989) *Beyond Feminist Aesthetics: Feminist Literature and Social Change.* Cambridge, Mass.: Harvard University Press.

RITA FELSKI (1995) *The Gender of Modernity.* Cambridge, Mass.: Harvard University Press.

LESLIE FIEDLER, in B. ROSENBERG AND DAVID MANNING WHITE (EDS.) (1957) *Mass Culture: The Popular Arts in America.* Glencoe, Ill.: Free Press.

JOHN FISKE, BOB HODGE AND GRAEME TURNER (1987) *Myths of Oz: Reading Australian Popular Culture.* Sydney: Allen & Unwin.

MICHEL FOUCAULT (1979) *The History of Sexuality: Volume One – An Introduction.* Trans. Robert Hurley. Harmondsworth: Penguin.

MICHEL FOUCAULT (1987) *The Use of Pleasure: The History of Sexuality Volume Two.* Trans. Robert Hurley. Harmondsworth: Penguin.

MICHEL FOUCAULT (1988) *The Care of the Self: The History of Sexuality Volume Three.* Trans. Robert Hurley. New York: Vintage Books.

MICHEL FOUCAULT (1988) *Technologies of the Self: A Seminar with Michel Foucault.* Ed. Luther H. Martin, Huck Gunman, Patrick H. Hutton. London: Tavistock.

MICHEL FOUCAULT (1991) Governmentality. In G. Burchell, C. Gordon and P. Miller (eds.) *The Foucault Effect: Studies in Governmentality.* Hemel Hempstead: Harvester Wheatsheaf.

SIGMUND FREUD (1938, first published 1919) *Totem and Taboo: Resemblances between the Psychic Lives of Savages and Neurotics.* Harmondsworth: Penguin.

JOHN FROW (1995) *Cultural Studies and Cultural Value.* Oxford: Oxford University Press.

JOHN FROW (1993) Knowledge and class. *Cultural Studies* 7(2), 240–81.

NICHOLAS GARNHAM (1987) Concepts of culture: public policy and the culture industries. *Cultural Studies* 1(1), 23–37.

ROBIN GERSTER (1990) Gerrymander: the place of suburbia in Australian fiction. *Meanjin* 49(3), 565–75.

KATHERINE GIBSON AND SOPHIE WATSON (EDS.) (1994) *Metropolis Now: Planning and the Urban in Contemporary Australia.* Sydney: Pluto Press.

JOHN GILCHRIST AND W.J. MURRAY (1971) *The Press in the French Revolution: A Selection of Documents Taken from the Press of the Revolution for the Years 1789–1794.* Melbourne: Cheshire, and London: Ginn.

PETER GOLDING AND GRAHAM MURDOCK (1989) Pulling the plugs on democracy. *New Statesman and Society* 2(56), 11.

HUGH GOUGH (1988) *The Newspaper Press in the French Revolution.* London: Routledge.

HOLLY GOULDEN AND JOHN HARTLEY (1982) 'Nor should such topics as homosexuality, masturbation, frigidity, premature ejaculation or the menopause be regarded as unmentionable': English, official discourses, and school examinations. *LTP: Journal of Literature Teaching Politics* 1, 4–20.

HARVEY GRAFF (ED.) (1981) *Literacy and Social Development in the West.* Cambridge: Cambridge University Press.

LYNNE SCHAFER GROSS (1990) *The New Television Technologies.* 3rd edn. Dubuque, IA: Wm. C. Brown.

JÜRGEN HABERMAS (1989) The new intimacy between culture and politics: theses on enlightenment in Germany. In *The New Conservatism: Cultural Criticism and the Historians' Debate.* Ed. and trans. S.W. Nicholsen. Cambridge, Mass.: MIT Press.

STUART HALL, CHAS CRITCHER, TONY JEFFERSON, JOHN CLARKE AND BRIAN ROBERTS (1978) *Policing the Crisis: Mugging, the State, and Law and Order.* London: Macmillan.

TOM HARRISSON (1978) *Living Through the Blitz.* Harmondsworth: Penguin.

JOHN HARTLEY (1992) *The Politics of Pictures: The Creation of the Public in the Age of Popular Media.* London and New York: Routledge.

TERENCE HAWKES (1992) *Meaning by Shakespeare.* London and New York: Routledge.

MICHAEL HECHTER (1975) *Internal Colonialism: The Celtic Fringe in British National Development, 1536–1966.* London: Routledge & Kegan Paul.

JOKE HERMES (1993) Media, meaning and everyday life. *Cultural Studies* 7(3), 493–506.

DAVID T. HILL (1994) *The Press in New Order Indonesia.* Perth: University of Western Australia Press/Asia Research Centre.

THOMAS HOBBES (1968, first published 1651) *Leviathan.* Ed. C.B. Macpherson. Harmondsworth: Penguin.

RENATE HOLUB (1992) *Antonio Gramsci: Beyond Marxism and Postmodernism.* London and New York: Routledge.

TOM HOPKINSON (ED.) (1970) *Picture Post 1938–1950.* Harmondsworth: Penguin.

IAN HUNTER (1988) *Culture and Government: The Emergence of Literary Education.* London: Macmillan.

IAN HUNTER (1992) The humanities without humanism. *Meanjin* 51(3), 479–90.

RONAL HYAM (1990) *Empire and Sexuality: The British Experience.* Manchester and New York: Manchester University Press.

HENRY JENKINS (1992) *Textual Poachers: Television Fans and Participatory Culture.* New York and London: Routledge.

BEVERLY JONES (1993) Cultural maintenance and change. *Media Information Australia* 69 (special issue on Art and Cyberculture edited by Ross Harley), 23–37.

JOHN KEANE (1995) *Tom Paine: A Political Life.* London: Bloomsbury.

[VISCOUNT] KEMSLEY AND OTHERS (1950) *The Kemsley Manual of Journalism.* London, Toronto, Melbourne, Sydney, Wellington: Cassell.

SØREN KIERKEGAARD (1989, first published 1841) *The Concept of Irony: with continual reference to Socrates.* Ed. and trans. Howard V. and Edna H. Hong. Princeton: Princeton University Press.

RUDYARD KIPLING (1977) *Selected Verse.* Ed. James Cochrane. Harmondsworth: Penguin.

JON P. KLANCHER (1987) *The Making of English Reading Audiences, 1790–1832.* Madison: University of Wisconsin Press.

JON KLANCHER (1990) British periodicals and reading publics. In Martin Coyle, Peter Garside, Malcolm Kelsall and John Peck (eds.) *Encyclopedia of Literature and Criticism.* London: Routledge, 876–88.

ERNESTO LACLAU AND CHANTAL MOUFFE (1985) *Hegemony and Socialist Strategy: Towards a Radical Democratic Politics.* Trans. Winston Moore and Paul Cammack. London: Verso.

LARRY LAMB (1989) *Sunrise: The Remarkable Rise and Rise of the Best-selling Soaraway Sun.* London: Macmillan.

MARCIA LANGTON (1993) '*Well I heard it on the radio and I saw it on the television*'. Sydney: Australian Film Commission.

TERESA DE LAURETIS (1989) *Technologies of Gender: Essays on Theory, Film and Fiction.* London: Macmillan.

F.R. LEAVIS AND DENYS THOMPSON (1933) *Culture and Environment: The Training of Critical Awareness.* London: Chatto & Windus.

Q.D. LEAVIS (1932) *Fiction and the Reading Public.* London: Chatto & Windus.

SOPHIE LEE (1995) interviewed by Catharin Lambert in *Australian Style* 12, 62–3.

MICHAEL LEWIS (1993) J-school confidential. *The New Republic*, 19 April, 20–7.

YURI (IURII MIKHAILOVICH) LOTMAN (1990) *The Universe of the Mind: A Semiotic Theory of Culture.* Trans. Ann Shukman. With an introduction by Umberto Eco. Bloomington and Indianapolis: Indiana University Press.

CATHARINE LUMBY (1994) Feminism and the media: the biggest fantasy of all. *Media Information Australia* 72, 49–54.

CATHARINE LUMBY (1996) *Bad Girls: The Media, Sex and Feminism in the 90s.* Sydney: Allen & Unwin.

JEAN-FRANÇOIS LYOTARD (1986–7) Rules and paradoxes and svelte appendix. *Cultural Critique* 5, 209–19.

CRAIG MCGREGOR (1984) *Pop Goes the Culture.* London: Pluto Press.

COLIN MACINNES (1959) *Absolute Beginners.* London: Allison & Busby.

CHARLES MACKAY (1841, 1852) *Memoirs of Extraordinary Popular Delusions and the Madness of Crowds.* London. Republished (1932) New York: Farrar, Straus & Giroux.

MARSHALL MCLUHAN (1962) *The Gutenberg Galaxy: The Making of Typographic Man.* London: Routledge & Kegan Paul.

C.B. (CRAWFORD BROUGH) MACPHERSON (1962) *The Political Theory of Possessive Individualism: Hobbes to Locke.* Oxford: Oxford University Press.

SALLY MANN (1988) *At Twelve: Portraits of Young Women.* New York: Aperture.

SALLY MANN (1992) *Immediate Family.* New York: Aperture.

KARAL ANN MARLING AND JOHN WETENHALL (1991) *Iwo Jima: Monuments, Memories and the American Hero.*

KARL MARX (1978) *Karl Marx: Selected Writings.* Ed. David McLellan. Oxford: Oxford University Press.

LAURA MASON (1989) Songs: mixing media. In Darnton and Roche (eds.), 252–69.

ANDRÉ MAUROIS (1937, first published 1927) *Disraeli.* Harmondsworth: Penguin.

KATHLEEN MEE (1994) Dressing up the suburbs: representations of Western Sydney. In Gibson and Watson (eds.), 60–77.

DENISE MEREDYTH (1992) Changing minds: cultural criticism and the problem of principle. *Meanjin* 51(3), 491–504.

ERIC MICHAELS (1985) Ask a foolish question: on the methodologies of cross cultural media research. *Australian Journal of Cultural Studies* 3(2), 45–59.

TOBY MILLER (1990) 'There are full professors in this place who read nothing but cereal boxes.' Australian screen in academic print. *Media Information Australia* 55, 5–13.

TOBY MILLER (1993) *The Well-Tempered Self: Citizenship, Culture, and the Postmodern Subject.* Baltimore and London: Johns Hopkins University Press.

JOHN MILTON (1974) *John Milton: Selected Prose.* Harmondsworth: Penguin.

WILLIAM J. MITCHELL (1994) *The Reconfigured Eye: Visual Truth in the Post-photographic Era.* Cambridge, Mass.: MIT Press.

JAMES MORAN (1973) *Printing Presses: History and Development from the Fifteenth Century to Modern Times.* Berkeley and LA: University of California Press.

MEAGHAN MORRIS (1988) At Henry Parkes Motel. *Cultural Studies* 2(1) (with a photo-essay by Ann Zahalka), 1–47.

MEAGHAN MORRIS (1988) *The Pirate's Fiancée: Feminism, Reading, Postmodernism.* London and New York: Verso.

MEAGHAN MORRIS (1988) Things to do with shopping centres. *Working Paper No. 1,* Center for Twentieth Century Studies, University of Wisconsin-Milwaukee.

MEAGHAN MORRIS (1991) Responses to Graeme Turner. *Meanjin* 50(2), 32–4.

MEAGHAN MORRIS (1992) A gadfly bites back. *Meanjin* 51(3), 545–51

MEAGHAN MORRIS (1992) *Great Moments in Social Climbing: King Kong and the Human Fly.* Sydney: Local Consumption Publications.

MEAGHAN MORRIS (1992) *Ecstasy and Economics.* Sydney: EMPress.

KATE MOSS (1995) *Kate.* London: Pavilion Books.

KATHY MYERS (1986) *Understains: The Sense and Seduction of Advertising.* London: Comedia.

JOHN LA NAUZE (1977) *Walter Murdoch: A Biographical Memoir.* Melbourne: Melbourne University Press.

DONALD J. OLSEN (1979) *The Growth of Victorian London.* Harmondsworth: Peregrine Books. First published 1976 by B.T. Batsford.

WALTER J. ONG (1971) Latin language study as a Renaissance puberty rite. In *Rhetoric, Romance and Technology: Studies in the Interaction of Expression and Culture.* Ithaca and London: Cornell University Press, 113–41.

TOM O'REGAN (1996) *Australian National Cinema.* London: Routledge.

GEORGE ORWELL (1941) *The Lion and the Unicorn: Socialism and the English Genius.* London: Secker & Warburg.

GEORGE ORWELL (1941) The roadman's day. *Picture Post* 10(11), 15 March.

THOMAS PAINE (1937, first published 1792) *Rights of Man: Being an Answer to Mr. Burke's Attack on the French Revolution.* Ed. Hypatia Bradlaugh Bonner. London: Watts.

THOMAS PAINE (1976, first published 1776) *Common Sense.* Ed. Isaac Krammick. Harmondsworth: Penguin.

PICTURE POST (1941) A plan for Britain. 10(1), 4 January (whole issue).

ROSS POOLE (1989) Public spheres. In Helen Wilson (ed.) *Australian Communications and the Public Sphere: Essays in Memory of Bill Bonney.* Melbourne: Macmillan, 6–26.

JEREMY D. POPKIN (1989) Journals: the new face of news. In Darnton and Roche (eds.), 141–64.

KARL POPPER (1950) *The Open Society and its Enemies.* Princeton: Princeton University Press.

KARL POPPER (1983) *A Pocket Popper.* Ed. David Miller. London: Fontana.

MARK POSTER (1990) *The Mode of Information: Poststructuralism and Social Context.* Cambridge: Polity Press.

MARK POSTER (1994) Baudrillard and TV ads. In *The Polity Reader in Cultural Theory.* Cambridge: Polity Press, 126–33.

DIANE POWELL (1993) *Out West: Perceptions of Sydney's Western Suburbs.* Sydney: Allen & Unwin.

ROBERT B. RAY (1990) Postmodernism. In Martin Coyle, Peter Garside, Malcolm Kelsall and John Peck (eds.) *Encyclopedia of Literature and Culture.*

London: Routledge, 131–47.

ROLF REICHARDT (1989) Prints: images of the Bastille. In Darnton and Roche (eds.), 223–51.

THOMAS RICHARDS (1991) *The Commodity Culture of Victorian England: Advertising and Spectacle, 1851–1914*. London: Verso.

THOMAS RICHARDS (1993) *The Imperial Archive: Knowledge and the Fantasy of Empire*. London and New York: Verso.

MARSHALL SAHLINS (1972) *Stone Age Economics*. London: Tavistock.

MARSHALL SAHLINS (1976) *Culture and Practical Reason*. Chicago: Chicago University Press.

CHERISE SAYWELL (1994/5) Post-sacred sex: melodramatic discourse and the erect penis in *Sophie Lee's Sex*. Paper presented to *Intellectuals and Communities*, conference of the Australian Cultural Studies Association.

ELLEN SEITER, HANS BORCHERS, GABRIELE KREUTZNER AND EVA-MARIA WARTH (1989) 'Don't treat us like we're so stupid and naive': Toward an ethnography of soap opera viewers'. In Ellen Seiter *et al.* (eds.) *Remote Control: Television, Audiences and Cultural Power*. London and New York: Routledge, 223–47.

RICHARD SENNETT (1974) *The Fall of Public Man*. Cambridge: Cambridge University Press.

THOMAS SHARP (1940) *Town Planning*. Harmondsworth: Pelican Books.

ANTHONY SMITH (1979) *The Newspaper: An International History*. London: Thames & Hudson.

LYNN SPIGEL (1992) *Make Room for TV: Television and the Family Ideal in Postwar America*. Chicago: University of Chicago Press.

J.V. STALIN (1954) *Marxism and Problems of Linguistics*. Peking: Foreign Languages Press.

HUGH STRETTON (1974) *Housing and Government*. Sydney: ABC.

ANNE SUMMERS (1975) *Damned Whores and God's Police: The Colonization of Women in Australia*. Ringwood, Vic.: Penguin Books.

DAVID TAFLER AND PETER D'AGOSTINO (1993) The techno/cultural interface. *Media Information Australia* 69 (special issue on *Art and Cyberculture* edited by Ross Harley), 47–54.

JOHN TAYLOR (1991) *War Photography: Realism in the British Press*. London: Comedia/Routledge.

LAURENCE THOMPSON (1970) 1941. In Tom Hopkinson (ed.), 88.

THE TIMES (1935) *A Newspaper History 1785–1935: Reprinted from the 150th Anniversary Number of The Times, January 1 1935*. London: The Times Publishing.

HENRY TUDOR (1972) *Political Myth*. London: Macmillan.

GRAEME TURNER (1991) Return to Oz: populism, the academy and the future of Australian Studies. *Meanjin* 50(2), 19–31.

GRAEME TURNER (1992) Suburbia verité. *Australian Left Review*, October, 37–9.

GRAEME TURNER (1994) *Making It National: Nationalism and Australian Popular Culture*. Sydney: Allen & Unwin.

LIESBET VAN ZOONEN (1994) *Feminist Media Studies*. London: Sage.

VOGUE PAR NELSON MANDELA: PARIS VOGUE 742, with English text, December 1993–January 1994.

VALENTIN VOLOSHINOV (1973) *Marxism and the Philosophy of Language*. New York: Seminar Press.

DROR WAHRMAN (1992) Virtual representation: parliamentary reporting and languages of class in the 1790s. *Past and Present* 136, 83–113.

IAN WARD (1995) *Politics of the Media.* Melbourne: Macmillan Education Australia.

McKENZIE WARK (1990) Vectors of memory . . . seeds of fire: the Western media and the Beijing demonstrations. *New Formations* 10, 1–12.

McKENZIE WARK (1991) From Fordism to Sonyism: perverse readings of the New World Order. *New Formations* 15 (Winter), 43–54.

McKENZIE WARK (1993) Suck on this, planet of noise! (Version 1.2). In David Bennett (ed.) *Cultural Studies: Pluralism and Theory.* Melbourne: Melbourne University Literary and Cultural Studies, vol. 2, 156–70.

R.K. WEBB (1955) *The British Working Class Reader 1790–1848: Literacy and Social Tension.* London: George Allen & Unwin.

ANGUS WILSON (1977) *The Strange Ride of Rudyard Kipling: His Life and Works.* London, Toronto, Sydney, New York: Granada Publishing.

ELIZABETH WILSON (1990) These new components of the spectacle: fashion and postmodernism. In Roy Boyne and Ali Rattansi (eds.) *Postmodernism and Society.* London: Macmillan, 209–36.

ELIZABETH WILSON (1990) All the rage. In Jane Gaines and Charlotte Herzog (eds.) *Fabrications: Costume and the Female Body.* New York and London: Routledge, 28–38.

Index